The social work
dissertation

The social work dissertation

Using small-scale qualitative methodology

Malcolm Carey

 Open University Press

Open University Press
McGraw-Hill Education
McGraw-Hill House
Shoppenhangers Road
Maidenhead
Berkshire
England
SL6 2QL

email: enquiries@openup.co.uk
world wide web: www.openup.co.uk

and Two Penn Plaza, New York, NY 10121-2289, USA

First published 2009

A catalogue record of this book is available from the British Library

ISBN-13: 978-0-33-522549-1 (pb) 978-0-33-522548-4 (hb)
ISBN-10: 0335225497 (pb) 0335225489 (hb)

Library of Congress Cataloging-in-Publication Data
CIP data applied for

Typeset by RefineCatch Limited, Bungay, Suffolk
Printed in the UK by Bell and Bain Ltd, Glasgow.

Fictitious names of companies, products, people, characters and/or data that may
be used herein (in case studies or in examples) are not intended to represent any
real individual, company, product or event.

Mixed Sources
Product group from well-managed
forests and other controlled sources
www.fsc.org   Cert no. TT-COC-002769
FSC   © 1996 Forest Stewardship Council

The *McGraw·Hill* Companies

Contents

Figures and tables

Figures

Tables

List of case studies

Acknowledgements

This book would not have been possible without the support of my family and friends, especially my mother Catherine. Thanks also go to my sister Claire, brother Joseph and, last but not least, my energetic nephew Jarv Lee. Special thanks remain for Victoria and Zachary, who both remain precious. Also a special welcome to Otis Leon.

Derek Clifford and Liz Foster each provided helpful references. Chris Jones, Tony Novak and Hugh Beynon have each offered advice in the past which I have not forgotten. Finally, I would like to thank my students who attended lectures for the dissertation module taught at Liverpool John Moores University. Either inadvertently or explicitly each helped me immensely with this project.

1 Social work research and the dissertation

Introduction

This book seeks to guide and support students who are undertaking small scale qualitative research as part of a social work course; including at undergraduate, post-graduate or post-qualification level. It sets out to help meet the many requirements for a dissertation: typically a distinct part of taught social work courses and one which requires a more extended period of personal study and application. However, this book can also be used by practitioners undertaking research as part of their social work role, or perhaps due to personal interest.

As well as literature based research this book also accommodates empirical research undertaken directly with participants, typically between one to twelve participants, although larger samples are possible. This approach is motivated by a belief that the limited time available to busy social work students means that involvement with larger samples can compromise the available time and therefore quality of other core aspects of a dissertation, such as the literature review or writing up. As Denscombe (2007) has also highlighted, substantive social research with smaller groups of people still leads to the researcher inter-acting with, and absorbing, all of the research processes involved with larger groups.

As Bell (1987: 1) suggests, within social research 'the problems facing you are much the same whether you are producing a small project, a MEd disserta-tion or a PhD'. Such 'problems' include a need to select and carefully outline a research topic, thoroughly review any relevant literature, apply a research methodology and method, and analyse and write up any findings. This book explores all of these processes in relation to small scale social work research.

How to use this book

Although it can be used unaccompanied this book will offer more substantive support if used in conjunction with related publications. Qualitative social research remains a discipline that has generated a wide range of course text-books. For any student or practitioner this will offer a set of valuable resources on which to draw. For this reason, at the end of each chapter there is a list of relevant reading that can supplement and extend any discussions regarding themes covered in each chapter.

The book is divided into ten chapters. Typically for social work and social research a book will not be read from cover to cover. This is because a variety of topics or research questions will be pursued by different students, and sections of a particular book will relate to some but not others. There is therefore a distinction between core chapters that relate to all dissertations and optional chapters that link to some topics but not others. Core chapters include this one and Chapters 2, 3, 4, 5, 9 and 10. Engagement with other chapters will depend upon your selected research topic, and related research method and methodology used.

The book's structure

This chapter looks at the requirements for a dissertation at different levels, including at degree, postgraduate and post-qualification level. The chapter identifies the nature and benefits of research for social work, and the prioritiz-ing of research ethics. Chapter 2 looks in more detail at research processes followed as part of a social work dissertation. These include essential require-ments such as selecting a suitable topic, undertaking a literature review, selecting and applying suitable research method(s), analysing data and finally, the writing up and dissemination of any findings.

Chapter 3 discusses general research concepts. These include a discussion of the distinct attributes of qualitative research, and the differences between applied and pure, and inductive and deductive research. Chapter 4 looks at social research theory and introduces the four main types of theory used in qualitative social work research – positivism, interpretivism, critical theory and postmodernism. Chapter 5 explores a vital stage within any dissertation – the literature survey or review. It is argued that alongside the setting of a research question with its related aims and objectives, and qualitative analysis completed throughout a study, the literature review represents a pivotal part of any dissertation. This is because the literature review is directly related to, and therefore supports, other aspects of a dissertation, including the application of research methods such as interviews and analysis, the writing up stage, and so on. The literature review offers a *foundation* on which the quality of much of the final dissertation is likely to rest. This chapter also details the specific requirements of literature based dissertations.

Chapter 6 explores the use of practical frameworks, philosophy and theory within social work research – usually identified as a research methodology that helps to frame and encourage meaning within any research project. This chapter also identifies examples of specific methodologies used within social work research. Chapters 7 and 8 explore research methods and methodology used within applied or conceptual and theoretical social work research. Chapter 7 looks at traditional methods that include the one-to-one interview, questionnaire and focus group. Chapter 8 examines newer and often more complex methodologies that include narrative research, discourse analysis and life history approaches.

Chapter 9 details qualitative analysis and this can sometimes be a more demanding aspect of a dissertation. Although much analysis takes place towards the end stage of a dissertation, it usually begins earlier (such as during the literature review) and proceeds throughout. Chapter 10, the final one, explores the writing up of a dissertation. Once again, although often assumed to begin towards the end of a project, writing can, and indeed should, begin earlier. This chapter also details the writing up of literature based dissertations and suggests some ways in which your research findings might be disseminated, including as part of social work practice.

The nature of research

Research has been defined as 'planned, cautious, systematic and reliable ways of finding out or deepening [our] understanding' of a selected topic or theme. It also involves some form of investigation, exploration of an issue, trend or social group; and typically entails theoretical and philosophical support and analysis (Blaxter *et al.*, 1996: 5). Research within social work may also seek to ask wider ontological (in philosophy, the nature of being or existence) questions that link to the experiences or attitudes of research participants, or a particular theme under investigation. Such questions may seek to unravel the ethical or moral dimensions of a form of social work intervention, or seek to ask difficult questions about why a particular 'service user' group has not received necessary support.

Although a definition of research is relatively easy to construct, the *processes* of research tend to be more varied and contestable. Research process is the way in which research develops or moves on: both in a physical sense of completing necessary tasks such as reading or interviewing, and in relation to the changing thoughts, ideas, beliefs and values of the researcher as their work proceeds. Regarding process there are also different types of research: for example, pure (theoretical and conceptual) and applied (practical combined with theoretical) research, commercial and academic research, covert (hidden) or overt (unconcealed) research methods, among others.

One of the most apparent distinctions within social research is that which divides qualitative and quantitative processes. Whereas quantitative social research tends to draw from large samples, uses statistics and often aims to be scientific, objective (unbiased) and value free, qualitative social research instead seeks to engage with one or more of the following:

- explores in great depth the attitudes, and/or behaviour and/or experiences of research participants;
- identifies, discusses and explains the often detailed opinions of participants;
- focuses upon the everyday and sometimes 'gritty' and 'real' life of select people. Explores the emotive opinions, experiences and actions that are linked to the research journey and sometimes called an *emic* perspective;
- remains *context*-bound, or attempts to be both ethically and politically sensitive to any research environment and settings, and looks for explanation, trends, themes, outcomes which help us to explain and understand;
- often highlights the political nature of social research and especially the impact of culturally relative influences such as gender, power, disability, class and sexuality, among others;
- maintains a close and sometimes personal and emotionally sensitive relationship between the researcher and participants;
- can attempt to change social and political systems through research, such as by empathizing with participants' needs or forms of disadvantage, and subsequently criticizing taken-for-granted assumptions within society;
- does not generally seek to be objective, distant and value free, but instead acknowledges the impact of the researcher upon participants and seeks to view each as equals rather than as subjects or distant objects 'under a microscope'.

(Adapted from Sapsford and Abbott, 1996; Holloway, 1997: 5; Dawson, 2007)

This definition relates to applied research in which direct contact is made with participants. However, literature based social research, which concentrates upon exploring related publications and theoretical concepts, still draws from the same research *culture* or outlook. A literature based dissertation will again aim to explore themes such as personal or group attitudes, needs or behaviour and political outcomes, or the impact of legislation and policy upon practitioners or service users. It may also seek to critically engage with established theory or practice, or compare different forms of social work practice including in different countries, and so forth. This distinction between quantitative and qualitative research is further explored in Chapter 3.

The benefits of research for social work students and practitioners

There remain various reasons why qualitative research is appealing and relevant to social work. To begin with, there are strong links between the culture of research and social work in practice. For example, Gilgun (1994) proposes that remarkable similarities persist between qualitative research and social work practice. These include a joint *recognition* of the impact of wider social, political and cultural factors upon the behaviour and attitudes of both service users and research participants. The shared importance of collecting detailed information from different sources – such as part of assessment processes for the social worker and the research interview undertaken by a researcher – provides another link. Engagement and empathy with service users or participants should be also central within both roles. Dominelli (2005) also highlights mutual attempts to stimulate change and empowerment.

A piece of research can also help any student or practitioner to:

- better understand the *context* under which they practise;
- offer a broader and more detailed *understanding* of social 'problems', needs and the impact(s) of social work interventions;
- gain new insight into themes such as those relating to policy, legislation and political, economic or cultural dynamics – for example, issues related to class, gender, power relations or the educational needs of practitioners or service users, etc. – that impinge upon aspects of practice;
- broaden any prior understanding of service user or carer needs, and possibly also those of future work colleagues;
- help achieve a greater sense of satisfaction and achievement, such as through increased confidence gained through a sense of accomplishment, especially if more appropriate social work interventions eventually follow as a result;
- provide better advice, guidance and other forms of support to people in need due to increased knowledge and skills gained;
- increase the capacity to use our imagination by stimulating thought and ideas.

Royse (1991: 9) has argued that social work research can not only make us better practitioners, it can also be exciting and represent a type of adventure:

Social science research is exciting because it studies a lively topic – people. As we learn more about people and their problems, we become better practitioners. Research is conducted by social workers in the field and in universities who are adventurers extending the frontiers of their field of knowledge.

Social work research is distinct from some other disciplines because many findings can be *applied in practice* almost immediately. Unlike some related disciplines it is not merely theoretically focused, but instead can have an instant impact on the lives of people who come into direct contact with social workers. In relation to this, the merger of research and practice is increasingly identified as essential.

Potentially, social work practice and, in particular, interventions, can have a profound impact on a service user's or informal carer's life. Inevitably more informed practice through good research (and the resources available to support it) may lead to more positive outcomes for vulnerable social groups who come into contact with social workers.

The social work dissertation

Dissertations within social work tend to be extremely varied. For example, Dellgran and Hojer's (2003) exploration of 589 social work dissertations (Bachelor, Masters and PhD level) completed in Sweden between 1977 to 1998, discovered a 'wide range of analyses of different social problems and interventions' undertaken by students. Despite this, research undertaken was predominately qualitative, and relied upon small samples which stressed an in-depth exploration of one of many areas of study. These dissertations also drew on different disciplines, most notably psychology, sociology, law and social policy. Trends which formed over the years included an interest in 'social problems and phenomena', the workings of organizations (including social work departments), and specific service user groups and casework. Also students' interest in community work, social policy and poverty had tended to recede over the years.

There is, nevertheless, a downside to being offered more choice within a multi-disciplinary subject such as social work. In particular, deciding a feasible topic from so many possible options can cause problems. The somewhat uncertain, if not nebulous, nature of 'social work' as a discipline also means that there is a greater danger that non-suitable topics can be selected. It is therefore paramount at the early stages of research that close contact with a tutor is maintained in order to ensure that any research topic is *suitable*. Generally it is also important to have a focused topic, be realistic regarding its feasibility and also ask to what extent any topic can be used to influence practice. These themes are explored further in Chapter 2.

Most social work dissertations tend to be around 8000 to 15,000 words in length, and there is usually an expectation of a significant amount of time spent in personal study prior to submission. For example, as part of a Masters dissertation module on a postgraduate social work course there is typically an expectation of at least 600 hours of personal study in order to complete. This figure helps to emphasize the amount of commitment that is usually required for a project that can generate considerable work. In relation to this, an early start is always advisable and, perhaps inevitably, leaving things until the last minute needs to be avoided wherever possible. One reason for this is that the process of social work research is rarely predictable or linear – again, as with social work practice, there are times when things do not go according to plan. This might include problems relating to access to participants or unplanned difficulties in accessing relevant literature, and so forth.

Although initially a dissertation can sometimes seem like an insurmountable mountain to climb, it is worth remembering that all dissertations adhere to a basic format and processes which are remarkably similar to other forms of assessed work. At either graduate or postgraduate level you are likely to have already passed numerous assessments which have indicated your ability to pursue a research project by the time you begin a dissertation. Although new roles (such as interviewing research participants) may appear as a challenge, they remain tasks which are within your capability, and which you may have already experienced when on a practice placement. The key difference for a dissertation is that the *scale* of the work is greater, and there is therefore more need to plan ahead and read more widely around related themes. Another distinct quality of the dissertation is that a student is expected to be able to bring together and utilize skills and knowledge, such as those gained on previous modules, *within one project* that is also managed much more independently. There is also an expectation of an ability to engage with more analysis and critical insight, relating to any topic or research question. Each of these themes is explored in detail in later chapters.

Bachelor, Masters and post qualification courses

In many countries there are three different course routes that involve a social work dissertation. For example, in the UK they include the Masters degree, and, much more recently, the Bachelor degree and post-qualification (PQ) routes. A dissertation (and other assessed forms of social research such as a 'long essay' or research project) will tend to be pitched at the highest level of any course. This is especially regarding formal institutional requirements and regulations, but also more informal expectations placed on students by tutors.

In Britain the expectations attached to all dissertations include an ability to:

- review, assess and apply to social work practice a coherent body of knowledge (such as a theory);
- draw from, and critically apply, ideas and concepts from a range of relevant sources (for example, books, journals, newspapers, the Internet, etc.);
- use and transfer research skills (for example, communication, interview, writing, and so on) within and across major social and human science disciplines;
- consider, assess and evaluate new concept(s) (theoretical and practical) and apply each to a piece of social research;
- be able to select and apply relevant method(s) to a research topic;
- be aware of, and seek to apply, the values and beliefs of anti-discriminatory practice;
- express, articulate and contextualize findings in a final report;
- show some initiative, and not rely solely on the advice and direction offered by tutors.

(Adapted from the Quality Assurance Agency for Higher Education, 2000; Training Organisation for the Personal Social Services, 2002; and the General Social Care Council, 2004)

The assumption for any dissertation module is that students will already have engaged in numerous research-*related* activities. This will include those relating to essays, presentations, seminars, reading, analysis, and so on. Qualified social work practitioners will already have prior experience undertaking similar academic assessment-related roles – for example, as part of a first social work qualification or an initial degree and/or Masters in social work.

What will be less familiar to many students and practitioners, however, remains a capacity to engage in *applied* research, as well as fulfil a longer and therefore more demanding piece of academic work. In practice, this will involve the capacity to decide and explore a research question of *one's own choosing* (Chapter 2), and more formal and sustained engagement and awareness of research methodologies and methods (explored in Chapters 5 to 8), qualitative analysis (Chapter 9) and the writing up of one's findings (Chapter 10).

Despite the same expectations listed above for all three types of social work course there are some distinctions between each. The different expectations for the three social work courses in the UK are summarized in Table 1.1.

There is a distinction between a Bachelor and Masters degree and also any PQ awards, including the PQ award for approved social workers. In general there are more expectations placed on Masters students and those undertaking further training within mental health services at PQ level. For example, there is

Table 1.1 Expectations at Bachelor, Masters and post-qualification level

Bachelor degree with Honours and the PQ awards in social work (for non-approved social workers)	Masters degree and the PQ award for Approved Social Workers
Critically review, consolidate and *extend* a systematic and coherent body of knowledge	Show *originality* in the application of knowledge, and the ability to tackle and solve problems
Understand and apply relevant research methods	*Design* and apply appropriate research *methodologies* and demonstrate expertise in specialised professional skills
Use specialized and professional skills across a major discipline	Display a *mastery* of a complex and specialist area of knowledge
Assess and evaluate new concepts and evidence from a range of sources	Use critical knowledge to understand, *promote* and *develop* service user and carer rights and empowerment
Transfer and apply relevant skills and exercise judgement in a variety of research situations	Use *independent* critical judgement to take a leading role in systematically developing personal practice
Codify and articulate research findings	Be able to *disseminate* results of research topics

Source: Adapted from the Quality Assurance Agency for Higher Education (2000) and the Training Organisation for the Personal Social Services (2002).

an assumption that at this level more evidence should be provided of critical and analytical insight regarding any topic of study, and also that there should be more evidence of originality (especially in the final write up). Therefore students cannot simply offer a 'guided tour' of any available published literature related to any one topic. They must also provide some new insight(s), and more rigorously investigate related issues which might draw from any primary research undertaken. Originality might emerge from recommendations made for future social work practice or suggested reforms to an established theory, policy or piece of legislation. Masters and some PQ students are also expected to be more versatile in understanding and applying research methodologies (theoretical frameworks or ideas orientating a researcher's work), a point explored in more detail in Chapter 6.

Because they have previously studied at a higher level, Masters and some PQ students are also expected to be able to take more initiative for their own learning. In other words, although they will still be expected to keep their tutors informed of progress throughout their research, in general they may be less likely to require as much formal supervision and guidance. It is also expected that such students have a relatively strong grasp of theory due to longer periods previously spent in study. Finally, Masters and some PQ students are expected to be able to disseminate (distribute or apply) their research findings – for example, by being able to present findings to an audience or draw directly upon findings and apply as part of social work practice (explored further in Chapter 10).

At Bachelors degree and standard PQ level there is more emphasis upon engaging with less theoretically informed roles such as assessing new concepts and applying research methods, alongside other relevant *skills*. There is also no formal expectation of a *fluent* use of theory; instead theory should be utilized wherever necessary. Despite a lack of formal expectation however this does not mean that theory may not be used fluently or dissemination proceed.

With generally unpredictable and typically diverse research processes within qualitative research it is likely that the distinctions drawn above may well blur from time to time. This will depend upon what it is you decide to research and how this is undertaken. In practice any such regulations should be seen as offering *general* guidelines and minimum requirements rather than strict and rigid rules to adhere to. For example, the lesser expectations relating to Bachelor and some PQ courses should be looked upon as potentially beneficial regarding a minimum set standard level to reach, rather than as a set of stipulated rules to aspire to. If in doubt it is important to consult with a personal tutor.

Levin (2005: 15–16) offers a helpful guide of basic expectations for any dissertation from an examiner's perspective. Key attributes include:

- command of the subject matter;
- ability to 'conceive of a purposeful, feasible and manageable project' and frame a concise and meaningful research question;
- ability to choose and apply a clear and appropriate research methodology;
- awareness of the subtleties of a subject, eye for relevance and significance and a capacity to 'see connections and to handle a complex subject matter without oversimplifying it';
- ability to see 'both the "big picture" and significant details';
- evidence that relevant literature has been read;
- some evidence of an ability 'to think critically and independently';
- evidence that work has been done carefully, with detail and without 'loose ends' remaining;
- evidence of advocacy regarding arguments and a capacity 'to put forward a point of view and argue for it'.

Each of these qualities, and others, are explored in much more detail throughout this book.

Research ethics

Research ethics refer to 'rules of morally good conduct' which should be 'grounded in moral and political beliefs' (Gomm, 2003: 298). Within applied or practical ethics priority has tended to be given to determined morally 'good' behaviour above all else; however what constitutes good and not good behaviour remains highly subjective and open to interpretation. As Vesey and Foulkes (1999: 105) remind us, 'there is much disagreement as to what constitutes the good life, and it is not clear whether there can be a definite resolution of such divergencies'. Despite this, according to Banks (2002), social work has tended to embed itself within core aspects of the ideas of the philosopher Immanuel Kant; especially the importance of maintaining dignity and respect for others, complying with universal moral rules and determining the qualities of *individual* actions.

Dominelli (2002) however, in drawing from feminism as well as the opinions of other critical theories and thinkers, argues that this is not enough, and that social workers should also seek to engage in struggles for equality and social justice, especially on behalf of less powerful groups including women, disabled people, minority ethnic group members, and so forth. Based on evidence that inequities of opportunity and outcome (regarding access to education, wealth, employment, housing, and so on) impact upon many people, and usually more so service users, it can be said that the aim to promote justice and equality can only be achieved through attempts to correct this imbalance. Within social research this may be achieved by drawing attention to forms of discrimination and disadvantage, especially the ways in which particular people experience its many forms.

The power that a researcher may have over participants (such as that gained through their knowledge or status), means that intended or unintended mistreatment, or even exploitation, is a possibility. For this reason (among others) we have research ethics, and more recently there have been attempts to develop specific research ethics or codes for social work. Codes of ethics encourage researchers to become more accountable for the dissemination of their findings, but also attempt to regulate research techniques, especially so as to avoid malpractice, incompetence or dishonesty and abuse. Ethics within social research therefore can go beyond the relationship between researcher and participant, and attempt to place 'responsibility upon the researcher to his/her wider research community' (McCauley, 2003: 98–9).

Up until recently research in the social sciences had been based around '*informal* codes of ethics' which often contained 'ambiguities and contradictions [that] mean[t] most social scientists could justify any course of research as "ethical" ' (Truman, 2003: 3, my emphasis). However, this culture is being reformed, and research undertaken as part of a social work course is now typically screened by ethics or research governance committees. They are created to 'regulate research and to quality assure that research proposals and processes are ethical' (McLaughlin, 2007: 55), and tend to decide whether or not to grant 'ethical approval' to a proposed piece of research. Increasingly for social work such committees or panels are led by staff trained within a health care discipline, and this can create problems for social work students and staff. In particular, there may be possible tensions regarding contrasting approaches of research, as Darlington and Scott (2002: 23) stress:

> Ethics review boards are often unfamiliar with qualitative research and this can create difficulties for researchers . . . Some of the most common areas of misunderstanding in relation to qualitative research relate to the often small sample size and the lack of specific hypotheses, control groups and predetermined questions, which can lead to the false assumption that the proposed study is not sufficiently rigorous.

Truman (2003: 12) is also critical, highlighting the impact of research committees on particular types of participatory research (in which participants play an active role in research design and process) and that are now popular in the social sciences and social work:

> The way that processes of ethical review have been formulated is particularly problematic for researchers working within a participatory paradigm since they add a further set of barriers to the creation of democratic knowledge whereby people who are the subject of research production can influence how knowledge about them is conceived, produced and disseminated.

Butler (2002: 243–7) has proposed a fifteen point code of social work research ethics. Amongst other qualities and attributes the author suggests that social work researchers should endeavour wherever possible to:

- take practical and moral responsibility for their work;
- seek to empower service users and promote their welfare;
- respect human rights and 'aim towards social justice', especially for service users;
- be anti-discriminatory at all times;
- serve the greater good, and seek to avoid any harm for service users;
- inform all participants 'of all features of the research' and 'respect the individual participant's absolute right to decline to participate in or withdraw from [a] research programme';
- ensure confidentiality at all stages for research participants and service users;

- allow research participants the right to withdraw from a project at any point;
- report research findings even if they 'reflect unfavourably on agencies of the central or local state, vested interests . . . as well as prevailing wisdom and orthodox opinion';
- acknowledge any part played by participants.

McLaughlin (2007: 52) suggests that this code can be used alongside Banks's (2002) four point ethical rules for practice that stress respect for people, the promotion of service user empowerment, the aim to support social justice and endeavours to maximize the interests of service users.

There are, however, some problems attached to any attempt to create a professional code of research ethics. For example, a paradox persists between (minority) professional interests (for example, power, status and financial reward) and what may appear as rhetorical claims to protect and support service users. Also most dissertations and pieces of qualitative research demand creativity, flair, and the use of initiative – qualities that are likely to be restricted within the confines of a rigid code. As Holdaway (1982, cited in Seale *et al.*, 2004: 8) argues, professional codes of ethics tend to 'deal with predictable and planned research, conditions which are not present in field-work'. Some researchers may also argue that a small piece of research that bypasses one or two rules relating to a code – yet which may lead to wider forms of social justice being achieved later on – is ethical due to the eventual political *outcomes* rather than the research *process*. As Seale *et al.* (2004: 8–9) propose:

> [critics] maintain . . . that covert research is ethical when the social actor observed plays a public/civic function or service for service users, customers and clients . . . Professional ethical codes for researchers are too often constituted as armchair criticism, distanced from the needs of the research practice. In addition, even if ethical codes aim to be universal, they are a product of a local culture and . . . are not easily exported outside the original culture.

For such reasons, as Butler (2002) himself acknowledges, codes of ethics tend to require continuous reform and revision. Despite possible deficits the code of ethics for social work does offer a useful summary of non-discriminatory practices, and also attempts to encourage critical research which may question state agencies and the authority of their representatives. As McLaughlin (2007: 54) suggests, such codes offer clear guidance 'on how to act and as a means to protect research subjects from malpractice or abuse'.

The following list seeks to offer a general guideline regarding some key ethical issues for a social work dissertation. They include the need to:

- always seek permission from a reliable and dependable source for any intended empirical research and inform research participants of what you are doing;
- discuss any potential concerns or uncertainties with your personal tutor or module supervisor regarding the ethics of an intended approach;
- maintain respect, honesty and trust with research participants and identify each as an *equal* rather than as an *object* of observation or study;
- avoid forms of discrimination or prejudice at all times, including pre-conceived assumptions or stereotypes relating to the cultural habits, behaviour or attitudes of particular groups of people (for example, older people or members of minority religious or ethnic groups);
- avoid covert and other forms of 'hidden' research – in general such potentially devious research is unlikely to be granted permission from an ethics committee or supervisor;
- avoid harm and risk to participants, and carefully consider any implications of undertaking direct research with vulnerable people, such as children or adults with a learning disability;
- ensure privacy, confidentiality and anonymity, especially regarding personal and other sensitive information gained from participants or elsewhere;
- aim for advocacy and empowerment;
- seek to encourage social justice within your overall research wherever possible;
- decide where data is likely to be stored and ensure that there is no risk of sensitive information being lost or gained access to.

By its very nature social research has always held a potential to encourage positive social change – such as by allowing disadvantaged groups to have a voice or drawing attention to forms of social injustice. For some people involved in social work research, such as Dominelli (2002) or Humphries (2008), this remains the only form of research that can be identified as being truly ethical.

Summary

This chapter has highlighted the benefits of small scale research within social work education, training and potentially practice. In particular, more in-depth and substantive research with smaller groups, or theoretically centred literature based research, can help us understand the social problems and issues that we will confront as part of social work practice. There are now different routes that lead to a social work dissertation via courses, but many tasks and themes within each are similar.

Among other benefits social work research can offer new insights, and at its most ambitious, research may also support us to become better social workers by allowing us to fully appreciate and understand the social needs that we aim to meet. It should also help us to become more aware of service users, as well as how best to meet their needs. Finally, qualitative research should also be able to help us to become more reflexive – that is to look critically at our own beliefs and practices, as well as the activities and principles of related organizations, colleagues, other professionals, and so forth. As Lynch (2000: 95) suggests:

> Those who have experiential knowledge of inequality and injustice can ally this understanding with academic knowledge to create a new and deeper knowledge of their world. This deeper understanding can [help us] challenge established 'wisdoms' and 'ideologies' around inequality and injustice.

Social work research also has some distinct qualities, including its attempt to apply different theories from diverse disciplines so to understand a variety of social needs. It also stresses the centrality of applied ethics, and most prominently the need to strive to protect and empower service users wherever possible.

The next chapter looks at the overall *process* of social work research for a dissertation.

Suggested reading

Corby, B. (2006) *Applying Research in Social Work Practice*. Maidenhead: Open University Press. (Chapter 2: Research and social work – an uneasy alliance over time)

D'Cruz, H. and Jones, M. (2004) *Social Work Research: Ethical and Political Contexts*. London: Sage. (Chapter 1: Research, social work and professional practice)

Humphries, B. (2008) *Social Work Research for Social Justice*. Basingstoke: Palgrave Macmillan. (Chapter 1: Introduction: research as contentious)

McLaughlin, H. (2007) *Understanding Social Work Research*. London: Sage. (Chapter 1: Why research for social work?)

Padgett, D.K. (1998) *Qualitative Methods in Social Work Research – Challenges and Rewards*. London: Sage. (Chapter 1: Introduction)

2 The research process for a social work dissertation

Introduction

This chapter explores eight stages followed when completing a social work dissertation. The remainder of the book discusses each in more detail. The stages are outlined in Figure 2.1. It is critical to recognize that any research process followed within social work, or indeed most forms of qualitative research, are rarely linear in practice. The stages followed are unlikely to be rigidly predicted or precisely planned in advance. Instead research process stages typically overlap and also spread throughout a project. As Padgett (1998: 30) notes: 'Qualitative researchers find themselves going back and forth between the stages of problem formation, data collection, data analysis, and write up. This process is rarely linear, but instead zigs and zags depending on where the data lead.' For example, although the writing up of a dissertation is usually assumed to take place towards an end stage, in practice this can begin *to develop* or be initiated much earlier. Also, despite an intense period dedicated to each stage, aspects of the literature review are also likely to be dispersed *throughout* a project. This is because each stage tends to be

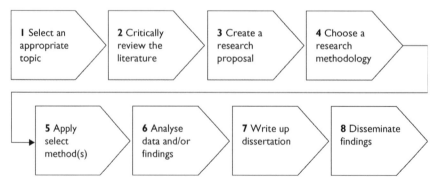

Figure 2.1 The stages of a dissertation.

dispersed into core elements of the overall research. Depending upon the topic there can also be differences in the amounts of time and effort that go into each stage for separate projects. For example, some dissertations may involve an extensive and ongoing literature review, while others may concentrate more on the collection and analysis of data. Each process is now explored in detail below.

1 Select an *appropriate* topic

A research topic is an area of particular interest or an issue that requires further investigation.

A research question is a statement that details a query which briefly summarises what it is you hope to investigate. It is a detailed question that will be answered to the best of your abilities during research processes followed for your dissertation. Typically a research question is summarized in one sentence.

The selection of a topic, or the asking of a research question, is sometimes assumed to be the most straightforward and least time-consuming stage of a dissertation. In practice, however, it can prove a more challenging task, and if uncertain for an extended period, it can potentially waste precious time. This is especially the case if an *inappropriate* topic is selected and a project is then started and abandoned later on.

Below are five questions you need to ask regarding a potential topic:

- Why is the research necessary? For example, is it likely to reveal anything that is not already known or established?
- Is the research relevant to your course? Does it link *explicitly* to social work practice and/or is it likely to improve the methods utilized by yourself or other practitioners?
- Is it likely to offer new insights regarding an aspect of social work theory or practice?
- Do you have some experience or knowledge relating to the topic? Without either the project may still be possible, but inevitably it may be more difficult to complete to a satisfactory level.
- Do you have adequate time and resources to achieve all of the likely aims and objectives of the research? If not, you might consider narrowing the focus of your topic.

Royse (1991: 38) suggests that research topics within social work nearly always emerge from a research question or the identification of a recognized social problem that needs to be improved or solved. In relation to this, Fairclough (2001) argues that human and social science disciplines such as social work should target social *problems* instead of asking research questions; especially with a view to critically assessing each and finding ways of overcoming them.

It is imperative to ensure that your topic research question and/or social problem are not too broad or over ambitious. This is a common error made not merely by some social work students but also by professional researchers. The more specific you are, and the more detailed your plans, then the better your research is likely to progress. Dawson (2007: 5) has suggested that as with an initial research question, all research topics should be able to be summed up in one sentence. If this is not possible then it is likely that your research topic 'is too broad'. This can be a useful exercise at the beginning of a project. In practice however it can take time for an initial idea to develop and become more focused – simply because further reading is sometimes required to develop and fine tune a topic.

Another tip is to avoid selecting a topic that is *too* narrow, vague, obscure, or just trivial. In order to support a dissertation you will need adequate published material to support the next (and key) stage, that of the literature review. Inevitably with little or no published material relating to a topic it is unlikely that your project can be sustained. Also, if you intend to investigate a social group through empirical research then deciding whether contact can be achieved (or not) may be important.

Bell (1987: 11) has argued convincingly that it can help to 'prepare the groundwork' before deciding upon any research topic. In relation to social work this might include scouring core journals such as the *British Journal of Social Work, Critical Social Policy* or *Qualitative Social Work*, so as to investigate whether or not adequate research has been undertaken relating to your topic. Looking through journals, or just scouring the shelves in the library, can also be a good way to stimulate ideas for a topic.

Once decided you should also consult your tutor to verify if your topic is suitable. Dawson (2007: 5–8) has proposed five core questions to ask prior to deciding whether or not to pursue a topic. They are:

1   What *exactly is your research attempting to achieve?* You should be able to summarize your core intention(s) for the project in a brief paragraph, and then reduce your title to a sentence. This sentence or statement contains the essence of what it is you are hoping to achieve and therefore can be returned to, and possibly revised, as the research proceeds.

2   Why *do you want to pursue your chosen topic?* Be careful to ask yourself whether or not a chosen topic will sustain interest and also be helpful for future practice and other intentions.

3   Who *will be your participants?* You will need to decide whether or not you want to interview or observe people for your research. For example, students sometimes interview practitioners while on a practice placement. This is feasible but it is imperative to check with a

tutor prior to any plans to interview. Alternatively, you can instead concentrate on the literature and focus much more on theoretical and conceptual concerns.

4   Where *are you going to conduct your research?* You may wish to undertake literature or discourse based research in the library. Alternatively, you may undertake empirical research in an organization where you work voluntarily. You could also approach practitioners at other placement or welfare employment sites, such as a hospital, clinic or school. In practice, projects based away from any practice placement base tend to be more difficult to complete, and there are also issues around any related ethic committee obligations. For example, if you are hoping to interview practitioners based in a hospital you may have to pass through a health trust committee as well as a university or college panel. In practice this will take up considerable time and permission may not be granted by one or either panel.

5   When *will you be completing most of the tasks?* If you intend to concentrate upon a literature based dissertation then it is likely that most of the tasks will be fairly evenly spread out from the beginning. Empirical research is much more difficult to plan and spread. This is because you cannot always know when it is that people are free to be interviewed, and their plans can change. Despite this, it is still imperative to make some rough plans and also not to leave everything till the last minute. If you need to gain ethical approval or write to other organizations for permission to access participants this may potentially take up a great deal of time, so try to begin as soon as is reasonably possible.

Possible topics

Possible research topics for a dissertation include:

1 Theory based
This may involve focusing upon the impact that one specific theory has had on social work practice. Such a theory might include one that has become neglected but which may still have much to offer. For example, you may wish to consider the impact of systems or labelling theory, or perhaps compare the impact of two theories over time. You could consider how any one theory has impacted upon practice with a service user group while you were on a practice placement, or compare the different influences that sociological theories have had in contrast to psychological paradigms. Potentially multiple possibilities persist, with placement settings and personal areas of specialist practice providing a good basis for a more focused study.

> **Examples:** *Contrast the influence of the medical and social model of dementia care upon social work practice with older people; the impact of labelling theory in social work with young offenders; utilizing feminist theory in residential care provision for young women with autism – case study; the changing use of theory regarding social work practice with families – a critical evaluation.*

2 Law

Ways in which a piece of legislation has influenced social work practice might be investigated. You may want to critically assess the effect of a specific Act of Parliament over a period of time on a service user group, or attempt to predict the eventual consequences of a new White Paper. Alternatively critically evaluating how legislation is interpreted in practice by social workers, such as while drawing from experiences on a practice placement, may be appropriate. Again many different permutations are possible.

> **Examples:** *Contextualizing the impact of aspects of the 1990 NHS and Community Care Act upon care managers within a local authority social service department; the 1983 Mental Health Act – a critical appraisal of core principles regarding young men in supported living; critical overview of core aspects of the 1989 Children Act; a critique of the sustained impact of the core principles of the 1834 Poor Law Amendment Act upon social work with vulnerable adults.*

3 Social policy

Another discipline strongly linked to social work is social policy. Again an overview of an aspect of social policy relating to social work could be undertaken or make up the basis for a reflexive review of the available published literature. Again this might be linked to personal experiences relating to a practice placement – perhaps with a view to constructive recommendations for future policy makers or practitioners being made? Another popular option remains comparing different policies applied in two different countries.

> **Examples:** *Comparing and contrasting adoption policy in Sweden and Scotland; the effect of community care policy upon a group of older men with a physical disability living in residential care in South London; the impact of asylum policy over the past five years upon a group of state social workers involved in adoption services in Liverpool, England; Sure Start: a critical assessment of support work with teenage mothers in South Birmingham.*

4 Service user groups

Students can explore and potentially gain a better understanding of the needs that particular service user groups require. A dissertation exploring a client group in depth may also offer an opportunity to address themes not covered on every social work course. For example, you may be offered only limited discussion of social work related topics around homelessness or HIV/AIDS, and a dissertation could offer an excellent opportunity to explore such issues in more detail.

> **Examples:** *The unmet needs of older men with depressive mental health problems – a case study; social work responses to young people living with schizophrenia in a rural community; statutory social work interventions with women experiencing alcohol addiction – a 'team' case study; supporting younger people with HIV/AIDS – a critical overview of the social work research literature.*

5 Types of intervention

Specific types of social work intervention, including those witnessed or experienced on a practice placement or as a part of previous work experience, might also provide the foundation to a dissertation. Instead you might wish to discuss the demise of some practices, such as group work or counselling within many areas of state social work in Canada and the UK (Carey, 2003; Baines, 2004). Your study might instead critically assess one of a range of current or possible future interventions.

> **Examples:** *The impact of group work on older men based in a residential care home; disadvantages of bureaucratic interventions in work with adults with a learning difficulty – a practice placement study; alternative 'social work' practices in a day centre – a case study.*

6 Social trends

A demographic or social trend that is having an impact upon social work practice might be investigated. For example, a dissertation that explored the effect of asylum seekers migrating to the UK, and how this links to social work practice, might be possible. Alternatively, a student might investigate the likely impact of a continued increase in the numbers of heterosexual older people diagnosed with HIV/AIDS.

> **Examples:** *Consequences of the increase in contingency social work in England and Wales; social work with young black women who self-harm in an inner-London borough; the 'problem' of the demographic time bomb regarding social work with older people – a critique.*

There will be other potential topics to explore. It is possible that your module leader or tutor may have particular preferences or interests which could help support a topic. Sometimes a dissertation can represent a compromise between your own interests and external factors that include potential access to a sample, the type of practice placement setting where you are based, course and module requirements, available resources or time, and so forth.

2 Critically review the literature

The literature review represents a crucial stage in the research process. As Alston and Bowles (1998: 64, my emphasis) stress:

> Conducting a literature review is a *vital* part of your research . . . A literature review allows you to discover what knowledge is already available about the issue you want to investigate, and to determine how your study will differ from existing work and hence add to our knowledge in the area . . . it [also] enables you to conceptually frame your work.

The literature review also supports all of the other stages of research – from proposal and methodology, right through to the write up and dissemination. This is because it provides a *foundation* of established knowledge that you can build on, develop and steer in a new direction.

As Royse (1991: 40) summarizes, a literature review is essentially an attempt to discover 'what others have written about a topic' so that you can go on to 'relate your problem or hypothesis to existing theory'. Importantly you do not simply gather together literature that relates to your topic and then read and internalize it passively. Instead you will also need to pull out key themes, critically assess points being made, and analyse the arguments while paying careful attention to how this knowledge fits with and influences your area of study. As an aid you can also look at the references that other authors cite – often you will discover helpful sources that relate to your dissertation. In practice a literature review will go on to not only influence the selection and construction of a set of research method(s) and methodology, but also will regularly alter any direction taken during a project. This will sometimes include a revision of the initial research question and topic.

3 Create a research proposal

For any dissertation there is usually an expectation that you complete a research proposal. This helps to *clarify* what it is you need to do and how you plan to fulfil any research expectations. A proposal also allows a tutor or supervisor to assess potential difficulties, and in response they may suggest some revisions to your initial plans. Bear in mind that a proposal is a *provisional* estimate of intended work. Therefore it is assumed that this is likely to change slightly, or occasionally more drastically, as the research progresses. The main sections that compromise the format of a typical proposal include:

Title

This should be brief and succinct – ideally you should aim to present no more than a sentence that captures and also explains your intended research and topic. At this stage the title is assumed to be provisional.

Background

In this section you will need to offer the reader a *brief* introduction to the topic and also convince a supervisor or tutor that you have adequately prepared following a literature review. Some references to key published sources that link to a topic are likely to help regarding this task. In addition, you also need to answer two key questions. First, why are you undertaking this research, and second, why is the research needed?

Aims and objectives

Like the title this remains a crucial section of any proposal and it is often the section that a supervisor will be especially keen to check. As Dawson (2007: 60–1) notes, the aims are 'the overall driving force of the research' and typically, like the title, they can be summarized in one sentence. The objectives refer to 'the means by which you intend to achieve the aims', and they represent the substance or building blocks of a dissertation. The objectives tend to be more detailed and are typically summarized in three or more separate sentences (as indicated in Table 2.1).

Although research aims and objectives often alter as research progresses, experience suggests that a good proposal often supports a superior dissertation. The example presented in Table 2.1 offers some guidance on how to link a title with research aims and objectives. It is extremely specific and clearly pinpoints the nature of the project in hand. It deals with broad issues (social work with older people and care management and use of advocacy skills) and a specific form of analysis that will be undertaken. As the research develops some of the objectives may be reduced or even discarded, and the topic may become even more focussed. This is a relatively common process, typically due to a glut of findings which the student does not have adequate time to process and evaluate.

Table 2.1   Example of a title and the aims and objectives for a dissertation proposal

---

Title: *The use of advocacy skills amongst care managers working with older people – an exploration of empirical research utilizing critical theory*

Aims: To critically explore the use of advocacy skills among care managers working within a Social Service Department

Objectives: The research seeks to:

1. Determine the nature, forms and extent of advocacy skills used in practice by care managers working with older people
2. Determine the ways in which theory, or other forms of knowledge, are utilized by care managers when applying forms of advocacy with service users
3. Determine the possible restrictions that hinder the use of advocacy in practice for care managers
4. Utilize aspects of critical theory within the methodology and apply these so as to understand and help explain the overall findings

---

Methodology and method

Both these sections are combined for some proposals. They allow a tutor to see exactly *how* you intend to undertake any research. As was first explored in Chapter 1, methodology is the *general principle* of any research which includes its philosophy and theoretic input, and this is an essential component of any proposal as it offers a theoretical framework or structure. Within the example in Table 2.1 the student has decided to draw upon the beliefs of critical theory to guide and frame their overall research. Due to this they are likely to explore, and possibly then question, the effectiveness of the care management policy in encouraging forms of practitioner advocacy. As was explained earlier, for Bachelor degrees and some Post-qualification routes, an explicit methodology may not be necessary; instead the identification of research methods may be enough to guide your research.

Method refers to the *tools* by which data or information relating to a topic is collected. For example, a method such as conducting interviews can be utilized as part of empirical or applied research. In the example in Table 2.1 the student eventually decided to use interviews with care managers in order to investigate and explore her research aims and objectives.

Finally you will need to also consider why you have selected a particular methodology and/or methods, and how each fits with a topic and research aims and objectives. In the example in Table 2.1 the student selected critical theory because the majority of publications she came across were critical of care managers' capacity to advocate on behalf of their service users. The student also believed that personal one on one interviews with her research participants would allow practitioners' personal feelings to be more openly expressed.

Timetable

You may need to indicate how long each research stage will take. In general try to be realistic and account for any likely problems such as difficulties gaining access to participants or the availability of relevant literature in the library.

The content that a supervisor will look for within a dissertation research proposal will include:

- that a topic links *directly* to the course;
- that a clear and feasible title is provided;
- that clear, succinct and *realistic* aims and objectives are offered;
- that there is a bond between the title, methodology and method(s), and the research questions can be answered by the methodology and/ or method;
- that the project can be completed on time and will not cost too much;
- that enough relevant detail and information is provided;
- that there is limited risk of possible problems;
- and that evidence of adequate background reading has been completed.

(Adapted from Jones, 1983: 112–14; Greene and Browne, 2005: 23–31; Dawson, 2007: 62–5)

Research committee applications

Each university or college tends to have their own procedure to follow regarding research committee applications. Personal tutors should be able to offer advice on how to follow any relevant procedures. Typically, for research that involves interviews or any other form of direct contact with participants, there will be a form to complete and submit for consideration by a committee, which will usually be made up of senior academics and possibly one or two practitioners.

For an archetypal application some of the following sections will need to be considered:

Title Provide a short and focused title relating to the proposed project.

Research question/aims and objectives Clearly present any research question; once again this should be compressed into one sentence.

The aims and objectives should be succinct, clear and realistic rather than broad, unclear or over ambitious.

Participants Detail who the participants will be and how many are likely to be approached and involved in the research.

Method You will need to identify how participants will be approached or recruited. Also, how will informed consent (permission based upon a clear understanding of the facts or consequences of an action) be gained and what will participants be asked to do as part of any research? Other questions, such as whether participants will be debriefed about the research, may also be asked. Finally, a committee is likely to want to know how any information or data collected will be handled safely and securely, and also how confidentiality will be maintained for participants.

It is imperative to think carefully about these questions and to make it clear that you have, or intend to, make some plans to accommodate each in advance. Many ethic committee members, especially those with a background in a health related discipline, like to see evidence of pre-planning and foresight, and some may wish to see examples of questions you plan to ask if this relates to your preferred research method.

Ethical considerations This may include issues relating to informed consent and how this might be gained from participants – for example, will there be a relevant form to sign? Confidentiality is also important: are there any plans to ensure confidentiality regarding any information collected from participants? How will any results from your research be used? For example, do you plan to publish any material or are the findings likely to only be used for the dissertation? Finally, will any vulnerable groups be used as part of the research process, and if so, how is this justified? These remain important questions that should be carefully considered and answered as succinctly and clearly as possible. Overall the panel will be keen to see at least some evidence that you have made some plans and are aware of ethical dilemmas relating to empirical research.

Benefit and potential risks to participants Ask yourself whether there are any ways in which the research might benefit participants. For example, will it allow excluded voices to be heard or perhaps draw attention to, or promote, a cause that has otherwise generated little attention within social work?

Potential risks to consider can include those that relate to physical or psychological harm in extreme cases; including if sensitive issues are to be discussed. Try to articulate how you intend to reduce the risks of potential negative outcomes if this is possible, and again try to show evidence of careful thought and planning relating to any such possible occurrences. In general, it is better to avoid discussing potentially sensitive issues with participants as part of any intended research, especially if groups are identified as vulnerable. If you feel that this is unavoidable or ethically just, then you will need to be extra vigilant when documenting this section of the form.

Systems for disseminating research findings back to service users, practitioners, etc. This section concerns whether any plans for formal dissemination to participants following analysis of your findings and possible recommendations have been made. This may not be compulsory but it could strengthen any case with an ethics committee or tutor or if you feel that it is an ethical priority. If so, such plans should be briefly declared.

Consent Has a consent form been created for participants? This section may be compulsory and will usually need to be signed by participants prior to any formal method being applied.

Appendices The committee may request that any relevant forms, such as those relating to a plan of interview questions, be attached.

It can be difficult to identify in advance the answer to some of these questions since it may be too early to know for sure how the dissertation is likely to proceed come the time of any empirical research. For example, a student may not know prior to undertaking empirical research how they intend to disseminate their findings (if at all) once they have been analysed.

It is advisable to answer as many questions as possible prior to submission and state clearly any reason(s) why a section or question cannot be answered. It is also advisable to talk to a tutor regarding any application to an ethics committee, and ideally they should have checked it before it is forwarded to a panel. Your tutor may also have copies of previous successful applications that may assist in your application. Although any application to an ethics committee can seem daunting at first, in practice this assessment process as part of any dissertation will help to clarify a research question and any subsequent research process. Such clarity is then likely to save considerable time that might otherwise have been lost with unclear plans. My own experience suggests that the ethical committee process is ideal for clarifying the focus of a topic and also helps to ensure that vulnerable groups are adequately protected.

4 Choose or construct a research methodology

Methodology is sometimes presented as a form of 'recipe' by which to guide a research project (Daly, 2003: 192). An aspect of this may relate explicitly to theoretical influences which inspire and direct your research. A methodology should also provide a philosophical *framework* around which to structure a dissertation – that is, it should be able to bind together into a coherent whole (as well as direct) your ideas, approaches, and methods utilized. A methodology can also accommodate wider themes beyond practice based research methods, most notably the ethical implications or dilemmas (discussed in Chapter 1) that are linked to all forms of social research.

A methodology can be represented by a theory such as feminism or anti-discriminatory practice. A methodology can also be represented by a substantial and wide ranging method, such as narrative research (explored in Chapter 8), or can encompass a particular set of research methods that form into a coherent whole – such as through evaluation research (explored in Chapter 6). Finally, a methodology can utilize research methods that are compatible to explore a specific topic, such as interviews or focus group research that aim to capture the attitudes of practitioners or informal carers regarding their role.

It is important to consider carefully how any data may be collected and what type of methodology may suit requirements, such as the need to collect information in order to be able to explore and answer your identified research question.

5 Apply select method(s)

A research method is a procedure, practice or set of techniques that are used to identify and explore research questions and a means by which to 'collect and analyse data, and present findings' (Payne and Payne, 2004: 149). The analogy of the 'tool' is often used, but such tools must recognize possible limitations. The most common method used in both social and social work research is the face to face interview, although other methods including focus group research can also been utilized (Shaw and Gould, 2001). Some methodologies are also a type of method, most notably narrative or discourse analysis, which offers not merely a general philosophy and ethical framework but also a technical means by which to collect information or data. The selection of appropriate method(s) can save time, improve the quality of work and also increase the chances of completion.

6 Analyse data and findings

The analysis of data or findings is vital to all forms of qualitative research. This process typically begins during the literature review and continues through to the end of a project. Analysis attempts to critically investigate and unearth meaning and understanding by rigorously exploring themes, perspectives, trends, issues or outcomes that relate to a research question and subsequent aims and objectives. Three examples of data analysis include:

1   *Thematic analysis.* This approach attempts to look for specific identified themes within data and other findings, which can include social trends, patterns or outcomes that can be used to generate debate and draw conclusions from.

2   *Comparative analysis.* This approach is sometimes used alongside thematic analysis. It identifies *contrasting* research themes, homes in on them and then compares and assesses any related data or findings. Typically two themes or case examples (a policy, type of social work practice, pieces of legislation, etc.) are compared and contrasted within one single topic or project. Sometimes comparative analysis can become a dissertation in itself, such as when two countries are compared regarding aspects of their social policy or legislation.

3   *Critical analysis.* This approach draws from a variety of influential theoretical sources including feminism, Marxism and interpretivism (each is explored in Chapter 4). The emphasis is very much upon discussing and explaining forms of social disadvantage, discrimination and forms of inequality or injustice, such as those linked to gender, 'race', disability or class. Critical analysis also tends to explore wider themes and link the 'micro' experiences of individuals with wider 'macro' forces such as those linked to language, culture, institutional practices and government policies.

(Adapted from Payne and Payne, 2004: 214–15;
Dawson, 2007: 112–22)

Analysis is explored in much greater detail in Chapter 9.

7 Write up your dissertation

The penultimate stage of any research process is sometimes not given the attention it requires. Swetnam (2000: 99) argues that writing up should be 'regarded as the tidying-up section', that is, the majority of research tasks should already be complete and the write up allows any ideas and discoveries to be brought together. As well as the exercise of writing itself, Swetnam also argues that dissertations or reports should be proofread 'at least twice'.

As with the process of analysis, writing should begin as early as possible. This is beneficial because it:

- allows time to develop your writing skills;
- promotes the development of thoughts and ideas;
- may encourage you to contextualize and analyse your research as it unravels;

Regarding structure and content there are two main types of dissertation – first an empirical and second a conceptual or theoretical (sometimes known as 'pure' research). Each type will be structured differently within a final write up, and Chapters 6 and 10 give examples of each.

8 Disseminate findings

As D'Cruz and Jones (2004: 169) highlight, dissemination, or ways in which we distribute and circulate our research findings, is 'not something we [should] hope to achieve simply by writing up our findings'. As is illustrated in the final chapter, there are other ways to disseminate research findings, including during social work practice itself.

Case examples

Table 2.2 and 2.3 show two examples of social work dissertations. In Table 2.2 – a thesis which involved empirical research and explored care management with people with a disability and subsequent assessments of need – has been broken down and presented in eight stages. In Table 2.3 the stages of a theory based dissertation are presented.

The empirical dissertation followed the usual stages for a thesis that involves interviews with social work practitioners (or care managers). It utilized a methodology based on critical theory which allowed the student to explore her research themes within a literature review as the interviews proceeded. The student undertook interviews at her practice placement setting with six care managers, each with a minimum of seven years experience regarding disability related social work and assessment. Each care manager was asked five core questions that linked directly to the student's research aims and objectives. Other questions were sometimes asked, such as if practitioner's answers were unclear.

As the empirical research progressed aspects of the findings contrasted

Table 2.2 The stages of a social work dissertation involving empirical research

Stage	Outcome
1 Topic/research question	How do care managers working with people with a disability believe that their assessment skills could be improved?
2 Proposal	Aims and objectives included a plan to interview care managers at practice placement setting about their attitudes and feelings regarding the assessment process. Plan to also use critical theory to build and develop theory around care managers' responses.
3 Literature review	Academic journal papers (for example, *British Journal of Social Work*; *Critical Social Policy*; *Disability and Society*, etc.); Textbooks (for example, covering community care policy, social work and disability; social policy, etc.); Magazines (for example, *Community Care*), etc.
4 Methodology	Critical theory
5 Methods	In-depth semi-structured interviews with 6 care managers specializing in the needs of adults with a physical disability
6 Analyse data and findings	Looked for key trends and themes amidst transcripts and notes taken during interviews. Compared any findings with previous published empirical research. All but one care manager argued that bureaucracy, performance targets and limited time available to spend with service users and carers influenced their assessment work
7 Write up	Chapter 1: Introduction; Chapter 2: Literature review; Chapter 3: Methodology; Chapter 4: Findings; Chapter 5: Analysis and discussion; Chapter 6: Discussion and conclusions
8 Dissemination	Conversations; professional and non-professional practice.

with some findings detailed in previous publications. In particular, management and training styles were not identified by practitioners as being as detrimental to the assessment process as excess paper work or limited time available to spend with service users. Over the course of a six month period the study became more focused as the student delved into the literature and gathered together and assessed any new data. This process of continued reading helped in the design of the questions asked to practitioners, which in turn facilitated the production of much clearer results.

The student made clear recommendations in her conclusion that drew from her findings. These included a need to increase practitioners' available time to spend with service users, reduce unnecessary bureaucracy and increase available resources for support services. The student also discovered that according to the care managers the opinions expressed by informal carers often played a key role throughout the assessment process. Finally, upon qualification the research findings influenced the student's practice: especially

Table 2.3   The stages of a theory based dissertation

Stage	Outcome
1 Topic/research question	Has the impact of an increase in the proportion of older people on the demand for social and other welfare services been exaggerated?
2 Proposal	Aims and objectives were to consider different sources of information, including government and critical journals or textbooks that evaluated and analysed predictions. Particular attention was targeted upon the likely impact upon social work practice of an increase in the numbers of older people.
3 Literature review	Student scoured government census data and reports; social trends; journal articles; reliable websites; media articles (via web searches, library documents, etc).
4 Methodology	Discourse analysis
5 Method	Discourse analysis
6 Analyse data and findings	Looked for key trends and overall findings from literature and compared with prior research. Research acknowledged likely increase in proportion of older people but disparities were noted in the *interpretation* of consequences. These included the discovery that media reports had tended to exaggerate and sensationalize many of the recent or likely demographic trends and, at times, reported factual inaccuracies. In particular narrative styles were emotive, biased and also seemed to endeavour to agitate readers. Small but growing numbers of retired people were employed part-time and paid taxes, etc.
7 Write up	Chapter 1: Introduction; Chapter 2: Methodology; Chapter 3: Older people, demographics and social services; Chapter 4: Interpreting government statistics and media reports; Chapter 5: Moral panics, older people and social work; Chapter 6: Conclusion: Future directions for social work with older people
8 Dissemination	Conversations; professional and non-professional practice.

how she approached the assessment process and communicated with service users.

In contrast to the empirical approach above the dissertation summarized in Table 2.3 involved a piece of research that was built around an extensive literature review. This dissertation began with a broad topic that linked together older people, social work and welfare services. Quickly, however, following the gathering together and reading of related published material, the topic became more focused. Consequentially, some initial themes that the student had hoped to explore were taken out, while others tended to expand in emphasis and became a key part of the aims and objectives of the dissertation. This process of giving more attention to specific themes continued as the research and reading evolved.

The student concentrated upon media and government related reports of an imminent 'demographic time bomb' that would generate considerable financial and other costs following an assumed increased provision of welfare support services (especially pensions, health related and social work). Through a methodology influenced by discourse analysis (discussed in Chapter 8), different texts were carefully read and analysed regarding emerging structures of grammar, syntax and the use of particular emotive words.

The tendency for misinformation and bias within reports that seemed to encourage a largely negative view of older people as welfare dependant, and sometimes a burden, were stressed. This, and other more critical sources which countered many of the arguments presented regarding seemingly 'dependant' older people, led the student to offer a more balanced account of current and future outcomes. Indeed many of the student's findings were more positive than the negative accounts portrayed by the media, which had tended to exaggerate likely needs and ignore contributions made by older people. This research later helped the student in her work with older people, and she was also able to disseminate her findings to colleagues.

Although each dissertation drew on different approaches (notably empirical and theory based research) each followed a similar process. For example, both began with quite broad ideas that narrowed in focus as the research progressed and reading intensified. Also each project was built upon a firm methodological base. Finally, each project unearthed some new and original findings that influenced each student's practice.

Supervision

Throughout a research project any allocated supervisor or tutor remains a valuable resource who should be able to offer advice, guidance and support. Supervisors typically:

- provide general support and, if necessary, direction;
- broaden the learning experience;
- offer specialist knowledge and advice, including regarding a topic;
- advise on related reading material (a particularly important role);
- endow overall guidance on the research process, including key stages such as the methodology, methods and writing up;
- ensure that you are focused and do not wander off unnecessarily from your initial topic;

- offer information regarding your institution's (and module's) regulations and rules relating to the dissertation;
- discuss your research and share ideas;
- help to link theory with practice for social work;
- if necessary, inspire and motivate you.

While drawing upon many years experience Swetnam (2000: 27) concludes that 'failures and non-submissions [of dissertations] are heavily dominated by those who have declined to see tutors'. My own experience supports this and also suggests that there is a link between regularly attending supervision and the submission of superior dissertations with higher grades. Despite this, any student still remains the key player at the centre of any research project for a dissertation, as Blaxter *et al.* (1996: 139, my emphasis) warn: 'investing *too much* authority or responsibility in key figures in your research life is likely to lead to disappointment. It is as important to develop your own sense of authority and responsibility'.

It is beneficial to utilize a supervisor when necessary and at certain junctures – such as regarding the points identified in the bulleted list above. You should also try to:

- make appointments in advance and keep to any dates and time planned;
- try to decide before any meetings what it is you need to ask your supervisor – possibly write down a list of questions to ask;
- *always take notes* when in supervision, especially regarding useful references, material and advice;
- allow your supervisor to see some of your findings and perhaps a sample of your written work following any draft stage;
- take responsibility for your work and avoid asking supervisors to fulfil tasks that are clearly not a part of their role.

Summary

This chapter has stressed that most if not all dissertations follow a similar set of rituals within an overall research process. Most projects proceed through eight stages – topic selection and research question; research proposal; literature review; choice of methodology; selections of method(s); collection and analysis of data; the write up, and finally the dissemination of findings. Despite this, qualitative research is distinct from quantitative research in that movement *between* stages, including back and forth, is relatively common.

A number of recommendations have also been made. Among others these include the benefits of personal planning and attending supervision sessions with an allocated tutor, as well as beginning any research as early as possible and endeavouring to reduce and focus your aims and objectives that link to any topic. Following general stages of research should allow your work to develop with a clearer structure, and also help you avoid problems such as having to complete too many stages at once towards the end!

The next chapter begins to consider some key qualitative research concepts.

Suggested reading

Bell, J. (2005) *Doing Your Research Project*, 4th edn. Maidenhead: Open University Press. (Chapter 2: Planning the project)

Blaxter, L., Hughes, C., Tight, M. (2006) *How To Research*. Maidenhead: Open University Press. (Chapter 2: Getting started; Chapter 5: Managing your project)

Dawson, C. (2007) *A Practical Guide to Research Methods*. London: How To Books. (Chapter 1: How to define your project)

D'Cruz, H. and Jones, M. (2004) *Social Work Research – Ethical and Political Contexts*. London: Sage. (Chapter 2: The research question)

Greene, J. and Browne, J. (2005) *Principles of Social Research*. Maidenhead: Open University Press. (Chapter 3: Framing a research question)

Padgett, D.K. (1998) *Qualitative Methods in Social Work Research: Challenges and Rewards*. London: Sage. (Chapter 3: Choosing a topic and designing a study)

3 Key concepts in social work research

Introduction

This chapter looks at some important concepts relating to social work research. This includes a further exploration of qualitative research and the strong emphasis it places upon meaning and understanding. The distinction drawn between applied and pure research, and reliability and validity, are then discussed. Other social research concepts such as data, evidence, triangulation and sampling are also examined. Finally this chapter concludes by discussing inductive and deductive reasoning.

Qualitative research

As discussed in Chapter 1, the two key methodological approaches within social work, and more generally the social sciences, are quantitative and qualitative research. Quantitative research concentrates upon 'numerical measurement of specific aspects of phenomena', and its tradition or research *culture* has close links to the natural sciences. For this reason it has a tendency to rely upon the use of statistics, often processing extensive amounts of detailed information and typically involves contact with large numbers of people (Daly, 2003: 192). Due to a long held tradition of working with small numbers of people at a time within casework, as well as the often sensitive, informal and confidential nature of the social work task, the impact of quantitative approaches on social work research has sometimes been more limited. There are also schools of thought (notably feminism) that perceive quantitative research as failing to adequately explore, and therefore fully understand, research participants, and any related social issues being explored.

Qualitative research held within a social work dissertation instead attempts to explore in great detail themes such as the attitudes, behaviour and experiences of specific social groups. It may also seek to investigate a social problem or set of ethical dilemmas relating to social work practice. Regarding empirical research intense interviews or observations with small groups of people are typically utilized and then compared with existing theories. As a methodology which embraces a set of creative methods to collect and evaluate information, qualitative research can also seek to examine and explain social trends and offer cultural and/or political meaning through an ability to contextualize knowledge and gather or observe facts (Crotty, 1998). As Daly (2003: 193, my emphasis) stresses, meaning and context are usually vital elements embedded within qualitative research:

> Qualitative research seeks *meaning* (rather than *generality* as with its quantitative counterpart) and contributes to theory development by proceeding inductively. Meaning is achieved not by looking at particular features of many instances of a phenomenon but rather by looking at all aspects of the same phenomenon to see their interrelationships and establish how they come together to form a whole . . . One does not . . . separate out something from its *context*. Rather the phenomenon is studied in its context with the view that it is impossible to understand it apart from it.

Although sometimes accommodating less information due to the use of smaller samples or less data, a qualitative research methodology is still as likely to be as complex as any quantitative survey. This is due to the rigorous nature of the inquiry and the tendency to explore the many interrelating layers or causes of social phenomenon. As Crotty (1998: 67) suggests, there has remained a tendency to seek *understanding* alongside the quest for *explanation* found within much quantitative research. Despite this, quantitative research has still influenced many of the processes followed within qualitative research – for example, the tendency to plan and follow a research process, or engage with research procedures such as the questionnaire or pre-planned interview that draw significantly from related quantitative methods and techniques.

As there are usually fewer people involved in qualitative social work research it is often the case that more time is spent exploring any topic with research participants. If empirical, qualitative social work research will usually take place in a natural setting, such as a place of work or in another organization or setting that participants are familiar with. Qualitative research can also involve the exploration of other people's research and publications, such as by exploring the use and structure of language within narrative or discourse research, or simply by fulfilling an extensive literature review with specific goals. Here qualitative research will again look for trends or tendencies from any empirical or literature based research undertaken.

Applied and pure research

As suggested in Chapter 2, broadly speaking social work dissertations can be divided into two types – those that are based on either applied or 'pure' theoretical and conceptual research. Applied research tends to look at the relationship between theory and practice, and is especially concerned with identifying and attempting to solve practical or social problems. In contrast, pure research is more concerned with knowledge, trends, theory and abstract concepts.

Within social work applied research is often critical of aspects of government policy or legislation, especially those that directly influence key roles which social workers undertake. It may also stress the *impact* of policy and legislation on service users or informal carers, and explores essential concepts that usually influence their lives, such as poverty or discrimination. As a consequence applied social work research often argues the case for greater levels of equality and social justice (Humphries, 2008). It is also often the case following applied social work research that recommendations are made regarding reform(s) suggested by the researcher. However, applied research does not necessarily need to concentrate upon only policy and legislation. It may also be used to explore other topics such as the identity of practitioners or health professionals, issues that relate to gender, age, or mental health and social work practice, or the effect of attachment theory upon social work practice with vulnerable people, and so forth.

In contrast to applied research, 'pure' or basic research is propelled by attempts to expand debate, ideas, knowledge and understanding. Theories can include those that influence social work practice, such as network, labelling or critical theory. Social concepts can include themes and issues that influence social work practice, such as ethics, poverty, housing, gender, the ageing process and discrimination, among many others. Relevant themes relating to ethics or political understanding, especially those that link to social work practice, are also common. This form of theoretical or conceptual research involves an in-depth investigation of published material that relates to a topic being studied. Usually this will lead to an exploration of relevant journals, books, legal documentation, the Internet and government or independent reports, among other sources. Traditionally pure research has tended to be less prevalent in social work for dissertations, due mostly to the applied nature of social work practice and education.

Qualitative data, evidence and triangulation

Data represents the most basic 'building blocks' of research and many dissertations. It is identified as 'facts' or 'things' within qualitative research, and tends to be extremely varied. Examples can include the words, opinions or actions of participants, interview transcripts, remarks made in a diary, historical records, personal memos or recollections, and so on. Contrary to quantitative research, qualitative data can be difficult to measure and can also remain more ambivalent and open to interpretation. For example, how might a researcher seek to accurately measure emotions or power relations between colleagues? As a consequence 'data' has a somewhat different meaning within qualitative research, and, although important, is often not as pivotal to a social work dissertation as it may be to a research project driven by a quantitative methodology.

Ideally a student should seek to define as early as possible what they understand to be their qualitative data. Some form of measurement is an inevitable requirement because without this we cannot hope to look for trends, relationships or tendencies during any analysis. Despite being more susceptible to interpretation, and sometimes less precise or easy to grasp or measure, qualitative data is still just as legitimate and 'real'. As Walliman (2006: 55) remarks: 'Concepts such as poverty, comfort, friendship, etc., while elusive to measure, are nonetheless real and detectable.'

There are two main types of data – primary and secondary. Primary data is generated from direct observation, participation, personal experience or a large source of data such as a National Census. It can be gathered throughout participant observation, during an interview or focus group meeting or relate to notes taken from a diary or assessment form. This type of data relies upon our senses and also subjective interpretation of what is happening around us. It may also be represented by the meaning that a person is trying to convey during a conversation, or within a diary or report. Secondary data is where primary data has been processed or analysed, typically by other researchers. Examples include academic papers, chapters in books, newspaper reports, etc. Although it has already been processed this form of data is still open to interpretation. In general 'pure' research such as a literature review dissertation will rely more upon secondary data sources, whereas applied research relies on a combination of both primary and secondary sources. This distinction is discussed further in Chapter 5.

Data provides an essential form of 'evidence' on which to build a thesis. Evidence is provided by forms of collected data that have been analysed and are presented to substantiate or confirm claims within a dissertation. Typically this evidence will be (critically) compared with, or evaluated alongside, contrasting evidence such as that presented by another researcher in a paper. It is a general requirement that when a point is raised, such as part of an argument within a dissertation, some evidence is provided to support claims. As is explored in Chapter 9, trends, themes, categories or patterns identified within data also make up the essence of analysis.

Finally, triangulation is when two or more sources of data, such as relating to two different research methods used to collect data, are used together to explore a topic. Ideally such sources or methods should compliment each other rather than be integrated or fused together (Bryman, 2004). For example, a questionnaire may be used alongside interviews with research participants to collect primary data. Also, national statistic data, such as from the Census or a Department of Health website, might be utilized alongside the findings from several academic journal papers to provide or help present more evidence of a trend that is being explored. Triangulation is one way in which quantitative and qualitative methods can be used to compliment each other, which is also known as a 'mixed method' approach.

Research concepts, issues and context

Closely linked to data and evidence remains the priority given within qualitative research to concepts. A concept is a theme, trend, idea, social group or construct, that is linked to a research topic and which has wide meaning within a discipline such as social work. Concepts include gender, ethnicity, class, poverty, service users, and so on. Typically each dissertation will link to two, three or occasionally more key concepts that will each help to locate, inform and direct a research project (Blaxter *et al.*, 1996: 37). For example, within a dissertation that seeks to explore social work practice with men with mental health needs, it is likely that a student will utilize the concepts of both gender and mental health, as well as how they relate, as part of any overall literature review and analysis.

Research issues are general concerns, subjects of debate or controversy, or significant trends or outcomes that link to a discipline or specific topic. Due to its applied and wide ranging nature, social work research is often saturated with social issues, many of which are held within ongoing debate or types of theoretical investigation. Examples of issues include questions regarding policy applied to asylum seekers, the legal rights of foster carers, whether levels of welfare benefits available to service users are adequate, or the forms of discrimination that people from ethnic minority groups often experience, among many others. Each dissertation will usually engage with one or more issues, as well as perhaps draw attention to new ones as part of the research process.

Context is pivotal to all qualitative research and draws from two main streams. First, context relates to a comparison with existing literature or ideas. That is, how does any research compare to existing theories or ideas, including those found within available published material? As Blaxter *et al.* (1996: 37) stress, 'research seldom, if ever, breaks wholly new ground; it builds upon an extensive history of other peoples work'. By contrasting your own research with other related material a topic is placed into context or given greater understanding and meaning. A research topic may also utilize material that is not *directly* related but still links to a topic. For example in exploring the mental health needs of a service user, a researcher may also need to consider other related influences, such as the impact of available welfare services or the effect of prior institutional support upon the current social needs of a participant.

Second, context links to understanding a topic from the perspective of related cultural, social or political factors that influence. For example, if exploring adoption policy within a particular country it may help to also look at attendant factors such as government initiatives relating to education or health policies of the time. This is likely to help explain some of the decisions made at this juncture and help clarify points or arguments that are signified to the reader of a dissertation. Often context also explores historical factors, such as earlier trends or legislation, which can play a significant part in the development of later policy or practice. The importance of context, especially regarding analysis, is further explored in Chapter 9, and is also referred to in part throughout this book.

Sampling

A sample is a small group of research participants or subset from which a degree of generalization can be made; sampling is the process by which a sample is gathered. Ideally a sample should be *representative*, and reflect the wider *population* or total number of people being explored through research. However within most qualitative research, and especially research undertaken for a dissertation, a sample is more likely to either be a *purposive* or *convenience* sample, neither of which are likely to be representative (Royse, 1991: 113–16). A purposive sample is selected because it is *purposeful* – here the priority is to gather enough people to be able to collect sufficient data and, more importantly, begin to interpret, explore and understand the topic under investigation. As Holloway (1997: 142, my emphasis) suggests, 'generalisability is less important than the collection of *rich* data and an *understanding* of the ideas of the people chosen for the sample [becomes the priority]'. Snowballing is a relatively common form of purposive sampling in which the researcher literally pieces together or builds almost like a jigsaw a sample by moving from one person to the next, with participants often identifying and introducing to the researcher other potential participants. This is especially useful for social groups that are considered to be difficult to reach. A convenience sample is one built from participants to whom the researcher has convenient access. Social work practitioners based at a practice placement setting are likely to provide such a convenience sample, and through snowballing each participant may also be able to offer potential access to people employed elsewhere.

As stated in Chapter 2 samples for social work dissertations tend to be very small – rarely any more than twenty participants, although often less. Such a

small group of participants is unlikely to be representative of the wider population, and in practice the sample may be both purposive and convenient. It is
imperative that an adequate explanation of why and how the sample was
selected and utilized as part of the research is provided within the methodology
section of a dissertation.

Reliability, validity and rigour

Reliability refers to the extent to which our findings are consistent and
dependable. In particular, reliability looks at repetition and the extent to which
a method can be repeated to produce similar results. For example, if we are
exploring the attitudes of support workers based in a children's residential
home towards social workers, are our conclusions likely to be the same if the
research were repeated with a different group of support workers at a later date?
Related to this, reliability is more likely to be achieved if each support worker
has been asked the same questions under similar circumstances.

Although reliability as an approach is founded and deeply immersed in
quantitative research – drawing as it does upon large scale survey or poll based
research – it still has relevance to qualitative research (Cohen *et al.*, 2007: 132).
However, qualitative approaches address a different set of issues which impact
upon the extent to which reliability can be tested. For example, the complexity of many different issues typically explored, as well as the different social
environments often explored, means that a repeat of the same research project
and questions elsewhere is unlikely to uncover the same results. As Payne and
Payne (2004) insist, rather than seek uniformity qualitative research instead
pursues more dynamic and innovative methods, which might include personal
reflexivity, in order to reduce uncertainty: 'By confronting the researcher's
own reactions and shortcomings, and comparing what different techniques
have produced [in other related studies], plausibility and coherence emerge
from dialogue and experience' (p. 198).

In general then reliability within a social work dissertation will be less
concerned with an exact and scientific endeavour to repeat future research
outcomes in another setting. Instead students will be more anxious to explore
and unpack the findings from their research and decide how they might be
applied to practice. Concerns linked to reliability should also stimulate reflexive questions about the extent to which personal planning, choice of a particular method, the setting where interviews took place, the sources of literature
utilized, and the choice of participants, etc., were all fulfilled with an *intention*
of maximizing the reliability of any findings. Certainly different participants
are unlikely to be asked different questions in different settings and sources of
literature should not be chosen randomly.

Validity refers to results or findings, and, in particular, the extent to which they are authentic, genuine and sound (Salkind, 2006: 113). Within validity a fundamental question to ask is what are the strengths of our findings and conclusions? For example, if a student is again exploring the attitudes of support workers based in a children residential home towards social workers, are her findings a *true reflection* of the group being interviewed? Validity is often seen to be much more achievable with qualitative research due to the many questions asked, themes explored, and longer period of time spent with a typically smaller group. In contrast survey research may only unearth a fraction of the findings, and even they may lack validity due to a lack of contact and exploration. According to critics, the downside of qualitative validity is that the findings may not be representative of the wider population, and also that the small sample may generate significant bias. In other words, what it gains in validity it loses in reliability, and vice versa for quantitative approaches (Cohen *et al.*, 2007: 150–5).

Ways in which to apply validity to qualitative research have been suggested. These include contacting participants at a later date following interviews and discussing results and conclusions with them – this is to increase any likelihood of knowing if findings are truly accurate (Bloor, 1978). However for many dissertations there may not be adequate time to undertake such additional work. Finally, although it will always help to recognize both reliability and validity as representing significant components of any methodology, it is also worth noting that other priorities may be just as, if not more important, within social work research. These might include a wish to draw attention to forms of social inequality or discrimination, or ensure that research is ethical and serves a clear purpose such as being able to better meet the needs of service users or informal carers.

Rigour refers to the extent to which research findings 'are authentic and its interpretations credible' (Padgett, 1998: 88). Attempts to achieve reliability and validity offer a form of rigour but this approach is often criticized as being too scientific and objective. There exists a paradox because this approach prioritizes authenticity and detachment from participants or social facts. Alternative interpretations of rigour have since emerged. For example, interpretive researchers argue that rigour should be based upon a researcher's capacity to articulate and understand research participants' meanings, feelings, events and experiences. This can only be achieved by encouraging closer and more subjective contact between a researcher and participant(s). Some feminists have also argued that rigour should be assessed according to the capacity of their research to confront and alter the disadvantages experienced by female participants (Ezzy, 2002: 55–7). Rigour then is a sensitive construct that continues to be debated within social research. It is closely related to ethics and the four main theories of social research discussed in the next chapter, each of which takes a different stance on rigour.

Inductive and deductive reasoning

There are two distinct ways in which reasoning, and therefore a thesis, is *constructed* and/or *tested* as a part of any research process. These approaches are known as inductive and deductive forms of reasoning, and both are discussed below.

Inductive reasoning

Most qualitative research is inductive, and it will seek 'to *discover*, not test, explanatory theories' (Padgett, 1998: 2, my emphasis). It is here that observations and/or assessments of data and other information are enacted or collected by the researcher. From this information and/or observations, patterns or trends are identified and from these a provisional hypothesis or set of statements are created. From the provisional hypothesis we then begin to develop and form a theory – a set of statements or proposals that helps us explain and understand what it is we have discovered. This process is summarized in Figure 3.1.

Ideally any process of induction should emerge direct from 'raw' findings which have been gathered through the research process. From such findings theory grows and develops, such as from the beginnings of a dissertation to the stage of writing up a final thesis. Accordingly more dominant theory should not *impose* itself upon the researcher prior to engagement with interviews or other methods of data collection. As Brewer (2003d: 155, my emphasis) argues:

> empirical generalisations and theoretical statements about the social world [are created by] *the data themselves* free of preconceptions,

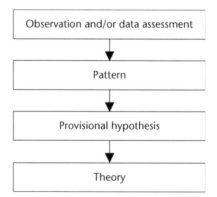

Figure 3.1   Inductive reasoning.

allowing subjects' perceptions, ideas and social meanings not only to speak for themselves but to speak in a broader way by generalisation and theory *without contamination.*

This type of process can also suit a literature based piece of research in which confrontation with a set of differing 'texts' or narratives leads to the formation of a revised or new theory.

In practice, however, inductive research does not necessarily process in the ideal manner identified in Figure 3.1. Primarily this is due to the unpredictable and multi-layered nature of qualitative research which largely defies *complete* control and pre-planning. Also the emergence and use of theory is not always as prominent as is ideally presented within the inductive approach. In practice the boundaries between inductive and deductive research are often blurred, and it is the latter form of reasoning that we now turn our attention to.

Deductive reasoning

As can be seen in the diagram in Figure 3.2 deductive reasoning *begins with a theory,* and then eventually leads to the rejection, reform or confirmation of that theory. Central to deductive reasoning remains the hypothesis, which represents a type of 'informed speculation' represented by statements of test-able facts (Bryman, 2004: 540). Such statements are constructed by the researcher from personal experience, but may also be built with the help of a theory which has already been established, and which is typically discovered during the literature review. From the hypothesis comes the next stage, that of observation, most commonly facilitated by method(s) of empirical research.

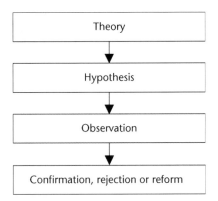

Figure 3.2   Deductive reasoning.

Finally, following observation, the hypothesis (and therefore theory) is rejected, accepted or (more often) reformed.

The process of deduction is generally assumed to be more suitable for science based 'positivism' (discussed further below) and quantitative research. Despite this, it is debatable whether any piece of social research can comply with a purely deductive approach. In contrast, social research is often influenced by a fusion of both deductive and inductive approaches. As Bryman (2004: 8–10) notes, deductive approaches do not always follow a 'linear pattern' as planned, and some stages followed may conflate or emerge earlier than planned. As induction and deduction processes conflate, this can also lead to 'a weaving back and forth *between* data and theory'. Indeed this is the case for most processes in social research – including the distinction made between qualitative and quantitative research, applied and pure research, induction and deduction, and so on. Although both sets of camps are often separate and sometimes opposed, typically each can influence and engage with the other in the more pragmatic and suitably 'messy' confines of the social research and *practice* arena, in which clear distinctions can become blurred, if not muddled (Dominelli, 2005).

This may appear a little confusing at first, but nevertheless the flexibility offered *in practice* is more often to the benefit of students rather than a *rigid* either/or process (which may be unworkable in practice anyhow). As Bryman (2004: 11, my emphasis) suggests, the many different processes in social research are 'possibly better thought of as *tendencies* rather than hard and fast distinction(s)'. It is important to be aware of the inductive and deductive distinction, but the priority is still to adequately confront and answer a clearly defined research question to the best of your abilities.

Summary

This chapter has considered qualitative social work research and especially its emphasis upon meaning and understanding, theory development, and subjective interpretation and explanation. Predominately as part of a dissertation forms of small scale qualitative research will be concerned with exploring the in-depth experiences of a handful of participants, as well as critically investigating related literature. In comparison to such applied research, pure research can also be essential to a social work dissertation, and this literature based approach can include topics and themes such as comparative analysis or theory development, among others. Qualitative social work research also tends to explore concepts and issues, which might include topical and pressing subjects or themes that link to social work practice.

This chapter has also stressed the distinction between reliability and validity, with social work and other forms of qualitative research tending to compromise upon reliability while strengthening the validity of any findings. The chapter has also briefly explored central concepts such as evidence and sampling, and noted the distinction between inductive and deductive reasoning while also recognizing that these approaches often blur when applied in practice.

The next chapter looks at the role of theory in social work research.

Suggested reading

Bryman, A. (2004) *Social Research Methods*. Milton Keynes, Open University Press. (Chapter 13: The nature of qualitative research)

Cohen, L., Manion, L., and Morrison, K. (2007) *Research Methods in Education*, sixth edition. London: Routledge. (Chapter 1: The nature of inquiry: setting the field; Chapter 6: Validity and reliability)

Hall, D. and Hall, I. (1996) *Practical Social Research – Project Work in the Community*. Basingstoke: Macmillan. (Chapter 1: Philosophy and practice of applied social research)

Padgett, D.K. (1998) *Qualitative Methods in Social Work Research – Challenges and Rewards*. London: Sage. (Chapter 8: Rigour and relevance in qualitative research)

Royse, D. (1991) *Research Methods in Social Work*. Chicago: Nelson-Hall Publishers. (Chapter 2: Basic research terms and concepts)

4 Theory and social work research

Introduction

This chapter introduces theory relating to social work research. Theory offers a vital contribution to the research process; in particular it supports our capacity to make sense of what it is we are doing and also helps us to explain and understand our findings. This chapter also discusses epistemology and the four main groups of social theory that can be used in social work research. This chapter also looks at social ontology, or the nature of being, and explores the relationship between ontology, epistemology, methodology and method with three case examples.

Theory and the social work dissertation

Theory offers a necessary contribution to all qualitative research – it offers a set of proposals, statements or ideas that link together coherent arguments which help us explain, conceptualize and understand what it is we are doing and why (Howe, 1987; Fook, 2002; Payne, 2005). A theory may be applied to help us explain a phenomenon or type of empirical reality. Theories may also be general abstract accounts that try to clarify and place into context social norms, events and the implicit or explicit workings of institutions or the behaviours and attitudes of people. They offer the researcher (or practitioner) meaning, focus, direction and consistency, and potentially can be used to assist and support service users or carers. More potent however is Althusser's (1971) proposal that positive social or political change is unattainable without the support of theory. Theory is often more explicit within qualitative rather than quantitative research, because potentially it is able to untangle convoluted strands of data and provide meaning from otherwise complex themes, trends and dynamics.

A principle obstacle that qualitative researchers often face is to establish a theory from their findings. As Bryman suggests (2004: 11): 'not only does much qualitative research *not* generate theory, but also theory is often used at the very least as a background to qualitative investigations'. For a dissertation, students are not required to create a new theory or transform an established theory. Rather an awareness of, and engagement with, theory that relates to the exploration and answering of a research question is expected. This may be represented by the confirmation of the validity or otherwise of an established theory (for example, anti-discrimination theory) or a critical revision or analysis of previous research undertaken in a related area of analysis. For example, an author may have previously expressed opinions about why older people with a disability prefer living at home to attending a day centre. Your own findings may differ slightly from this 'theory' and a subsequent revision of this author's related proposals may provide the foundation of your dissertation. Here a thesis has developed following interviews with research participants, from which the researcher can debate the merits or otherwise of an established theory which has previously attempted to explain and understand the topic under investigation. Not unusually new social work research will lead to one of three possible outcomes, that include the:

- confirmation of a theory;
- rejection of a theory;
- or critique and reform or extension of a theory.

The confirmation or rejection of a theory is usually an unequivocal response to previous ideas and findings based on your own new research data and/or conceptual ideas. The third type of response which involves criticizing and making a (typically slight) revision of an established theory is the most common outcome of most academic research. In all cases, however, evidence must be presented to support whatever stance is taken.

Levin (2005: 85–6) postulates various questions and processes that a students may ask and follow about a theory or theories within a dissertation. These may include:

- description of theory – foundations, origins, postulates, etc.;
- the place of any theory in current academic thinking;
- why a theory needs to be tested and whether it is still valid?;
- review of publications relating to a theory, as well as critiques and commentaries;
- review of publications setting out alternative theory to that being considered;
- testing of a theory (such as against new empirical evidence or contrasting theory);
- internal consistency or validity of a theory;

- discussion and evaluation of the usefulness or otherwise of a theory;
- how theory might be revised or improved.

Several of these questions and processes might be used to assess a current form of social work theory – such as anti-discrimination or evidence based practice – as part of a dissertation. Alternatively two or more theories might be compared in relation to their effectiveness with a specific service user group or regarding any impact in solving a social problem that social workers have traditionally experienced in their role.

Epistemology and social research theory

At its most basic epistemology is the 'theory of knowledge'. More generally epistemology relates to the different forms and types of knowledge that exist. This will include assumptions made about the differing ways of acquiring knowledge (Holloway, 1997: 54). Finally, the manner in which knowledge is created and formed, and also goes on to alter and change over time, can be seen as central to epistemology. This aspect can be valuable for social work research, especially if (as is often the case) an established theory is questioned or reformed during the research process. Theories exist as the essential components of epistemology, because they are the building blocks of knowledge.

Inevitably since social work research is linked directly to knowledge production and enhancement (as indeed all research is), so epistemology remains a key (if not inevitable) component of any research process. This is most evident within the literature review (discussed in Chapter 5), a key stage which itself is dependant upon established forms of knowledge that have been created via previous forms of research. Regarding epistemology, Corby (2006) has argued that there are four theoretical schools which have influenced social work research. Each is considered below.

1 Positivism and post-positivism

Positivism (also known as realism) attempts to apply scientific methods drawn from the natural sciences to the study of people and society. Up until the 1960s positivism remained 'the orthodoxy in social science' (Brewer, 2003a: 235). As a widespread or grand methodology it helped to articulate attempts to construct and apply scientific laws to human behaviour, as well as promote measurement, objectivity and a lack of bias in social research. Positivism assumes that the social life of people remains '*independent*' of human consciousness' and therefore that *empirical* 'evidence' can be collected and measured by researchers (Jones, 1983: 118, my emphasis).

Such claims were criticized and presented as unfounded and unattainable from the 1960s onwards. In particular the importance of the uniquely personal and subjective interpretations and understanding on behalf of the researcher were stressed, as well as the complex, cluttered and unpredictable nature of social life for participants. Despite this, positivism has always retained a subtle influence within social research, most notably within empiricism and forms of applied research. This is because one of positivism's central philosophical propositions is that research should respond to (objective) *experience*, rather than simply rely upon theoretical propositions (Hughes, 1990).

Positivism tends to encourage approaches which:

- individualize or 'atomize' human behaviour. That is attempt to isolate, and, for the 'psy' theories attached to the influential discipline of psychology especially, carefully study or scrutinize a personality (or 'case') with only limited reference to other forms of influence, including group behaviour or structural influences (schooling, family, language, culture, etc.);
- rely upon a search for objective and uncontaminated truth(s) as part of the research process; with an assumption that the political and cultural neutrality of the researcher can be maintained;
- attempt to be able to influence and predict future human behaviour from prior collected 'data' and establish laws and/or procedures to enhance this process;
- neglect or ignore the impact of wider structural forces on human behaviour and attitudes. This will include 'factors' or 'variables' such as poverty, gender, 'race', class, etc.;
- gather social *'facts'*: collect information or data relating to a topic through observation or interviews and attempt to classify or code the findings;
- study or collect *statistical information* or 'variables' and seek to process, standardize and analyse this;
- identify *correlations*: that is, find links between two or more 'variables' and discuss them in a report or dissertation;
- isolate and discuss *causations*: that is, try to discover what might be causing a phenomenon or dynamic which is being studied.

Despite a retreat from the explicit use of positivism within social work research it has still maintained an influence as a *philosophy*, and indeed has also played a crucial part in the development of social work practice and education. For example, Jones (1983: 89) has underlined the detached and impersonal relations established between many early social workers and service users. Throughout the late nineteenth and early twentieth century, the social work profession also developed education and training strategies to mould practice into a 'science', with a stress on maintaining the 'neutrality, authority and righteousness' of the practitioner. Similar views are still being expressed today (for example, Goppner and Hamalainen, 2007). Although not as explicitly associated, traditional Marxism, including some support within social work, has also been strongly influenced by aspects of positivism, especially regarding aspirations to create a more scientific study of history and society (for example, Gough, 1979). Such examples underline that positivism has moved beyond representing just a methodology or theory – it is also a philosophy and ideology which encourages assumptions and beliefs to be made by us about the world around.

In science based disciplines, including health and medicine, the dominance of positivism has never really been challenged, and social work's more recent closer relations with health professions, among other developments, has led to the gradual promotion and resurgence of at least some aspects of positivism within social work research and practice. Indeed some commentators have identified positivism as central to some key methodologies now promoted within social work, especially evidence based practice (see Webb, 2001). Like positivism evidence based practice encourages social workers to draw from a scientific and empirical knowledge base and seek to be objective, including in attempts to evaluate the impact or efficacy of any interventions applied to service users. Despite this, and as Jones (1983) and Healy (2005) have noted, there have remained core aspects of positivism within social work practice long before the emergence of evidence based practice.

Post-positivism retains aspects of the sentiment of positivism but differs in two respects. First, it accepts that objectivity and truth within research can never be guaranteed. Despite this, there is still a (contestable) supposition that an unequivocal 'truth' can be acquired from social research 'if all procedures to establish *validity* have been followed' (Holloway, 1997: 123). Second, post-positivists concede that social research cannot necessarily be value free – that is the beliefs, opinions and prejudices held by researchers prior to undertaking their research will almost certainly influence their findings. Crucially post-positivists (or critical realists) believe that there are forms of reality or existence that are independent of our own existence, and which can be studied and captured by the social researcher. Primarily this can be achieved by the most accurate forms of research methods available, and ideally as many as possible if the researcher is to capture forms of 'reality' around them. Finally, post-positivists acknowledge that all forms of theory require regular revision, typically following more research, and no one theory will necessary be able to capture the 'truth' for long periods.

The *explicit* use of a positivistic or post-positivist methodology in practice tends to be limited in qualitative research, including within social work. Most dissertations or research projects within social work rely upon an in depth analysis of a small sample of participants, or a thorough investigation of an aspect of specialist literature. This research tends to be difficult to control, regardless of how much pre-planning has taken place. In addition, the unpredictable and complex *qualitative* nature of the social work role, as well as the altruistic, ethical or political principles that are often apparent within practice and research, provide a further set of hurdles (Corby, 2006: 145). Nevertheless, Feyerabend (1975) has argued in his critique of research in general, that the underlying principles of science and positivism tend to be at least subtly embedded within all the key *processes* of research. From this radical perspective, at least some engagement with positivism cannot be avoided when undertaking any form of research.

2 Interpretivism

Interpretivism attempts to uncover the meaning and 'reality' (or interpretation) of people's experiences in the social world. The researcher endeavours to *understand* the opinions, emotional responses and attitudes articulated by participants; and then link these to peoples' behaviour and actions and, finally, contextualize, or place into perspective, the views and conduct of participants. Interpretivists argue that researchers should try to unearth people's *interpretations* of the worlds around them, as well as the concomitant *beliefs* and *actions* that emerge as a consequence; especially the impact that participants *themselves* have upon creating the environment and world around them (Sumner, 1994; Scott, 1995).

While discussing the related work of the social anthropologist Evans-Pritchard, Layton (1997: 115, my emphasis) details his interpretivist methodology:

> Social life . . . has a pattern because humans are reasonable creatures and must live in a world in which social relations are ordered and intelligible. Fieldworkers should therefore aim to understand the people they stud[y] *in their own terms*; to think in their concepts and feel in their values. These experiences must then be translated into the conceptual categories and values of the [researcher's] own culture.

Interpretivism has provided one challenge to the previous dominance of positivism within social research, and indeed has become part of a wider (yet diverse) movement (along with feminism and postmodernism) that has stood to question the scientific aspirations of positivistic logic from the 1960s onwards. Interpretivists reject any claim that researchers can *objectively* predict the behaviour of social actors or groups being studied. Conversely, a *subjective* personal understanding of people and their interpretation of the 'worlds around them' becomes a goal. Also, interpretivists do not aspire to define or acquire measurable 'facts' as in the positivistic tradition – instead the dexterous (and sometimes tedious) skills of listening and/or observation take priority.

There are different interpretivist theories but each shares common themes and qualities. These include a tendency to:

- enter and try to understand the diverse and unique social worlds of research participants and/or social group(s) being studied;
- concentrate upon the individual and the personal *strategies* of research participants; including participants' use of language and behaviour so as to understand how the world appears to each;
- stress the centrality of participants' responses to external stimuli (symbols, knowledge, language, etc.) and aim to capture participants' subjective meaning of their own world;
- empathize with, and therefore try to better understand, research participants;
- allow participants to take a lead role within the research process rather than be directed by the researcher. As Jones (1993: 138, my emphasis) elaborates, 'unlike the positivist . . . [interpretivists] do not want our actors to go where *we* lead them. We want to go where *they* lead *us*';
- neglect (rather than ignore) the influence of social structures (for example, access to employment, housing, education, health care, alongside other supports services) upon participants' behaviour and values.

Interpretivism has different schools which include ethnomethodology, symbolic interactionism and phenomenology. Symbolic interactionism has tended to have the most influence upon social work theory and practice, and this is discussed further below.

Symbolic interactionism

This theory scrutinizes the ways in which people 'employ symbols of what they mean to communicate with one another', as well as the impact that 'the interpretations of these symbols have on the behaviour of parties during a social interaction'. Symbolic interactionist perspectives look at how people are perceived by others and respond within social settings (such as a school or workplace), and also 'the active role which humans play in the creation of their social selves'. This is believed to lead to forms of self-reflexivity on behalf of participants in social settings, which may include personal strategies that social actors manipulate 'in order to present the person we wish others to think we are' (Jones, 1993: 83–5).

Both Chaiklin (1993) and Forte (2001) have advocated the possibilities offered by symbolic interactionism for social work practice and research. As Payne (2005: 181) notes, symbolic interactionism may respectively help practitioners and service users understand their role and social circumstances better – which may also help us to empower participants:

> Focusing on interactions and symbols may be less demanding emotionally for both client and worker than the traditional close relationship . . . these ideas assume the basic normality and competence of most people, rather than assuming illness or maladaption and an inability [of service users] to control their own destiny.

Labelling theory is a form of symbolic interactionism that has been influential in social work, especially with seemingly 'deviant' service users. This emerged from theorists such as Lemert (1951) but gained widespread attention following the innovative and critical work of Howard Becker (1967, 1982). Labelling theory investigates the social rituals and processes that lead to individuals or social groups being ascribed a specific cultural and social classification or label, and one that usually has negative understanding and consequences. As Crotty (1998: 78) suggests, labelling theorists ask two key questions that include 'why is it . . . that society wants to exclude some members from full and free participation in its life?' and 'what are the mechanisms it uses to do so?'. The researcher will endeavour to look at how participants that have been negatively labelled (such as lone parents or 'single mothers' and 'juvenile delinquents' or 'hoodies') respond and are affected by such a label; but more importantly why and how this happens.

   In keeping with the tradition of symbolic interaction, and especially following the influence of Becker's work, labelling theorists have tended to defend the rights of the socially excluded or oppressed. Seemingly socially ascribed criteria target and often force negative attributes onto so called 'deviants'. Ironically perhaps, the socially constructed deviant is then more likely to aspire to such enforced labels and norms and continues to develop a 'deviant identity'. Deviancy is therefore seen as intensifying or even as being created through the actions and values of socially powerful groups (including professionals within the law, medicine, the police, social work, etc.), and is generated through the labelling process. However, positive labels can also lead to detrimental consequences. For example, Rogers and Pilgrim (2001: 136–7) note how positive labels that assume no or low-risk to suicide for black men (in contrast to white women) may prevent many medical professionals from providing a necessary support service to such a minority (yet significant) social group.

   Labelling theory has been criticized on numerous grounds, most prominently regarding its tendency to sometimes exaggerate and simplify the impact of labels, as well as ignore the moral choices open to people who have been labelled (Sumner, 1994).

   Interpretivist theories hold great potential for any social work dissertation.

Among many others, examples where interpretivist theory might support a dissertation include those that seek to explore:

- the experiences of social work practitioners regarding their role;
- the thoughts and reflections of social workers regarding their identity, or relations with colleagues or service users;
- the impact of stigma or labelling upon groups such as service users, informal carers or possibly even social workers themselves;
- the feelings of health professionals regarding their relations with social workers;
- a theoretical investigation of how a group of service users may become excluded from particular support services;
- a critical appraisal of labelling theory in social work with people with mental health needs.

In general interpretivist approaches can be used in isolation, or alternatively they can be combined with some critical or postmodern approaches (each of which is discussed below). In practice, in-depth interviews tend to be the preferred method used within interpretivist methodologies; however, participant observation can also be used as part of an interpretivist approach. Interpretivism is a flexible methodology and may also be used as a part of evaluation research (explored in Chapter 6).

Case study 4.1 is an example of a dissertation that I supervised which drew from interpretivist theory.

3 Critical theory

Critical theory presupposes that social research represents more than a series of tasks that collect, analyse and report data, so as to better explain and understand society. Conversely, social research is identified as 'a political activity, working either for or against the status quo', and it should investigate, query and critique established practices, institutions, conventions, policy and traditions, if social injustices or forms of inequality are identified. It should also seek to change society for the better (Porter, 2003: 60).

This tradition has been influential to varying degrees within social work since the 1970s, during the heyday of so called 'radical social work'. However the origins of 'activist' social work go back much further, including to the turn of the last century and the 'settlement movement' that sought to educate and empower people within disadvantaged communities (Hugman, 1991). Along with interpretivism, critical theory offers a contrasting cultural and political response to positivism. However it not only rejects the feasibility of applying scientific methods to social research, but also asks questions about the moral consequences of any such potentially insensitive and damaging research pro-

---

Case Study 4.1

Interpretivism in action: Relations between social workers and mothers of children with a disability

For her dissertation Jenny wanted to discover how younger mothers of children with a learning disability 'experienced' contact with their allocated social workers. Jenny was especially keen to unearth the types of relations built up between social workers and informal carers, and also wanted to look for possible ways in which contact might be improved. The methods she used were unstructured interviews with three mothers, and then interviews with the same number of social workers. The interviews lasted around an hour each and were then transcribed. Jenny then carefully scrutinized the transcripts and read each several times over.

A number of trends emerged from the findings. For example, Jenny noted how all of the mothers had benefited from contact with their social workers, and each was positive about the support received. Despite this, there were themes that both the mothers and social workers identified as problematic and that sometimes impaired any relations. For example, both groups were at times frustrated with the bureaucracy that sometimes dominated their meetings, and each agreed that less paper work would improve any service provided. Despite this, it also emerged that both parties recognized the importance of creating a strong working relationship and bond, especially so as to enhance the well-being and development of each child. An interpretivist methodology influenced Jenny by allowing her to concentrate upon and carefully analyse the personal *opinions*, *attitudes* and *experiences* of each person interviewed – especially when articulated through verbal and non-verbal communication during interviews. The many complex layers of meaning taken from each interview transcript were used to generate a discussion around relationships of support and identity.

---

cesses for participants. Although there are different, and sometimes separate, schools of critical theory, there are general links between each school, and critical theory is recognized as a relatively consistent (yet diverse) methodology that includes a tendency to:

- draw significantly from feminist and Marxist theory to emphasize the impact of economic and political power differentials, and other forms of inequality. It is proposed that exploitative relations reduce the possibilities and choices available to large numbers of people;
- try to explore and explain the *causes* and *impact* of social inequality and other forms of exclusion and oppression;
- appreciate and emphasize 'structural' forms of disadvantage and

exclusion: such as service users' restricted and limited access to resources, including those that relate to circumscribed employment and education opportunities, housing, health and social service support, among other types of 'life chances' or opportunities;

- highlight *cultural* forms of disadvantage such as by identifying ways in which language and knowledge production is used to maintain dominance and control for privileged groups and exclude and oppress others;

- try to *politically* and *historically* investigate, understand and draw attention to specific forms of social oppression. In particular, disadvantage on the basis of age, gender, 'race' and ethnicity, class, disability, and sexuality, have been explored;

- combine or link critical theory with *practice* to develop forms of *praxis* in which each informs one another, and theory directly influences action;

- within social work, draw from anti-discrimination and anti-oppressive theory and practice, both of which have been influenced by feminist and, to a lesser extent, Marxist theory. Each endeavours (in theory at least) to identify, confront and alleviate forms of domination and control, in which social research has a role to play;

- attempt to link the personal and individual experiences of service users or practitioners with wider structural forms of disadvantage. For example, by exploring the personal statements and experiences of service users, such as regarding their past relations with professionals or wider institutions such as schools or the social care system;

- wherever possible try to link social and human studies – including sociology, anthropology, history, political science, economics, and so on – in order to utilize all critical resources to highlight forms of inequality and injustice;

- recognize the importance of dominant ideas, beliefs and related practices – or ideology and discourse – in maintaining and justifying forms of discrimination, exclusion and structural inequality and poverty;

- offer alternative ideas and practices, especially those that seek to alleviate discrimination and emancipate oppressed social groups.

(Adapted from Jones, 1983; Harvey, 1990; Dominelli, 2002; Fook, 2002; Crossley, 2005)

Porter (2003: 57–8) isolates three major German thinkers that have helped to construct the philosophy of critical theory. First, Immanuel Kant's assertion that we should avoid 'taking our reason and knowledge for granted' remains paramount; instead we should endeavour always to question the 'conditions which make such reason and knowledge possible'. This claim has stood to justify many of the core principles of critical theory, including the belief that all knowledge, and related 'taken for granted' assumptions, should be exposed to rigorous forms of enquiry. Second, the philosopher G.W.F. Hegel's proposal that superstition and other 'distortions of knowledge' should be exposed has been utilized by critical theorists again to validate their approach. Ideally this process should help us 'move towards an authentic knowledge of reality'. Finally, among other thinkers, Karl Marx has influenced the profound impact of socio-economic dynamics on people's everyday beliefs and behaviour, and also highlighted the exploitative nature of capitalism as a dominant form of political economy.

These interrelated principles have led to the proliferation of specific methodologies and a culture of research which is distinct from others. There is a distrust of not only positivism but also many of the liberal-humanist (and sometimes conservative) values that undermine some interpretivist approaches. Critical theorists also look at the values of the researcher, which are identified as always influencing the research process, and tend to reveal their own beliefs, and how any initial beliefs and values might have changed throughout any study.

The key to a good critical methodology is the capacity to use related theory to *contextualize* any findings. An ability to explore, investigate and delve into any research problem, while also linking any findings to related discussions in the academic literature (following your literature review), is seen as vital to the process of analysis. Traditionally, the interview (explored further in Chapter 7) has been the most common method used within critical theory – this is because it allows the researcher to talk to, and explore, relevant interests on a *personal* and *confidential* level, and usually in great depth, with practitioners, other professionals, carers, etc. Despite this, other methods, such as questionnaires (Chapter 7), or focus groups (Chapter 7), can be just as effective in achieving the same aims.

Critical theory then has become much more detailed and elaborate and looked to move beyond a crude Marxist or feminist attempt to overemphasise merely economic factors or those that isolate gender alone. As with interpretivism, critical theory is appropriate for either 'pure' or 'applied' research within a dissertation. Among many others, possible topics for a dissertation utilizing critical theory might include:

- explaining and analysing disadvantage experienced by a specific group of service users;
- investigating and examining either literature or utilizing empirical research to explore an identified form of structural exclusion relating a particular group of service users. For example, the limited employment opportunities available for service users with a disability or mental health related need;

- assessing the impact of poverty affecting service users upon a group of practising social workers;
- considering how attitudes regarding 'gender' may affect the decision-making processes followed by a team of social workers;
- reviewing and linking a selection of the critical literature linking globalization with a form of social work practice;
- exploring how poverty impacts upon the assessment processes undertaken by a group of mental health social workers.

Case study 4.2 provides an example of research influenced by critical theory.

Despite its popularity and regular use, critical theory is not without criticism. It has been accused of *encouraging* bias within research (Leach, 1982; Holloway, 1997). Also, although critical theory is effective at exploring the structural causes of disadvantage it can be weak in helping us understand their true impact upon *individual* people. For example, it can struggle to cope with the *emotional* needs that many people who come into contact with social services experience. Finally, critical theory can sometimes appear grandiose and preoccupied with sporadic themes – such as historical trends and often 'unseen' political forces such as 'Globalization' – which can seem detached from the everyday world of day to day social work practice.

4 Postmodernism

One important development in social work research since the 1980s has been the many questions asked by critical academics that are labelled 'postmodernist'. Such a loose knit brand of thinking takes as its premise a 'laid-back pluralism of styles' and a concomitant celebration of a diverse range of social beliefs and cultures (Norris, 1995: 708). Of significance for social work has been the postmodern stress upon the need to appreciate previously excluded voices and opinions, including those of people with a disability, black and ethnic minority groups, and older people and women, among others. As Dominelli (2004: 2) argues:

> The view that there is one hegemonic version of truth can be sustained only at the expense of ignoring other voices, particularly those that are suppressed or considered inferior or irrelevant. In these constructs, the dominant discourse does not have to be specified as dominant, it is *assumed* to be so through its normalisation, i.e., being treated as 'normal' or 'natural' and therefore beyond question. Thus, for example, in racist discourses on skin colour in the West, 'white' is the colour of privilege and so does not have to be referred to as such in referring to white people, only 'black' is explicitly seen and treated as a colour in reference to people and an inferior one at that.

Case Study 4.2

Critical theory in action: *Participant observation at Sure Start*

Through the use of an overt form of participant observation, Foster (2007a/b) was able to intimately and critically explore the impact of a new government initiative, *Sure Start*, that aimed to support disadvantaged children under 5 years of age. The research was undertaken within a 'post-industrial' town in the north west of England. Foster utilized arts based research, an innovative method of research which allowed participants in her sample to become actively involved in the research process by engaging in the planning and fulfilment of activities related to art, drama and poetry. Through this process, which was also influenced by feminism, Foster was able to investigate and eventually highlight the benefits and deficiencies of the Sure Start programme, as well as attempt to change the seemingly often negative and dismissive views held of 'poor working-class women'.

As the parents themselves revealed, although families benefited in part from the support they received at Sure Start, there were also numerous (structurally induced) obstacles that restricted any such assistance. For example, Foster argues that at times the project involved the monitoring and surveying of the behaviour and 'lifestyle patterns' of the mothers by employed staff, and also implicitly aimed to encourage the mothers to enter paid employment, sometimes regardless of circumstance. Foster also stressed the importance of the dissemination of her, and the mothers', findings: 'we felt it imperative that the "researched", along with the wider community, were given an opportunity to view, and to comment upon, [the] research findings in a thought-provoking and entertaining way'. This was achieved in the hope that the conclusions would bring about change in how the women were viewed beyond the confines of the buildings in which the Sure Start policy was being disseminated.

Special attention has also been given to a greater understanding of discourse, or as Fook (2002, cited in Bowles *et al.*, 2006: 11) identifies, 'the ways in which we make meanings of and construct our world through the language we use (verbal and non-verbal) to communicate about it'. As Bowles *et al.* (2006: 11) add, discourse:

> includes not only beliefs and ideas, but also social practices, our ideas of who we are and power relations . . . dominant discourses are like tinted lenses that colour our world, without us knowing that we are wearing glasses. They incorporate the ideas and power relations that we take for granted.

The role of the researcher is to explore, uncover and challenge forms of dominant discourse. The potential relevance of this argument cannot be over-stated for social work research, especially if forms of discrimination, exclusion and neglect are to be identified, interrogated and challenged. Opportunities persist through research to:

- *question established truth(s) and convention(s)* This might include critic-ally exploring taken for granted and dominant beliefs and procedures within social work, or other disciplines that ultimately stand to main-tain the status quo. Examples include assumptions made by some people about the success or otherwise of services provided to service users, the over-reliance on dominant theories (such as systems or attachment theory) within social work practice or the role played throughout social work by a specific component of practice (for example, bureaucracy, procedure, casework, etc.). In essence, any-thing taken for granted or established as legitimate is open to rigorous exploration and critical questioning.
- *criticize 'scientific' or quasi-scientific logic and routines* This could include looking reflexively and critically at core elements of social work, edu-cation or health care practices which draw from a rational tradition – such as managerialism or particular schools of thought such as the medical model or pathological theories linked to psychology or psy-chiatry. Postmodernism has been critical of 'welfare' practices such as those held within health and education services, as well as social work and social security. Such sectors of welfare are accused of fulfilling a role of processing information as part of a wider goal of surveillance and control; especially for people that do not conform to narrow expectations regarding apparent 'normal' behaviour. This refers to people who threaten established orders, such as through a lack of engagement with education or employment sectors, or becoming involved in crime and deviance or having mental health needs, etc.
- *allow excluded voices to be heard* Postmodernism seeks to support excluded groups and especially people from minority communities who are traditionally not listened to. A social work dissertation draw-ing from this tradition might concentrate upon interviewing, or assessing the literature on, gay men with a disability and their rela-tionship with social work, or older people who volunteer and their personal experiences of support services. A student may seek to investi-gate a group that has been marginalized by social work in the past, for example, older people or service users who self-harm. This approach would seek to interview minority groups and allow them a voice, such as by representing views and direct quotes in the final write up.

Just as radically postmodernism also seeks to undermine the principles of modern society (or 'modernity'), which in social research are identified as being encapsulated within the philosophy of positivism. These principles include the assumption that science knows best and is always correct and leads to social improvement; that progress through rational developments (greater planning, organization, bureaucracy, etc.) are inevitable within society; and that clear distinctions can be drawn between what is right and wrong, good and bad, competent and incompetent, etc.

A spate of postmodernist thinkers has also proposed that:

- societies are now much more fragmented than in the past;
- socially and culturally there now persists less of a consensus, with more and more differences emerging including those relating to employment arrangements, social needs, expectations and traditions linked to class, gender, ethnicity, disability and sexuality, personal tastes, etc;
- language is seen as central to the formation of taken for granted assumptions, traditions, practices, and is believed to be closely linked to disparate power relations;
- language by its very nature and structure is ambivalent and unstable, and meaning is always open to a range of interpretations and, in relation, science based and established 'truth', especially those inscribed by powerful elites, should always be open to question;
- knowledge and language are utilized by typically elite groups to sustain power over others, such as by professionals and other 'experts' over service users. For example, authors such as Stenson (1993) propose that social workers utilize language to regulate and control service users – such as through the assessment process and concomitant state and legal powers used to punish, correct and normalize seemingly 'deviant' behaviour or values;
- dominant language or narratives can be deconstructed, or scrutinized and the logic and structure taken apart, and reconstructed (such as in a dissertation) so as to present an alternative and more realistic version;
- essentialism – or the idea that every woman, older or disabled person should be treated as homogenous members of the same sect or class – should be avoided in favour of a recognition and celebration of difference. Similarly, ethnocentricity – or 'being unable to conceptualize or imagine ideas, social beliefs or the world, from any viewpoint other than that of one's own particular culture or social group', while believing that 'one's own ethnic group, nation, religion . . . is superior to all others' – should be avoided and/or confronted within social research;
- processes of subjectivity and normalization are complex and rely upon elaborate, sophisticated yet often implicit and subtle forms of

discipline. For example, the coherence of both 'care' and 'control' approaches within social work practice. Or the impact of institutional or more parochial forms of socialization ranging from the school to the family to peer pressure, and so on.

(Adapted from Harvey, 1990; Parton, 1994;
Banyard and Hayes, 1994: 130; Sanders and
Liptrop, 1994; Norris, 1995; Dominelli, 2004)

Despite being identified as part of the problem by critics such as Foucault (1977) – especially regarding its apparent role of information processing and surveillance – authors such as Fook (2002) and Healy (2005) argue that social work has a role to play as part of any postmodern agenda for progressive change. Examples include its *potential* capacity to question dominant power relations and rituals as well as its ability to utilize its expertise and status to empower disenfranchised and disadvantaged service users. Through critical social research, social work has the potential to allow excluded voices to be heard and the needs of minority groups to be highlighted. An example of this approach is provided in Case Study 4.3.

Gibbs (2001: 690) has drawn attention to ways in which postmodern theory has influenced social work. These have included its ability to:

- help challenge universal ideas and knowledge;
- question established and dominant theories;
- contest taken-for-granted concepts and perspectives;
- challenge simplistic dichotomies and binary opposites (service provider/purchaser, professional/'service user', manager/employee, etc.);
- encourage new ideas and approaches to emerge;
- help to re-evaluate social work practices, assumptions and ideologies.

The diverse postmodern agenda has received widespread criticism, including within social work literature. It has been accused of implicit conservatism regarding its disparagement of welfare states (and their apparent drive to monitor and survey the population) and has been identified as inadvertently adding support to the demands of right wing governments, and their calls for a greater role for the free market within capitalist states (Harvey, 1989). Bishop (1996: 58) also notes that in arguing for a greater celebration of difference postmodernism has deflected attention from often more important concerns: 'The postmodernist . . . has been criticised for fostering a self-indulgent subjectivity, and for exaggerating the esoteric and unique aspects of a culture at the expense of more prosaic but significant questions.' The strong emphasis placed upon language and narrative by postmodernists has also been questioned. Might this draw attention from other forms of oppression such as those that link to poverty or class?

Case Study 4.3

Topic: Deconstructing and reconstructing media interpretations of 'frail' and 'redundant' older people through conversation analysis with 'service users'

Barry decided to explore the social construction of older people. He initially studied newspaper articles over a 3 month period and denoted examples in his dissertation of how the 'elderly' were presented to the public through a major form of communication – the mass media. As Barry illustrated in his findings the majority of articles presented older people either as 'figures of fun' and ridicule – such as when expressing surprise when an older person completed a half marathon or climbed a mountain – or as being frail and dependant upon 'expensive' welfare support services. This paradox was explored in one of Barry's chapters in the first half of his dissertation.

Following this, through interviews with six 'service users' who accessed a local advocacy organization, Barry was able to discover and reveal how peoples' exploration of their own lives and identity contrasted with many of the depictions of the 'elderly' represented in the mass media. Barry was able to present through the spoken viewpoints of the 'service users' a set of lived experiences that were little different from people thirty years younger; especially regarding participation in physical activities (DIY, sport, leisure walking, etc.) and part-time employment and/or volunteering. Also the people interviewed were allowed to discuss at great length their own understanding of what being older meant to them. Through the creative use of the published and spoken 'text' and 'narrative', Barry was able to both deconstruct and reconstruct the image of the seemingly 'frail' and 'redundant' older person.

Despite such criticism, the extensive debate around postmodernism has been useful in re-prioritizing the needs of neglected groups, encouraging us to (again) question dominant ideas, beliefs and conventions, and also highlighting the complex forms of oppression generated by dominant interests, including those that are so closely tied to discourse, power, language and culture. Like critical theory, postmodernists also draw attention to the importance of using different disciplines within any social research process.

Recent developments in social work theory and practice

The impact of the perhaps somewhat protracted debates regarding points raised by postmodernism – as well as the continued relevance of interpretivism, critical theory and the more recent resurgence of positivism – have led to notable trends emerging within social work theory and practice. More general trends include:

Scepticism of objectivity and truth Rather than a complete rejection of researcher objectivity there is instead a questioning and ongoing debate about the feasibility of neutrality and associated claims by researchers to discover and depict an all-embracing and uncontested true representation of their findings. Nevertheless, although a more humble and contested stance is encouraged it is still advisable to have confidence in a thesis.

Importance of culture, relativism and context The recognition and existence of disparate cultures at a local level – including within regional localities, organizations, groups, families, etc. – is often seen as preferential to an over reliance upon 'reductive' generalizations that can compress meaning and understanding into neat categories such as those that prioritize class or gender and assume that each is relevant to everyone across time and space. Despite this, in other respects reductive tendencies have intensified elsewhere – for example, the promotion of skills and competency based training within social work education (Jones, 1996).

Scepticism of knowledge itself There is recognition that knowledge production – including that which is created by the researcher or professional – is never neutral but instead reflects power and potentially forms of domination and control. This assumption generates more questioning of knowledge claims, and also seeks to recognize the importance of the voices or experiences of disadvantaged groups who are often held outside the arenas of knowledge production. Perhaps somewhat paradoxically, however, there have also emerged advocates who promote the benefits of traditional, and arguably elite, professionalism (for example Healy and Meagher, 2001, among others),

Critique and reflexivity A culture of questioning and scepticism, especially of taken for granted, dominant or 'common sense' assumptions, traditions and practices has been promoted within social research (Lather, 1991; Humphries, 2008, among many others). This persists alongside the querying of personal attitudes and possible prejudices, as well as any applied role enacted within the research process.

Centrality of history The work of Foucault but also Marx has helped to stress the need to look beyond the present and future and recognize the centrality of previous events, traditions and policy, etc.

Elevation of inter-subjectivity and inter-professionalism Many of the traditional boundaries that separate different disciplines and applied practices have become more blurred, and indeed in some cases have begun to disappear. For example, closer links exist between disciplines such as health and social studies, and this has also led to the encouragement of closer working relations between social work, education and health professionals. This process, however, is open to criticism such as regarding the prioritizing if not dominance of a health and science based ideological discourse, and a subsequent undermining of social work.

Promotion of international perspectives This approach utilizes comparison and critique in order to analyse social work, social problems or interventions with particular reference to how each has been applied or experienced elsewhere: especially other countries that have some links with any host nation-state. An underlying assumption is that we might learn more or be able to understand and contextualize social problems better by looking at similar or alternative examples elsewhere. This perspective is discussed further in Chapter 9.

In general choice and flexibility have tended to expand regarding approaches used in research alongside a less dogged commitment to a single theoretical school, such as psychoanalysis in the 1960s, systems theory in the 1970s and Marxism in the 1970s and 1980s. There is encouragement of a more diffuse and diverse range of approaches that encompasses a wider range of theories, disciplines and perspectives. The use of different theories (often combined) to explain specific events uncovered within research permits greater choice and flexibility, and also possibly accuracy, to the researcher. Such dynamism may also sit alongside a more introspective questioning by the researcher of their own values and research strategy.

Ontology and ontological approaches

Alongside the four epistemological stances or theories already explored, there is one more aspect of research philosophy, or more generally methodology, to be considered. This is social ontology which deals with 'the nature of being' or of social entities (Ezzy, 2002; Elliott, 2005). Although closely linked to epistemology, ontology asks wider and more general questions that are philosophical, abstract and penetrative. Within social research, ontology is directly linked to epistemology because it helps generate questions to ask and therefore helps us to construct a research methodology (Holloway, 1997: 113). The link between ontology, epistemology, methodology and method is explored further below.

Ontology, epistemology, methodology and method

Any dissertation will contain, and draw from, four interrelated themes. These include ontology, epistemology, methodology and method. Each is briefly summarized below:

- Ontology reflects the nature of social reality and what the researcher understands reality to be like.
- Epistemology concerns the nature of knowledge and knowledge production, including what the researcher counts as knowledge.
- Methodology relates to the theoretical and philosophical assumptions linked to a topic and the ways in which any such topic will be investigated.
- Methods are the techniques and procedures followed in order to gather data relating to any topic under investigation.

Each section is linked by a bond that exists between ontology and epistemology; especially the assumption that knowledge production is imperative in order to explore any ontological stance. The bold statements that can epitomize ontology, and which are usually represented by a research question, require some investigation and evidence to either prove or disprove their feasibility; this is how and why, in order of priority, ontology, epistemology, methodology and method(s) follow within any research process. Epistemology, or knowledge and its production, will typically represent the ways in which an ontological statement will be assessed. Methodology and methods represent the organization of specific *processes* within knowledge production by which an ontological question will be assessed. Typically methodology can be supported by a distinct theory and/or field of philosophy while methods are represented by specific and practical techniques. Methodology is discussed in much more detail in Chapter 6.

Figures 4.1 to 4.3 give three examples of three separate yet related social work dissertations. They are separate because they have each asked different research questions, yet they are also related because they were each concerned with exploring a similar ontological question; that of the nature of social caring.

In Figure 4.1 the researcher has drawn from ontology to assume that caring is predominately a human response to a naturally occurring biological instinct. This is a bold statement which suggests that not only is caring natural for some people but also that culture and forms of socialization (for example, the influence of the family, schooling or the media) have very little impact upon our need to care for other people. This stance will have to be tested and the student has decided that the most appropriate way in which to do this via

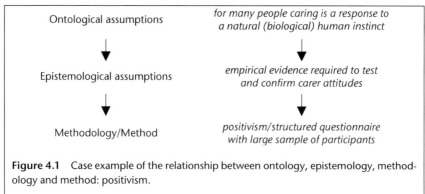

Figure 4.1 Case example of the relationship between ontology, epistemology, methodology and method: positivism.

Source: Adapted from Jones, 1993: 114–17; Foster, 2007b.

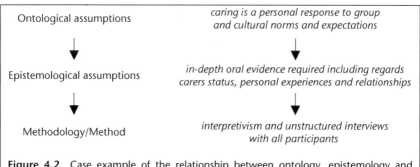

Figure 4.2 Case example of the relationship between ontology, epistemology and method: interpretivism.

Source: Adapted from Jones, 1993: 114–17; Foster, 2007b.

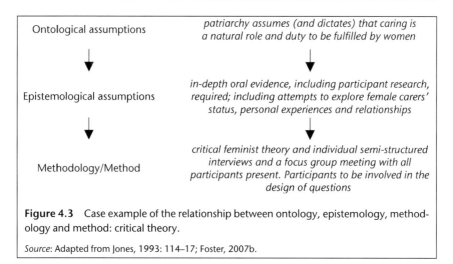

Figure 4.3 Case example of the relationship between ontology, epistemology, methodology and method: critical theory.

Source: Adapted from Jones, 1993: 114–17; Foster, 2007b.

knowledge production will be to make direct contact with a large sample of carers. This fits with a quantitative methodology due to both the size of the sample required and the beliefs inherent in the ontological assumption, which clearly draw from a scientific (biological) view of human action and values. The student has understandably decided that this research can best be accommodated by positivism, and has also decided to use the related method of a postal questionnaire sent to a large sample of potential participants.

In the example in Figure 4.2 the researcher has made a very different ontological statement, arguing instead that caring reflects a personal response to wider cultural and group expectations and norms, and *not biological*, factors. In order to test and confirm this through knowledge production the researcher has decided that in-depth and detailed evidence is required to allow her to investigate contributing factors. The student has used an interpretivist methodology because it rigorously explores personal details and meanings. Unstructured interviews fit with this overall approach as they permit space and time for participants to engage with the research process, and also allow the researcher to explore meaning, experience, self-identity and context with the participant. Overall, it is hoped that evidence collected from such inter-views and previous published research will allow the researcher to under-stand and explain the attitudes and beliefs of each participant regarding their carer roles.

Finally, the example shown in Figure 4.3 takes a much more critical stance, and assumes that caring reflects not only wider structural factors but more *generally* and *specifically* wider forces of patriarchy; or the influence of forms of male domination and control. The student has felt that this stance can only be tested via *in-depth* oral evidence. The methodology draws from critical feminist theory and the methods include more person-centred inter-views and a focus group meeting. This research also included an attempt to engage participants directly in the research process, such as by allowing each member to influence the design of any research questions. This reflects both the emancipatory values inherent within critical feminism and also allows the potential for more accurate data to emerge, due to closer contact and greater trust formed between the researcher and participants.

As can be seen above, three different viewpoints (or ontological stances) regarding the role of informal care held by three separate researchers has led to different outcomes regarding the use of epistemology, and the application of methodology and method. Each example illustrates the link between separate ontological stances and the differing ways in which research is planned and applied. Nevertheless each researcher is united in their search to discover whether or not their initial assumptions are correct.

Summary

This chapter has looked at the four main types or schools of theory used in social research – positivism, interpretivism, critical and postmodern. Each theoretical school has unique qualities and differing stances regarding how to undertake research and explain and understand findings. For a dissertation a student will typically commit to one alone as part of their methodology; however, there are times when one theory can link with another within a single methodology, such as when forms of interpretivism link with, or are influenced by, aspects of critical theory. Again boundaries can blur because of the unpredictable and sometimes 'messy' nature of social work research which can be better explained by a more flexible approach to theory. This chapter has also illustrated the distinction between ontology, epistemology, methodology and method, and highlighted how each binds together when applying social work research in practice.

The next chapter looks at the literature review.

Suggested reading

Alvesson, M. (2002) *Postmodernism and Social Research*. Buckingham: Open University Press.

Butler, C. (2002) *Postmodernism – A Very Short Introduction*. Maidenhead: Open University Press.

Corby, B. (2006) *Applying Research in Social Work Practice*. Maidenhead: Open University Press. (Chapter 4: Paradigm wars)

Crotty, M. (1998) *The Foundations of Social Research – Meaning and Perspective in the Research Process*. London: Sage. (Especially Chapter 2: Positivism: the march of science; Chapter 4: Interpretivism: for and against culture; Chapter 6: Critical inquiry: the Marxist heritage; Chapter 8: Feminism: re-visioning the man-made world; Chapter 9: Postmodernism: crisis of confidence or moment of truth?)

D'Cruz, H. and Jones, M. (2004) *Social Work Research – Ethical and Political Contexts*. London: Sage. (Chapter 3: Different ways of knowing and their relevance for research)

Humphries, B. (2008) *Social Work Research for Social Justice*. Basingstoke: Palgrave Macmillan. (Chapter 7: Critical theory)

5   The literature review and literature based dissertations

Introduction

A literature review represents a substantial component of any social work dissertation, and for some topics it can represent the most critical stage. Generally the literature review supports most of the key stages of any dissertation; from the development of a proposal to the final write up and dissemination. It should provide valuable information about a topic, offer related (and often contrasting and diverse) viewpoints from a range of authors, and may offer historical, theoretical and methodological themes that link to any subject matter. This chapter looks at the literature review in general and suggests key sources of information on which to draw. The chapter also provides practical tips on undertaking a literature review and looks specifically at literature based dissertations.

The literature review

Holloway (1997: 99) summarizes a literature review when she declares that 'Researchers trawl the relevant and related literature, summarise the main ideas from these studies as well as some of the problems and contradictions found, and show how they relate to the proposed project.' Just as significant are attempts to *critically engage with* and *analyse* any findings. As Walliman (2006: 182) underlines:

> Doing a literature review means not only tracking down all the relevant information, but also taking a critical position on the ideas contained therein . . . providing a description is not enough; your task is to give your own personal and professional appraisal of the content and quality of the text in question.

This process is especially significant in qualitative research; perhaps even more so within an *applied* discipline such as social work in which ethics and values play such a central role.

There are many reasons for undertaking a literature review, which include that it:

- helps to stimulate ideas;
- illustrates what other researchers have done in your area;
- broadens perspectives and places work into context;
- supports and expands upon personal experience;
- helps to fulfil the expectations of a supervisor;
- offers familiarity with different research methodologies and methods used by other researchers;
- improves research skills and knowledge;
- improves reading;
- may improve writing style by offering examples of how to construct and present arguments or a theory;
- helps to better understand a discipline and subject area.

(Adapted from Blaxter *et al.*, 2006: 93)

Typically a literature review for qualitative research will develop in two stages. This includes a relatively brief *initial* review, followed by a longer *ongoing* review. The former begins prior to, or soon after, a research question has been formulated, and includes a search for a handful of key related publications that will help develop a proposal. This initial stage will also help to narrow any focus so to construct a methodology and possibly begin to plan potential research methods to employ. The ongoing review begins when the initial stage has ended, and will include a more substantial and detailed overview of related material. As the latter phase takes place over a longer time scale – possibly including the application of a research method, analysis and even the writing up stage – this permits a more thorough search for related material.

It is unlikely that all published material related to any one topic can be identified, located and read. This is because there is likely to be far too much material that links to most subject areas, and only limited time available. As Bell (1987: 18, my emphasis) suggests, you will instead need to be able to 'provide evidence that you have read a *certain amount* of relevant literature' and also illustrate that you 'have [at least] *some awareness* of the current state of knowledge on the subject'.

Warburton (2004: 9–22) offers some general guidelines when reading around any topic. In particular it is advisable to:

> *Avoid being a passive reader* By taking notes and thinking carefully about the arguments or points raised by an author much more can be

gained from reading. Questions such as 'Is the author right?' or 'Has adequate evidence been provided to support an argument?' will allow a considered approach to each literary source and also assist the development of any study.

Get an overview Try to identify the core arguments within any article or book. The title, abstract of a paper or summary towards the rear of a book will help, but keeping notes and making references will also support a literature review. Identifying key passages and themes also support this process.

Avoid getting bogged down with details Re-read material if it is not clear or you don't understand it but remember that the central points that link to your topic are usually the priority and if you do not understand other sections this may not be a concern. First and last paragraphs are often important within an article as they often contain core details that relate to an article or academic paper.

Look for signposts These are typically indicated at the beginning of a paragraph and are represented by statements that explicitly detail the direction in which the author is taking us. They can help us better understand the arguments and general points within an article or book.

It will be of benefit to keep in mind your research question and ask whether any published article is helping to explore and answer the question itself. Ask yourself if it is helping to fulfil the objectives set out within a research proposal. Available literature should link to such core sections within a proposal and also begin to allow the development of a research method – for example, likely questions to ask research participants.

It will also help to explore material relating to qualitative research methodology as part of a literature review and help you to:

- gain an understanding about research methodology;
- understand how different approaches are applied in *practice* by other people;
- grasp and fully appreciate research approaches that differ from your own;
- extend your research knowledge base and skills;
- learn how to present and detail a methodology from examples set by professional researchers.

Walliman (2006: 184) has argued convincingly that there are four components to a literature review. Below is an attempt to link each with social work research:

1   *Research theory and philosophy* This represents an endeavour to 'establish the intellectual context(s) of research related to your subject'. For example, what theories have been used by other researchers to help explore the themes that you are attempting to address, and could they also be of use to your own research?

2   *History of developments in your subject* This section of a literature review seeks to explore the 'background to current thinking'. For example, how did we come to practise in the way we do *today* as part of child or adult protection? How has this changed in the past decade? How has a specific form of practice developed over the past century? In a discipline such as social work historical trends are often prioritized because of their impact regarding policy, legislation and the subsequent influence upon social and cultural trends. For most topics there will also be a need to consider both older publications and more recent works.

3   *Latest research and developments in your subject* This explores 'current issues' and 'latest thinking and practice', and will integrate current debates within social work. Ultimately you should try to bring the reader up to date with any major developments in social work practice or research that link to a topic under investigation. As ever there will be a need to use your discretion and be succinct if you have limited space to explore any individual themes.

4   *Research methods and methodology* Again it will help to consider your own methodology alongside approaches utilized by other researchers in the field. Looking at how other people design their research processes is always a useful way to stimulate ideas.

The extent and type of literature review undertaken will tend to vary between topics. For example, a review for a literature based dissertation will take much longer, and tend to be more rigorous than many that are linked to empirical research. This is primarily due to a need to adequately answer the research question, but it is also influenced by the amount of available time to undertake such work. For empirical research there are more research stages as part of the research process – these may include gaining access to participants such as for interviews, completing any such research method(s), processing and assessing your empirical data, and so on. Such practice based tasks often take up an extensive amount of time so your literature review will inevitably be briefer.

In general, the more focussed a topic then the more manageable a literature review will be – a broad and non-specific topic is likely to generate a literature review that is time consuming and laborious, and which may prove difficult to complete. Finally, and as was first discussed in Chapter 2, there are two relatively common problems experienced by some social work students regarding their literature review. They are that there exists either too much literature related to any topic or simply not enough. If there is too much literature this is easier to manage and accommodate, such as by reducing the project and overall objectives or by concentrating upon fewer themes in relation to the subject area. If there is not enough material this tends to be much more difficult to support. In such circumstances it will be of benefit to meet with your tutor to discuss possible ways forward – usually a topic will need to be altered or broadened in ambition and scope. Sometimes, however, a topic which lacks related published material will need to be reconsidered and another selected.

Primary and secondary sources

As was briefly explored in Chapter 3, either primary or secondary sources of information provide the basis for a literature review. Table 5.1 offers a list of examples of primary and secondary sources. Information from primary sources tends to be collected from 'hands on' experience and research methods such as interviews or focus group meetings. Less common sources such as statistical data bases and film or video material may still be suitable if they are closely linked to a topic. In practice, however, core secondary sources such as journal articles, textbooks, chapters in textbooks, and monographs will constitute the key resources which most dissertations will rely upon for a literature review. The next section offers more information regarding secondary sources.

Table 5.1   Primary and secondary sources of information

Primary	Secondary
Observation	Journal articles
Experience	Chapters in books
Relevant people	Monographs
Statistical data	Textbooks
Historical records and texts	Government publications
Organization records	Popular media
Personal documents (letters, diaries,	Research reports
reports, etc.)	Previous dissertations
Film/video	Specialist magazine articles
Original works of literature and art	Internet articles
	Databases (for example, the Census or Social Trends)

Key sources of secondary information

Sources of secondary information or 'data' include the following.

Journals

Articles in journals often represent the most reliable sources of information for any topic as part of a social work dissertation. This is because journal articles tend to be more up to date, focused, detailed and briefer than other sources such as most course textbooks or Internet sites. Journal articles are also usually peer reviewed and contain a rich source of empirical and/or conceptual or theoretical findings. There are a variety of journal formats including those dealing with local, national and international issues, interdisciplinary and subject specialties, as well as applied and practitioner-led approaches. Core social work journals such as the *British Journal of Social Work* or *Qualitative Social Work* should always be checked first for articles that are linked to a topic area. Following this, core journals in related disciplines such as social policy, sociology, psychology, law, etc. can also be searched. Table 5.2 lists some of the key journals relating to social work.

For an initial literature review and proposal you should be able to rely upon a handful of journal articles, key textbooks and chapters in books that *closely relate* to your topic. The advantage of this strategy is that you are able to rapidly familiarize yourself with current thinking around a topic, and should also be able to gain some historical perspectives from the articles themselves. As journals usually represent the best and most reliable sources of information for a dissertation you should aim to have between a quarter and a third of all references sourced from journal articles cited in the reference list of your dissertation. This will not always be possible depending on the nature of the research question being explored but remains a rough guide to aspire to.

Finally, it is important to remember that although journal articles typically provide the bedrock of quality research they also tend to vary in quality. For example, some journals are more rigorous in their peer review of articles than others. It may help to consult with your supervisor about reliable journals.

Monographs

A monograph is a published academic thesis (usually presented in book or booklet form) that explores in detail a single subject or series of related topics. It can be historical, political or explore a theme such as informal or institutional care for people with mental health needs. This format differs from most course textbooks because of the extent of detail and rigorous

Table 5.2 Some examples of social work and related subject journals

Discipline	Journal
Social work	*British Journal of Social Work*
	Journal of Social Work
	International Social Work
	Child and Family Social Work
	Child Abuse Review
	European Journal of Social Work
	Australian Social Work
	Practice
	Social Work Education
	European Social Work
	Social Work and Social Sciences Review
Social Policy	*Journal of Social Policy*
	Critical Social Policy
	Social Policy and Society
	International Journal of Sociology and Social Policy
	Contemporary Crises: Crime, Law and Social Policy
	Benefits: A Journal of Social Security, Research, Policy and Practice
Sociology	*Sociology*
	British Journal of Sociology
	American Journal of Sociology
	Critical Sociology
	Work, Employment and Society
	Organisation
	International Review of Sociology
	Ethnography
Psychology	*British Journal of Educational Psychology*
	British Journal of Developmental Psychology
	Psychologist
	Self and Society: a Forum for Contemporary Psychology
Law	*Journal of Law and Society*
	British Journal of Law and Society
	Gazette
Research methods	*Qualitative Social Work*
	Research on Social Work Practice
	Sociological Research Online
	Action Research
Other	*Ethics and Social Welfare*
	Children and Schools
	Disability and Society
	Journal of Inter-professional care
	Health and Social Care

academic examination that usually takes place. More often than not the content will include extensive analysis throughout. Sometimes a monograph may develop from research undertaken for a PhD or simply follow one academic's area of interest.

Introductory and overview textbooks

Course textbooks tend to dominate the market of published academic material in book form. This is because they offer a general and relatively easy to follow guide to a discipline and are therefore popular with students and practitioners. Although this can be beneficial in offering an initial overview it is advisable not to over-rely on such books. This is because much of the material contained within is wide ranging and one of the key purposes of a dissertation is to critically explore the *more specific nuances* of a series of debates or set of themes.

Edited collections and subsequent chapters

An edited collection is a set of articles held in a textbook that link to a specific topic (community care, mental health needs and social work, foster care, etc.). Articles typically comprise contributions from different authors. There are many edited collections linked to social work and related disciplines such as social policy. The writing style, content and presentation in such a format are usually held *between* an academic journal paper and an introductory textbook. Edited collections can be helpful in supporting any thesis – especially if the collection of articles is closely tied to a research topic.

In general there are two major types of edited collection – those that encompass broader trends in social work and other disciplines (for example, Parton, 1996) and publications that are more specific and explore one aspect of a subject in great detail (for example, Symonds and Kelly, 1998). Like all publications, edited collections come in all shapes, sizes and standards regarding quality – it is up to you to assess whether they are of relevance to your work and what the strengths and weaknesses are of each contribution.

Government publications

A number of government publications relate to social work research. Many can be found in an academic library or can be ordered or downloaded from websites. For example, in the UK the following websites are helpful for accessing government related publications:

> **www.parliament.uk** The House of Parliament website offers reports, findings from research, copies of acts of legislation and other information.

www.opsi.gov.uk The Office of Public Sector Information offers informative video streams, legislation from 1987 onwards, and also provides a register of unpublished information and feeds to other legislation in the UK.

www.dfes.gov.uk and the **www.doh.gov.uk** The Department of Children, Schools and Families and the Department of Health websites provide statistics, research findings, legislation and other information.

Remember that government material is likely to be slanted in favour of a political party and may also contain rhetorical claims.

Legislation

Major acts of legislation including Green and White papers in Britain and forms of Guidance are usually accessible from academic libraries or the websites identified in the previous section above. There is also a range of critical textbooks and journal articles that deal specifically with legislation, social policy and related disciplines. If you are concentrating upon the impact of a specific act of legislation upon a form of social work practice it is essential to read as widely as possible from different sources, including critical responses to the impact of the policy upon service users and practitioners. Typically, published legislation alone will only offer one side of a series of complex arguments and political stances.

Popular media

Newspapers tend to be kept in most university and college libraries and potentially can provide a good source of up to date information relating to specific topics. Inevitably some sources are more reliable than others and established 'broadsheet' publications tend to be more reliable regarding their factual accuracy and less biased reporting of facts. It is not advisable however to over-rely on the popular media as a source of information since it is generally acknowledged that any such reports are politically biased. The television and Internet can also be used as a source of information relating to popular media outlets.

Independent reports

Voluntary organizations, university departments and salaried researchers and independent organizations sometimes engage in research that leads to subsequent publications. Such reports may link to social work and specifically your topic – common areas to be studied include service user needs, support service evaluations or the impact of legislation on a particular service user group. Large voluntary organizations such as Age Concern or Barnardos in the UK tend to publish their own research findings, as does the Joseph Rowntree foundation. Many reports are also available via the Internet. Some reports will be published and some are stored in university libraries. It may be advisable to consult with your librarian or check the library index for any related reports.

Previous dissertations

Many university libraries or colleges typically stock dissertations completed by previous students. It is always worthwhile checking through some of these – especially to offer guidance on how to arrange and structure your thesis.

Specialist magazines

Professional magazines such as *Community Care* and *Care and Health* can offer practical, up to date and (sometimes) critical guidance on current research, policy and practice in social work. Such weekly or monthly magazines usually have their own websites complete with a search engine to help you find articles from previous editions.

Key authors' references and websites

Most topics will link to researchers and authors that specialize in this area of interest. It is sometimes worthwhile searching for other material published by such authors just to check if there are any publications or related material you may have missed. Personal websites kept by authors can help and you may again wish to scour the reference lists at the rear of any of their published work to check for material that links to your topic.

Reliable Internet sources

The Internet can offer an invaluable resource for literature based and empirical social work research. There are, however, a number of problems that relate to any *over-reliance* upon Internet sources. This is chiefly due to the almost infinite number of websites now available and also the lack of regulation attached to the Internet as a whole. Consequentially, it is imperative to be selective about using the Internet as a potential source of information.

There are a number of websites which may help support a social work dissertation. Alongside those already specified in Chapter 5, some of the best can be found in the Appendix (see page 185).

Keeping records and taking notes

It is beneficial to keep a record of all of the literary sources you access. This may assist a quick recollection of previously explored information and knowledge and also support any writing process or final reference list within a dissertation. The main details to keep a record of include:

- names of author(s)
- title of paper, book, etc.
- date of publication
- publisher and place of publication
- source details – for example, name of journal and volume, number, etc.
- a summary of key points raised in the article, paper, chapter, etc.

Although it may suffice to keep general notes regarding such information index cards can help provide a more comprehensive system. Such organized note taking allows key points and authors to be quickly compared and contrasted, as well as different arguments, theories or general ideas. Just reading material and highlighting themes may limit your capacity to conceptualize arguments and analyse themes.

The literature review process and critical analysis

The capacity to undertake a critical analysis of previous research is fundamental to any literature review. Blaxter *et al.* (2006: 104, my emphasis) maintain that within academic discourse 'being critical' is the capacity to offer 'a considered . . . and justified *examination* of what others have written or said regarding [a] subject in question'. As a social work student this means offering a personal and professional assessment of the quality of any related published work consumed.

This may be achieved by a combination of methods in which each article, book, report, etc., is appraised with special attention given to:

- the quality of the *evidence* presented to support the general thesis and arguments – for example new data or the coherence and logic of new arguments;
- whether or not any evidence originates from, and is supported, by *credible sources*, such as other people's research, data or arguments;
- the *arguments* presented and especially whether they are sound and consistent;
- whether the use of *supporting theory* is viable and sound and how this

compares to competing theoretical standpoints. For example, the conflict between Marxist and postmodernist standpoints regarding class, gender or power relations;

- the strengths and weaknesses of any *findings* and *discussion*. For example, the research may highlight the impact of unemployment upon a particular group of service users but neglect the effect of race and ethnicity;
- what the author(s) are presenting that is *new* or *different* regarding any debate. Is this unique or distinct stance adequately supported by evidence?
- the *wider context* of the publication, such as the influence of related historical trends, discourses and ideological forces, and ongoing debates, etc.;
- how the work *compares* with other publications, arguments and research findings. For example, is it more convincing, thorough, better argued and presented, or deficient and lacking in evidence? What is the relevance of the work in comparison to others?
- how each *links* to your own research question and topic;
- the *research methodology* utilized, including in comparison to others.
  (Adapted from Harvey, 1990; Dominelli, 2002; Walliman, 2006)

As detailed in earlier arguments, trends or 'facts' should never be accepted at face value, and instead should remain open to careful yet justified criticism (with evidence) by a student. This might include looking carefully at an author's methodology for possible weaknesses, or maybe considering carefully their presentation of arguments and conclusions for possible inconsistencies or deficiencies.

Literature based dissertations

Literature based dissertations have a number of advantages which include an opportunity to:

- explore a topic in great depth;
- examine theoretical and methodological approaches in more detail;
- spend more time surveying published research including prior empirical approaches utilized in social work and other disciplines;
- scrutinize an aspect of the social work course that has previously generated interest. For example, an aspect of interdisciplinary practice, international and comparative social work or a form of specialist social work practice, such as relating to mental health or poverty related service user needs;

- investigate the ethical and philosophical aspects of social work practice in more detail;
- explore the theoretical aspects of different or alternative social work approaches.

The pattern of literature based dissertations will differ from empirical research because there is usually no new primary data to be collected, such as from a practice placement arena. The key advantage that this offers is more time available to explore any published literature in greater depth. Consequentially, there will be an expectation that your review of secondary sources will be more extensive, rigorous and thorough. Despite differences there are still links between a literature based dissertation and a dissertation based around empirical research; this will include an expectation to pursue the same process of selecting a topic, scouring the sources of literature, narrowing your research objectives, and analysing and writing up your findings.

As with all dissertations your first task will be to select an appropriate topic to research, such as one that is built around a research question. Examples of possible topics are much the same as those explored in Chapter 2. However, some areas are perhaps more suited to literature based dissertations and obvious examples include the following:

Specialist practice This might involve an exploration of an area of personal interest relating to a specific group of service users. For example, older people, children with special needs, adults with mental health needs, and so on.

Theory and practice Investigating the link between theory and practice will offer another potential source of research. For example, you might want to explore whether labelling theory still has relevance in work with people with mental health needs, or enquire whether the social model of disability offers a viable alternative to current social work practices.

Comparative Comparing different approaches in social work provides another viable option for a literary review. For example, you may wish to interrogate the impact of two contrasting theories on practice or explore how a particular theory differs when used in work with separate service user groups (for example, older and disabled people).

Historical Usually this type of research involves studying over time the changing impact of specific ideas, practices, or policies, etc., including those that link to, and have an effect upon, social work practice. Any study of historical trends may help to contextualize and better understand current practices.

Legislation and policy Typically this will allow a student the opportunity to explore critically any act of legislation or policy. Hence, you may wish to investigate the long term impact of an older act of legislation (such as the Chronically Sick and Disabled Persons Act, 1970), or assess the possible implications of more recent policy (such as the *Every Child Matters* initiative in Britain). Often this type of research is comparative as well as critical – it may look to reflect upon international differences or differing responses to any specific reform based on previous and/or more recent empirical evidence gathered from social research.

Once you have a rough idea of a research question to investigate, your next task will be to undertake an initial literature review. As discussed earlier, this usually involves a survey of a small number of related key journal articles, course textbooks and chapters in books, etc. This initial search is a kind of 'mini literature review' and tends to be used to clarify and fine tune your research objectives and aims. Next you proceed by widening your literature search. This will help you to build upon the initial literature review by accessing many sources discussed earlier in this chapter. Arguably, this stage makes up the most demanding part of any literature based dissertation because you will need to physically search for, read and internalize much information. As well as critically assessing literature you will also need to look for key themes and trends that link to your topic. Finally, as any reading progresses, you may again need to fine tune and reduce your objectives further, especially if there is a glut of material that is associated with your research question.

Structure

Literature based dissertations tend to be structured differently compared to any thesis that involves empirical research. Although there are always introduction, methodology and conclusion sections, the chapters in between tend to concentrate upon core findings and analysis relating to background reading. This inevitably includes addressing, exploring and unpacking themes and issues that relate to your topic. Because findings tend to vary between each literature based dissertation, the structure will also tend to differ more. Literature based dissertations are therefore often less standardized than empirical dissertations. The four examples in Table 5.3 highlight this trend. The first example follows the traditional structure for an empirically based dissertation – that of the introduction, literature review, methodology, findings, analysis and conclusion. This contrasts with the first literature based dissertation, in which the student has decided to concentrate upon three core themes that relate to their research question. This makes up the section that will contain much of the material explored within the literature review, and follows an

Table 5.3 Differing structures of empirical and literature based research dissertations

Empirical based research dissertation	Literature based dissertation 1	Literature based dissertation 2	Literature based dissertation 3
1 Introduction	1 Introduction	1 Introduction	1 Introduction and methodology
2 Literature review	2 Methodology and background	2 Methodology	2 Background
3 Methodology	3 Theme 1	3 Literature review – previous research and trends	3 Main issues/analysis 1
4 Findings	4 Theme 2	4 Literature review – themes 1/2 and discussion/analysis	4 Main issues/analysis 2
5 Analysis and discussion	5 Theme 3	5 Literature review – themes 3/4 and discussion/analysis	5 Discussion
6 Conclusions	6 Discussion	6 Supposition and recommendations	6 Conclusions
	7 Conclusions	7 Conclusions	

introduction and conclusion section, a discussion of the methodology and previous research undertaken (by other researchers) so to give the reader a feel of the background to the topics that are later explored in sections 3, 4 and 5. The discussion section towards the end has offered an opportunity to bring together and debate themes identified within the three tier theme chapters.

In the second literature based dissertation, the student has begun with an introduction and methodology chapter. They have then split the literature review into three main chapters – the first offers an overview of prior research while the next two chapters explore, analyse and detail two themes each that link to, and explore, the original research question. The student has then offered a final chapter of suppositions and recommendations. Finally, in the third example, the student has decided to introduce their methodology in the introduction chapter as part of a general discussion. They have then gone on to offer a chapter of background details relating to prior research before concentrating upon several issues that relate to their topic within two separate chapters, before finally presenting a discussion and conclusion chapter.

In general then literature based dissertations offer more variety and flexibility regarding how any final work is presented, developed and structured. How this is done will depend upon your chosen topic and also your findings and analysis (discussed in Chapter 9). It is also possible to have a greater number of smaller chapters, especially if this will allow more succinct yet in-depth discussion of more themes that are part of answering a research question or exploring a social problem.

See Case Study 5.1 for an example of a literature based dissertation. Literature based dissertations are discussed further in Chapter 10 regarding any write up.

Case Study 5.1: a literature review dissertation

Topic: Critically evaluating preventative 'treatments' of older service users with depression – a literature review

Tony wanted to undertake a critical review of the welfare support treatments received by older people with depression. He was keen to assess which support services had proven to be 'successful' in the long term, especially those which had a strong emphasis upon preventative and therapeutic work. His assessment of any support services was to be based upon previous empirical and theoretically informed research. Initially he had hoped to concentrate upon the UK.

As part of his initial literature review Tony searched the relevant social work and health discipline journals for related material. He found a number of closely related studies in social work, health care (such as public health, physiotherapy and nursing) and social policy journals, and then began to look at textbooks, Internet sites, government reports, and so on. As his literature review developed Tony's study became more focused. For example, he began to reduce the total number of support services that he assessed and eventually concentrated upon 'innovative' and 'alternative' forms of therapeutic social work, primary health care and newer types of public health policy.

Tony began to appreciate the benefits of looking at *some* examples of policy in different countries, including America and Sweden. Overall he read more than thirty journal articles and a similar number of publications from other sources. Tony's reading and analysis using an adaptation of postmodern theory led to a clear set of conclusions and recommendations of how some forms of preventative social work, primary health care and public health policy with older people with mental health needs could be 'deconstructed' and 're-applied'. For example, he argued that therapeutic and preventative social pedagogical approaches – traditionally used in Germany in social work with children – had relevance for work with older people if slight revisions were made to their planning and application.

Summary

This chapter has stressed the central role of the literature review in all dissertations. In practice, most dissertations tend to be strongly influenced by the extent and thoroughness of a literature review – this is because the literature review represents the *foundation* of any research project or thesis. A slender or hurried literature review may lead to incomplete or inappropriate interview questions, and may also yield limited insight, analysis and conclusions. Literature based dissertations have a number of advantages. These may include more time to investigate and explore secondary sources, as well as provide an opportunity to explore in more depth a topic not adequately detailed on a social work course.

The next chapter begins a series of three that look more closely at differing research methodologies and method. Chapter 6 begins with a look at three research methodologies.

Suggested reading

Blaxter, L., Hughes, C., Tight, M. (2006) *How to Research*. Maidenhead: Open University Press. (Chapter 4: Reading for research)

Fink, A. (2005) *Conducting Research Literature Reviews – From the Internet to Paper*. London: Sage.

Gash, S. (1999) *Effective Literature Searching for Research*. Aldershot: Gower.

Hart, C. (1998) *Doing a Literature Review – Releasing the Social Science Research Imagination*. London: Sage.

Ridley, D. (2008) *The Literature Review – A Step by Step Guide for Students*. London: Sage.

Wilkinson, D. (2005) *The Essential Guide to Postgraduate Study*. London: Sage. (Chapter 6: Reading and searching for information and seeking advice)

6 Social work methodology

Introduction

This chapter explains how methodology can be used to direct and guide a dissertation. As was briefly explored in Chapter 2, the use of an *appropriate* methodology is beneficial because it encourages direction and meaning in a research project. The chapter offers four examples of methodologies that can be used within social work research – case study, evaluation, feminist and grounded theory approaches. There are other methodologies and some of these – including narrative and life history approaches – are explored in Chapter 8. Finally this chapter also looks at critiques of methodology, mixed methodology, and highlights the importance of linking research methodology to the use of theory and research method(s).

Social work methodology

The term methodology has attained two different meanings. First, it is often used (inappropriately) 'as a synonym for [research] methods'; possibly because, as Payne and Payne (2004: 150–1) insist, methodology represents an articulate word that 'rolls off the tongue' or simply 'just sounds better' than methods! Unfortunately conflation with research *method* procedures can result in uncertainty for the student and sometimes the reader of a dissertation. Although a research methodology will accommodate specific research method(s), it will also support much more – including a wider strategy, and a set of theoretical, philosophical and ethical stances that help to bind together a research project.

A second and more accurate definition of methodology identifies it as a 'grander scheme of ideas orientating researchers' work' (Payne and Payne, 2004: 150–1), and sometimes the analogy of a 'recipe' or 'framework' (Daly, 2003: 192) is used to encapsulate the means by which it brings together, frames, supports and directs the activities and processes involved in a dissertation. Figure 6.1 illustrates the relationship between methodology and other stages of the research process – as can be seen a methodology should 'surround' and hold together any dissertation.

Another advantage that a methodology provides is that it can help bring together *into a coherent whole* the procedures followed with any research project. This is because the methodology should bring with it a coherent set of beliefs and values. This may also enable the research and findings to make much more sense to the reader. As Payne and Payne (2004: 151) underline: 'If we are told that the writer has adopted a feminist methodology, or a constructivist methodology, we have some idea of the sets of values the researcher brought to the study, why it took a particular form, and how the interpretation has developed.'

Crotty (1998: 66) also notes the theoretical imperatives enclosed within methodology and how they play a role in *influencing* subsequent stages of any research process:

> [W]henever one examines a particular methodology, one discovers a complexus of assumptions buried within it. It is these assumptions that constitute one's theoretical perspective and they largely have to do with the world that the methodology envisages. Different ways of viewing the world shape different ways of researching the world.

Research methodologies can therefore be utilized to organize and plan your dissertation *overall* in a broad sense, while also being able to appreciate the more subtle nuances inherent within the research process. For example, a methodology influenced by interpretivism will emphasize the importance of meaning, identity and personal experience to research participants, and will therefore seek to use a method such as the interview which is able to explore personal experience in great detail. Without the support of a methodology,

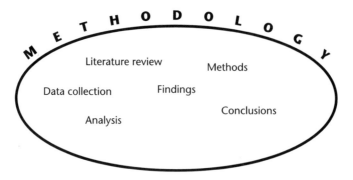

Figure 6.1   Social work methodology and research procedures.

social research can potentially be reduced to an almost mechanical process of undertaking research methods, and then completing the task of analysis and writing up *without looking at wider theoretical and philosophical concerns that impinge upon the process and outcomes of research.*

As well as offering a framework for theoretical understanding and debate, methodology also embraces a concern with ethics, or the moral dilemmas attached to the culture of social research. For example, a critical research methodology proposes that objective research – in which bias can be removed from the research process and the researcher can independently study people almost as an abstract and distant physical object – is largely unattainable. Such a methodology (and related set of theories) also claims that the priorities of research are to investigate, contextualize and highlight forms of disadvantage, discrimination and social exclusion. Use of such a methodology will indicate to the reader that a clear philosophical framework and structure have been present from an early stage.

In practice it is possible to decide a suitable methodology immediately after a research question and general topic have been decided. In such circumstances a methodology may reflect personal beliefs or will be appropriate due to the context of the research. Despite this, it is more common to decide a methodology after the literature review has begun. This is because the literature review can often alter the nature and context of a research project by throwing new light and providing different insights (including from the views of other published researchers) regarding the topic of research.

Finally, and in relation to this, although not common it is still possible for a methodology to be revised during later stages of the research process, and to adapt it as new findings emerge. It is also possible to construct your own methodology to suit the topic that you intend to research, for example, combining participant observation – in which close contact and engagement is maintained with research participants – with a feminist ethical stance when researching women working in a specific social care arena. Such a 'mixed methodology' approach is discussed towards the end of this chapter.

Four examples of methodologies that can be utilized in social work research are discussed below.

Case study research

The case study approach is where a single case example is explored in relation to a specific research question or social issue. A case can be represented by the study of:

- one person's life experiences and/or attitudes regarding a predetermined (and sometimes very specific) topic;

- a social role fulfilled by a person such as a social worker, teacher, carer, community nurse, etc.;
- a small group of people (or group case study) who share something in common, such as having a collective status, or similar experiences regarding the fulfilment of a certain role. For example, it could be a group of carers who each have a relative that has been diagnosed with a form of dementia and who support that person on a full-time basis.
- a specific social issue to investigate such as the different housing needs of young disabled males or older men;
- an organization such as a social care service provider or voluntary sector organization;
- a form of government policy such as that relating to adult protection or a subsequent piece of legislation that links to an aspect of social work practice;
- a nationwide social trend or national social policy.

This approach aims to identify and then explore a determined case in great depth and detail, so as to understand and appreciate the characteristics or unique qualities embodied within. Also cases are often identified as representing more general principles, qualities or issues, and may be used to generalize and make recommendations, such as regarding forms of future social work practice. The case study is an ideal approach for a social work dissertation because it offers an immediate focus on an identified subject of research. As Payne and Payne (2004: 32) also note:

> It is the limited scale, and manageability, of the case study that is often the real reason that it is chosen as an approach. By concentrating on one case, it is possible to complete work more quickly, and in much greater depth and detail, than if the researcher were trying to cover several cases.

Humphries (2008: 87) notes the attraction of case study research to social work students, but highlights the difference between this approach and casework as part of social work practice or education:

> Social work students are often attracted to case study research because it seems easy and sounds familiar. It is however quite different from the use of case studies in teaching, where a single case can be used to draw lessons for practice . . . Case study research attempts to approach a real-life phenomenon from the inside, using a range of methods. The study seeks to examine the phenomenon in depth in order to analyse thoroughly details that might be lost in any other type of research such as a larger survey.

For a social work dissertation it may also be possible to contrast two or more case examples, such as part of a comparative analysis of an aspect of contrasting social care service providers (comparative analysis is discussed in more detail in Chapter 9).

Punch (2005: 145) identifies four characteristics of any case study. They include the following:

- *The prevalence of boundaries that clearly delineate a case.* For example, if exploring one country's policy relating to adoption then it is important to clarify this early, and distinguish it from other related yet distinct policies, such as fostering or other forms of childcare.
- *Specify clearly what the case constitutes and entails.* For example, if studying an organization it can be beneficial to narrow any focus to a few easily assessed criteria for analysis, rather than attempt to study a number of broad and difficult to quantify themes.
- *Elicit research aims and objectives.* Try to be clear about what it is you hope to achieve and how. These questions should always link directly to any case and it is a priority to establish how 'evidence' from any case study might be used to explore research aims and objectives.
- *Establish the means of data collection.* Empirical research methods such as interviews and participant observation can be used but other approaches such as focus groups are possible depending upon the study. For other case studies, such as an exploration of an aspect of a (single) countries policy, it is inevitable that published literary sources will be relied upon.

Hitchcock and Hughes (1989, cited in Cohen *et al.*, 2007: 253) consider seven hallmarks of case study research which can include:

- a rich and vivid description of events or other themes relating to a case;
- a chronological narrative of events relevant to a case;
- a description of case related events or themes blended with an analysis of them;
- a stress upon individuals or groups of individuals and attempts to understand their perception of events;
- the highlighting of specific events or issues that are relevant to a case;
- the researcher becoming intimately involved with and immersed in a case study;
- the richness and distinct qualities of a case being highlighted in a final write up.

In Yin's (1994: 21–7) explorations of case study research, five elements of research design are identified. First, a study's research question or topic must be defined as early as possible (although once again this can be revised later on). Again it is advisable to try to avoid uncertainty, vagueness or over-ambition. Second, the formulation of research propositions, or preconceived assumptions or statements about the study case, may help to gain focus within a project. Third, a 'unit' of analysis must be identified as early as possible. For example, if studying a practitioner's personal experience of the assessment process, then it is the practitioner's *viewpoints* that become the unit. As with the research topic, clarity and focus are again imperative for any unit identified. Fourth, there must be a clear and tangible link between the data (on which any assessment is based) and the research aims and objectives of the study. Finally, some criteria for interpreting and evaluating the case study should be recognized – for example, on what basis will a case be assessed, and compared with other related research?

Yin (1994: 27–32) also stresses the central role of theory in case work (as in all social research). A number of related points are raised which include the need:

- to gain awareness of the established theories that relate to your topic, which should in turn influence the focus of your topic and help clearly define your aims and objectives. Also case study research can be helpful if attempting to test, refine or build theory.
- to link any established theory to your study and use it to analyse your findings and analysis.

Yin offers but one interpretation of the case study approach. However, in practice differing methodologies can be applied. For example, a prominent feature of case study research is the possible use of more than one method or source of evidence to collect data. Such 'triangulation', which can include the use of interviews, focus groups, and/or a combination of various literary sources (government reports, academic papers, Internet sources, textbooks, etc.), is more possible due to the benefits of having fewer cases to explore, and therefore more time available to undertake research. Because they are engaged in exploring one or two cases, the researcher may be able to vigorously examine the case study from many different angles and perspectives by using a variety of methods and theories (if appropriate).

Humphries (2008: 90–1) highlights the need for a strong rationale for selecting any case; that is, a researcher will need to be clear about 'what can be learned from the single case' in question. Rather than being selected for convenience the case should be able to permit a critical investigation of complex themes:

> There is a temptation for researchers to 'tidy up' cases and to see them as homogenous units to make them manageable, as in experiments where variables are closely controlled. A 'case' for study may be a group of disabled activists, but such a group cannot be abstracted from its context or the contexts of the lives of the people who belong to it. The meaning of membership of the group is tied up with structures, not only of government and organizational policies, not only of the meaning of the notion of 'disability' in any given society, not only of class, 'race', sexuality, age and gender, but with recognition of relationships, continuities, discontinuities, resources, in an attempt to understand the whole . . . identifying boundaries [of the 'case'] is a complex process.
>
> (Humphries, 2008: 90–1)

For such reasons analysis remains a key process that should be explicit within all case study research. It is not enough to merely describe attributes that link to any one case: any investigation will need to unearth and extrapolate, understand and place into context emergent themes that are associated.

Case studies for a social work dissertation

There is a wide range of potential case study topics to explore as part of a social work dissertation. Examples include:

An exploration of the long term impact of an older form of social policy upon one service user group; with careful evaluation of its success and/or failings

An analysis of one countries unique approach towards foster care and the benefits this approach may provide to other countries

A study of one voluntary sector organization's innovative role in providing a form of alternative social pedagogical support to a small group of children over a period of time

An evaluation of the views of an experienced social work practitioner regarding an aspect of their role, and comparing and contextualizing such data in response to other research findings and/or theory

An exploration of management styles applied within one organization and how these compare to other studies or theories of management

Each of these examples is likely to follow the traditional research process inherent in most social research projects (which is summarized in Chapter 2). They are likely to begin with a relatively broad set of aims which then become more focused as reading and research begins. It is also likely that competing arguments and stances will emerge. For example, in the first case study there may be more positive interpretations of the impact of a piece of social policy from some quarters, in contrast to more critical stances taken in some academic literature. It is the role of the student to understand these arguments, place them in a historical and political context, and consider their own views, engage with analysis and perhaps make possible recommendations for the future.

Criticism of case study research

Because of its reliance upon one or more studies in isolation the case study approach has sometimes received extensive criticism. For example, some types of case study have been accused of being too narrowly focused, and therefore lacking in potential to make more general claims. For social work this may limit the potential of case study research findings to be applied in some forms of practice. Flyvbjerg (2004: 390) notes how the case study approach is also sometimes dismissed as being trivial, and suitable 'for pilot studies but not for fully-fledged research schemes'. Like other forms of small-scale qualitative research a case study methodology is sometimes also assumed to be *too* subject-ive; seemingly having a tendency to give 'too much scope for the researcher's own interpretations'. Finally, research boundaries can be difficult to define for some topics which can mean that any case may be conflated with themes that do not necessarily link with the initial research aims and objectives.

What a case study lacks regarding any potential for objectivity, or possible generalization, can usually be made up for by the *depth* of any investigation available. Potentially a high level of analysis is also possible due to the smaller sample and additional time available to survey a rich supply of findings relating to each case. Overall the case study approach is ideally suited to the dissertation format because it represents a small and manageable project which involves extensive research and in-depth analysis.

Evaluation research

As part of the evaluation approach the researcher (sometimes also known as 'the evaluator') attempts to assess and evaluate the worth, value, effectiveness and impact of community or other organizational programmes, interventions or support services (Green, 2000; Robson, 2000). As Bryman (2004: 40, original emphasis) reflects, this approach also tries to gain an 'in-depth *understanding* of the *context* in which an intervention occurs and the diverse viewpoints of the stakeholders [service users, staff, managers, carers, and so on]'.

Hall and Hall (1996: 46–9, original emphasis) underline how evaluation research can be applied in a variety of formats. These include a traditional approach, which encompasses a 'specification of the goals or intended purposes of [a] programme'; and more critical interpretations in which 'programme participants [for example, service users and informal carers] are involved in gathering information' and may 'identify . . . *their* needs and priorities and . . . draw up action plans in collaboration with the community'. Originally this method utilized quantitative approaches to assess the *feasibility* of a programme, and this quasi-scientific process took place in close collaboration with a funding organization. Evaluation research can be influenced (and restricted) by an organization's own agenda, which may include those articulated by senior managers, share holders, or trustees. This tendency can be more pervasive if the organization or service provider has funded any research undertaken.

Humphries (2008: 173–4) argues that the use of evaluation in social work research is distinct because it is applied, practical, action orientated and much more political. It can therefore provide 'quick answers to pressing questions'. Humphries also highlights the crucial role of comparison: especially the researcher's priority of comparing what a service or organization is *meant to achieve and provide* (such as within mission statements, organizational brochures or regarding statutory or legal requirements) and what it actually does *in practice*. Engaging with this process can help to encourage good habits for students, such as the capacity to draw upon previous experience, and learn new, critical skills and knowledge that will be indispensable upon qualification.

Alongside an evaluation of a support service or aspects of the workings of a social care organization (including those provided by social workers), qualitative-led evaluation processes can include a capacity to explore and assess other phenomenon. These might include the impact and context of a piece of legislation, a new policy initiative or specific procedures applied in work with service users, informal carers or fulfilled by social work practitioners based in any organization that provides a service. A social work student may seek to evaluate the success or otherwise of a service or piece of legislation, such as when on a practice placement or by assessing a support service that is utilized or 'contracted out' of a social services department. The involvement of participants is often a central aspect of evaluation research and this offers potential – not least due to participants' likely *direct* personal experience of the service, policy, Act of legislation, etc., being assessed and evaluated.

Sanders and Liptrot (1994: 32) advocate a focused interpretation of evaluation. They suggest three possible approaches:

- Evaluation of something *before it has started* This may include a new service or initiative within an organization, and can be achieved by interviewing support staff or service users, professionals or managers regarding their opinions. Factors such as likely cost, impact on service users, and so on, may also be considered. Fundamental questions as part of such a feasibility study might include 'will it work?' and 'is it worth doing?'

- Evaluation of *change as it occurs* Again this can include the assessment of a new service or initiative but instead looks as progress, growth or general process over time as it happens. Again a practice placement or voluntary sector work environment is likely to be ideal for asking questions such as 'how is it doing?' or 'how is it changing?'
- Evaluation of the *effect or impact of something* This is sometimes referred to as 'outcome analysis' and raises retrospective questions such as 'was it worth doing?' or 'did it work?'

Important factors to consider when undertaking evaluative research include:

- identifying if a service/organization/piece of legislation, etc., can be *adequately* evaluated by the use of qualitative methods such as interviews, focus groups, and so on;
- isolating which group is most likely to help you evaluate the service/organization/piece of legislation, etc., that you are seeking to assess. For example, will it be practitioners, service users, carers, or other professionals?
- trying to isolate exactly *what* it is you are attempting to evaluate regarding a support service, piece of legislation, etc. It is unlikely that you will be able to assess everything in the limited time you have available so try to be realistic and clearly focused regarding your aims and objectives;
- making sure that you adequately review relevant literature relating to the organization and any topics you intend to evaluate;
- considering *how* you will gain access to your research participants. Also bear in mind that as with all empirical research formal permission regarding access can take weeks or even months to attain from official bodies or related organizations;
- deciding which method(s) you will use to evaluate the service/organization/piece of legislation, etc? Is it to be the interview, focus group, or questionnaire, or another approach? Inevitably questions for any participant sample will be involved at some stage in which case it is essential to be careful how you construct and deliver each (see Chapter 8 for further details).
- trying to decide what 'evidence' will be used to assess the topic of any evaluation. For example, will it be represented by feedback from practitioners, service users or some other criteria set in advance that relates to any research question?

Humphries (2008: 176–8, my emphasis) distinguishes between the significance of *outcome* and *process* within evaluation research. The former reflects the 'effectiveness' of aspects of an organization or policy and principally whether it is achieving what it claims to be, especially for service users? In contrast, process targets attention upon the 'actual *running* of [any] programme' under evaluation. This is usually more suited to qualitative research methods such as interviews or focus group research and can address an assortment of research issues: these may include relations between service users and service provider organizations or representatives; provisions or non-provisions regarding service user needs, including those that relate to 'social problems such as poverty, sexism and racism'; and perceptions, or the working reality, of any particular support service. Humphries stresses the role of service users within evaluation research projects but other advocates, such as Robson (2000), tend to highlight instead the leading role of practitioners and trained researchers.

It is important to recognize that although evaluation research can be utilized as a methodology you may still need to find a related theory that helps to better contextualize your research and findings. For example, Guba and Lincoln (1989: 8–11) stress the differing constructions and understandings of 'reality' for evaluators in deciding the *context* in which any assessments take place. Here discovering how evaluators make sense of what it is they are assessing remains pivotal, as do considerations of any social, cultural and political circumstances that impact upon evaluation and service provision. Most theories that link to any topic in question can be used alongside evaluation research to help explain, understand, analyse and, most significantly, contextualize any findings.

Recommendations tend to constitute a central component of qualitative evaluation research. These will often be presented towards the end of any dissertation or report, and should be in response to the views articulated by research participants, as well as the informed opinions of the researcher and based around a literature review and an analysis of any empirical research.

Finally, depending on circumstance it may sometimes be possible to evaluate a service or organization from your own perspective without undertaking interviews. If you are attempting to do this, such as if evaluating a service that you have regular engagement with on a practice placement, you should consider points such as a need to:

- undertake a literature review relating to the topic, organization and service;
- identify what it is you are evaluating and why;
- be clear how you will achieve this and what your rationale is for any assessments regarding the impact of a service or policy on people who provide and access them

Evaluation research is not without problems or criticism. Among others these

---

Case Study 6.1

Topic: the meaning of 'adequate support' for residents with a learning disability based in supported living accommodation

Paul wanted to evaluate the extent to which a communal 'supported living' house for adults with a learning disability provided adequate support to residents. More specifically he was keen to investigate whether there were differences between residents' understanding of their support needs and those of house staff and social workers. Paul decided to use in-depth interviews as his method of data collection.

As well as four residents Paul interviewed two social workers and three support staff that had regular contact with the property and service users. From the interviews in which the same questions were asked to all participants similarities and differences emerged, most notably a contrast between residents and staff regarding what service user needs were being met.

Drawing from his analysis Paul argued that although staff where keen to support residents there was sometimes a tendency to underestimate their needs. As part of his dissertation he was able to list and unpack the areas where any tension was most apparent, especially drawing upon the detailed feedback offered by residents. For example, service users wanted more privacy within the home, and, at times, felt that they were patronized by some support workers, or 'treated like children' as one resident proposed. For residents this point had been somewhat difficult and uncomfortable to express in the past. Interviews were made anonymous and a copy of the final dissertation was given to both the manager of the local social work department and the supported living accommodation. The findings were influential in changing the practices of staff. Paul utilized pedagogical theories of disability to support his analysis.

---

include the potential problem of recruiting participants (although this is not compulsory), the need to keep any staff being evaluated informed and comfortable with what can be perceived as an intrusive set of circumstances and activities, and the competing interests, and therefore potential conflict, generated by differing participant groups. In addition, organizations that request or accommodate evaluation research can potentially dominate proceedings, or simply ignore recommendations that counter their interests.

Above (Case Study 6.1) is an excellent dissertation which I supervised and which utilized evaluation research.

Feminist methodology

Feminism offers a broad and disparate set of theories, ideological components, social movements and practices which are difficult to adequately summarize and encapsulate. Nevertheless some common yet general themes can be isolated and they include:

- the recognition of forms of gender inequality and exclusion with priority given to women's subordination to men. This includes women's subordinate role within the family and workplace and in attempts to gain access to education and health support services, engage with political processes, and so on;
- a realization of both implicit and explicit forms of discrimination as well as subjugation to often punitive social policies, including those initiated within, and by, social work, the medical profession, the police, among others;
- an intention to emancipate women from forms of male supremacy and a range of forms of economic, political, social and cultural forms of disadvantage and exclusion.

These traits deal with critical feminism although liberal-humanist, and some conservative factions, are also influential within social work as elsewhere.

One important aspect of a feminist discourse to emerge since the 1970s has been a distinct research methodology. Although this would not claim to offer a unified methodology there are general attributes and beliefs that have become an influential aspect of a more general feminist methodology. For example, most feminists again draw upon, and indeed have significantly added to, the widespread critique of positivism evident within the social and human sciences (as elsewhere) since the 1960s. Key elements of a feminist methodology also seek to:

- highlight and contextualize through empirical and theoretical methods the exclusion and discrimination typically experienced by women. Also efforts are made to 'turn *personal* woes into *social* issues', locate 'the personal-in-their-social context' and link the personal to the structural for women through practice, research and consciousness raising (Dominelli, 2004: 84–7, original emphasis);
- engage in strategies to include women in key decision-making processes and activities, including those relating to social research;
- attempt to overcome dominant patriarchal research cultures, including the assumption that men should be the only or majority subjects

of research from which assumptions can be made regarding all of the population;

- critique seemingly established male social research methodologies, ideologies and cultures, including a search for (unobtainable) scientific and objective 'truth';

- question attempts to reduce research participants to 'subjects' to be studied almost like a substance in a laboratory, and instead endeavour to allow participants to actively engage with research processes;

- encourage a *reflexive* approach to research in which the researcher critically recognizes and confronts their own biography, values and beliefs, including potential personal prejudices, and prior personal conduct. Often this involves 'a process of looking *inward*, and thinking about how our own life experiences or significant events may have impacted upon our thinking, or on the research or assessment process' (Wise, 2001: 101, original emphasis);

- encourage consciousness raising, in particular the capacity of people to raise awareness of social injustice and political exclusion to others, and also advocate on behalf of disadvantaged groups;

- offer 'insights into gendered social existence' that otherwise would not exist. Also critically evaluate 'theories of gender and power, their normative frameworks, and their notions of transformation and accountability, even though these are not uniform' (Ramazanoglu and Holland, 2002: 147);

- look to engage with more meaningful and less superficial forms of social research, including sometimes more spiritual and evocative encounters within what otherwise can become mechanical and superficial routines for both a participant and researcher.

(Adapted from Stanley and Wise, 1983; 1993; Reinharz, 1992; Ramazanoglu and Holland, 2002; Fernandes, 2003; Dominelli, 2004; Foster, 2007a)

Whitmore (2001: 84–6) draws significantly from feminism and identifies four main characteristics of what she refers to as an emancipatory methodology that is ideal for some forms of social work research. First, a researcher should be aware of the impact of 'social, political, cultural, economic, ethnic, gender and disability values' inherent in the research process. This includes the differing values between research participants and the researcher, meaning that the student should be able to understand that participants typically emerge from distinct 'social and institutional "locations" ', which influence how they understand and interpret the world.

Second, and in close relation to the first characteristic, emancipatory research recognizes the importance of power differences between the student social worker and research participants. It attempts to include otherwise excluded voices in the research process, and tries to avoid dismissing those involved as 'subjects' who stand merely to be monitored and assessed. Third, the researcher should aim to understand the cultural differences between themselves and participants. In practice, this means 'connecting with what people know, learning to listen in unfamiliar ways and thinking outside of our customary understanding' (Reissman, 1987, cited in Whitmore, 2001: 85). In practice this may alter the type of research methods utilized following advice from participants. However, contrary to some popular misconceptions, this process does not necessarily compromise rigour, but instead may prove more valid and accurate due to its attempt to empathize with and understand people held under the gaze of the research process. Finally, participants should be actively involved in any research to the point that they are included in decision-making processes. Consequentially the student should ask themselves: 'Who creates knowledge? Who controls the research? Who conducts research on whom and for what purposes? Who benefits?' (Truman, 2000, cited in Whitmore, 2001: 85). Ideally participants should also be *actively involved* in knowledge production related to the research, have a degree of control over proceedings and influence who is to be studied and for what purpose. Participants should also be allowed to affect who benefits from any findings.

Such traits as those codified within a *general* definition of 'feminist research' have been widely debated and often contested. For example, the potential benefits and ethics of actively involving participants within research processes have been questioned by some feminist academics (De Laine, 2000). Also there is now recognition of the benefits of some forms of quantitative research, despite such seemingly 'scientific' forms of research receiving intense criticism throughout the 1970s and 1980s (Ezzy, 2002). Broad criticism of researcher objectivity as an ideal (for example, Stanley and Wise, 1983) has also not always been accepted within feminism, and some advocates suggest that this principle may still be beneficial (for example, Harding, 1986).

Like Whitmore (2001), Clifford (1994) draws from feminism but instead proposes core elements of what he identifies as an 'anti-oppressive' methodology. This includes a theoretical and political framework which:

- remains *anti-reductionist* and avoids over simplistic 'one reason' explanations for social trends and problems; that can be truncated and presented within overtly deterministic biological, economic or psychological accounts;
- is *historically specific* and able to contextualize accounts regarding the many cultural, political and social trends prevalent at a given time frame;
- integrates the *personal and the political* and truly understands and contextualizes the individual regarding the social, cultural and

        personal impact of their class, gender, ethnicity, disability, age, and so on;

- takes account of *materialist* dynamics and themes and, in particular, personal inequalities in access to wealth and income, employment opportunities, cultural resources and general 'life chances';
- understands and analyses social, political and cultural *difference*;
- remains *internationalist* and recognizes the impact of globalization, migration, the Internet and more generally the increasing tendency for nation states to conflate due to technology, transportation, communication and financial systems, etc;
- is *reflexive* with the researcher taking responsibility for their influence, and socially and culturally constructed beliefs and prejudices within the research process.

Ramazanoglu and Holland (2002: 11) stress how feminist methodology will tend to 'vary depending on experiences, our truths and realities'. In addition to the impact of personal beliefs or experience methodology is also affected by any restraints that potentially impinge upon the research process. For any social work student it may be difficult in practice to comply with some of the more general feminist inspired research techniques. For example, the involvement of qualified practitioners may be more feasible under some circumstances rather than service users. Despite some possible difficulties however, the use of a well defined feminist methodology does hold potential benefits. As well as offering a form of practical support to achieve positive change for some women, such a methodology also offers a clear, and relatively easy to define, theoretical structure by which to support any dissertation. Linked to this remain the benefits of a now substantial amount of prior research undertaken within the nevertheless loose-knit feminist movement.

    There are now many resources on which to draw within the feminist framework such as related textbooks, specific journals, magazines, websites, etc. As a broad church, feminism is also extremely accommodating of specific theories and methods. For example, feminism has drawn significantly from interpretive, critical and postmodern theoretical schools. Therefore it will help if you try to be as specific in your methodology about which school of thought (for example, liberal, Marxist, postmodernist, etc.) you are drawing direct influence from. It is however possible to draw from different schools as part of any feminist methodology.

    A feminist methodology will be able to accommodate literature based research as well as empirical – indeed in some cases this may be easier to apply simply because of the volume of literature now held under the general framework of feminist social research. Again when faced with more sources of literature it is especially important to define early on what it is you hope to achieve and how, as well as endeavour to narrow any focus so to make any aims and objectives achievable. The most common critique of feminism as a methodology relates (once again) to similar accusations also directed at other forms of qualitative research; namely that it can have a *possible* tendency to be highly subjective, and therefore is vulnerable to bias and factual inaccuracy. Such potential concerns should be acknowledged within the methodology section of a dissertation and considered throughout the research process.

Grounded theory

Grounded theory is a form of (radical) *inductive* reasoning in which research concepts are slowly built from observations, interviews or other methods. Each 'layer' of empirical evidence – such as based on investigations related to case studies, observations or focus group meetings in the field – are gradually built up, and slowly lead to the construction of a theory that directly links to the subject of research. The essential component of grounded theory is that theory *emerges from data*. This represents a distinct approach to social research in which a steady and measured process of theoretical formation is undertaken.

Strictly speaking such a research process departs somewhat from the method initiated by the pioneering American sociologists Glaser and Strauss (1967). As Gibson (2003: 134) laments, grounded theory *in practice* has at times 'tended to become whatever people claim it to be'. That is, its original methodological approach has been reformed and sometimes usurped by a spate of *qualitative* research techniques that have led to a revised research methodology. Nevertheless, many important aspects of traditional grounded theory still remain, and the essence or cultural tradition of the approach has much potential for social work research.

Grounded theory has unique qualities and processes – in particular, following the selection of a topic, empirical research and analysis begins once a sample has been found, and is ongoing along with observations, interviews and/or focus group meetings. Also, depending on the topic, the literature review will be ongoing, usually alongside any data collection. Essentially, the inductive method discussed in Chapter 3 (see Figure 6.2) is more stringently followed in comparison to other qualitative methodologies.

The empirical processes followed when using grounded theory as a methodology can be reduced to six stages. Below is an attempt to relate these to a suitable methodology for social work research. The six stages are as follows:

1   Once a topic has been selected, *a sample is identified and the researcher begins to collect and analyse information or data in the research field.* For example, the attitudes of social workers towards service users who experience severe depression based in a team specializing in work

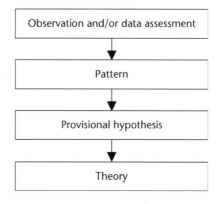

Figure 6.2 Inductive research.

with older people. A brief or smaller scale literature review may be undertaken around this topic prior to interviews with practitioners.

2   *Research 'cases' are continuously compared and contrasted. The findings are then utilized to form concepts in response to specific discoveries built from interviews and/or observations, etc.* Findings or concepts discovered from interviews with social work practitioners may be numerous and therefore a set of codes, or numbers linked to a possible list of answers or findings, may be developed in order to ease and support the process of analysis. For social work students however, any system of detailed notes, such as those linked to observations and/or interviews will suffice to support a dissertation. From here onwards the priority is to identify, compare and explore emergent themes from any data collected, especially those that link to an initial research question.

3   *Notes are kept regarding further individual 'cases' of observation/interview – analytical concepts or trends should continue to emerge from such new data which should subsequently be revised as a consequence.* For example, further observations and interviews with the social workers special-izing in work with older people should lead to a revision of any initial findings.

4   *Some less significant concepts or trends, especially those that do not link directly to the original research topic, may be discarded as the research proceeds with the addition of further information.* For example the social workers may consider the role of other family members to be less important when they are attempting to assist older people who experience depression. Therefore other more dominant themes that emerge, such as the significance of contact maintained with friends or neighbours, may be prioritized for discussion during further interviews.

5   *The researcher begins to gradually develop a conceptual scheme which leads to the emergence of a core theory.* From this point additional data is compared with this core theory. For example, all or a majority of the social workers may highlight the importance of day centre support in their attempts to alleviate depression amongst service users. Do all of the interviews confirm this thesis?

6   *At some point a state of 'saturation' is reached. Ideally this is where no more new findings or a repetition of outcomes emerges in observations or points raised by those interviewed.* At this stage the researcher should exit the field and continue their analysis alongside the literature review.

(Adapted from Strauss and Corbin, 1990; Hall and Hall,
1996; and Gibson, 2003)

For a social work dissertation the only way of interpreting grounded theory as part of the research process is by the use of recurrent and in-depth individual interviews, observations, or alternatively a combination of the two. Possibly a focus group meeting towards the end may help provide evidence to test the theoretical claims, although in practice this is probably unnecessary.

Because social work students accommodate smaller samples and have limited time and resources, they can be restricted in the extent to which grounded theory can be followed to rule. The extent to which grounded theory is *meticulously* applied, or otherwise, will depend very much upon factors such as the original research question asked and its related topic, the likely or intended sample, the expected time that data gathering will take, and so on. Again, the extent to which a literature review is undertaken will depend upon your own requirements. Also, in practice it is unrealistic to expect a social work student to build a sophisticated 'new' theory following brief contact with a small sample, and this will not be an expectation of any dissertation module taught at a university or college of further education. It is important to use your discretion regarding such dilemmas and also consult with a tutor if unsure.

Typically grounded theory relies on much bigger samples in comparison to those that are usually available to a social work student, and it also tends to proceed over a longer period of time. Despite this the cultural process and some core techniques – especially the intention to build or develop a rough or general theory from data and allow preconceived interpretations to be reduced – can still be applied on a smaller scale for a dissertation.

Grounded theory offers a sophisticated and elaborate qualitative methodology. At heart it attempts to combine both inductive and deductive research methodologies so as to allow recognition of subjective processes on behalf of the researcher, while also preserving the significance of structure and organized processes within research. You may have to simplify the process (by using a smaller sample, undertaking an initial literature review, revising or confirming current theory instead of creating a new paradigm, etc.) in order to fit the methodology to the requirements of your dissertation. However, some of the longer practice placements now held within some social work courses may allow an approach that is closer to the original intentions of Glaser and Strauss (1967), or one of their many protégés.

Critiques of methodology and methodological pluralism

Feyerabend (1975) has argued against the use of any fixed methodology when undertaking research. Such planned approaches are questioned as being narrow and restrictive, as well as reflecting the most flawed aspects of positivism – namely that they are rigorous and set within an exact and seemingly contrived framework. Although less nihilistic, Seale *et al.* (2004: 7–8) echo aspects of this argument and suggest that the concept of methodology draws from rationalist and scientific discourse. In contrast they suggest the adoption of a more flexible methodology – one that remains in dialogue with, and is adapted to, the research process as it forms and changes shape and direction. Related to this, Emerson (2004: 428) highlights the complex link between methodology, theory and findings:

> Fieldworkers never start without concepts, but they will inevitably abandon some initial concepts, significantly modify others, and develop and elaborate new and often unanticipated concepts, all as the result of close consideration of first-hand observation and data. In this respect, field researchers not only fit their analyses to critical features of what they study, but also modify what they are studying and the kinds of data collected so that the data bear on and advance these emerging analyses.

Hindess (1973) has added to this debate by arguing that methodologies remain contradictory, and often maintain only a tenuous link to what researchers later do and apply *in practice*. Rather than advocate a form of methodological anarchy however, such detractors are usually suggesting that a research methodology should be able to alter according to specific or unplanned circumstance, so that they more readily relate to the discovery of new information. This more flexible approach can help permit more discretion, as well as allow the researcher to remain in control of their project (rather than be at the mercy of a predetermined methodology). Other approaches might avoid any link to a specific school of theory, and instead compare or combine emerging ideas with different sources (such as other peoples' research findings), build theory from data or use theory as a *negative* reference point. Implicit within these research models are attempts to allow findings and data to take priority, possibly with a hope of exploring or generating new ideas, theory or practices.

In addition to the methodological approaches discussed in this and other later chapters, there are also different combinations of theory and methods that can be used to form a methodology. This is sometimes known as 'methodological pluralism'. For example, theories which are different yet have key elements in common, such as varieties of interpretism and postmodernism, or systems and anti-oppressive theory, can potentially be combined to form a distinct methodology that fits with a specific topic. It is also possible simply to use one or two methods and build up or reform a theory as the research progresses. In such examples, methodology represents not so much a 'recipe' but a selection of 'tools' to complete a specific task.

Methodology should not reflect a static or fixed set of approaches, or one narrow way in which to rigidly undertake research. Instead methodology should be seen as providing a supporting foundation and parameters that 'hold' any research process together, or at least provide some coherence and consistency. The often uncertain and unpredictable nature of qualitative research means that flexibility and discretion is usually, if not always, necessary to some degree in practice. Part of the learning process for any student undertaking a dissertation will be a capacity to be able to accommodate and adapt different approaches if and when required.

Summary

This chapter has highlighted the central role played by methodology in helping to support any social work dissertation. A methodology can offer a scheme of ideas, a framework in which to organize a project, a recipe of method(s) and a strategy, as well as a theoretical and philosophical structure around which to support a dissertation. It should also be able to help direct any research. There are numerous possible general methodologies which can be applied within social work and there is also the possibility of designing your own, or at least adapting a methodology within reason as your research evolves. Despite this methodology should not be used to dictate or suffocate research but should instead be used to support and assist any research process and data collection.

The next chapter looks at traditional methods used within social work research.

Suggested reading

Alvesson, M. and Skoldberg, K. (2000) *Reflexive Methodology*. London: Sage.
Dawson, C. (2006) *A Practical Guide to Research Methods*. Oxford: How To Books Limited. (Chapter 2: How to decide upon a methodology)

D'Cruz, H. and Jones, M. (2004) *Social Work Research – Ethical and Political Contexts*. London: Sage. (Chapter 4: Methodology)

Dey, I. (1998) *Grounding Grounded Theory: Guidelines for Qualitative Inquiry*. San Deigo: Academic Press.

Gomm, R., Hammersley, M. and Foster, P. (eds) (2000) *Case Study Method*. London: Sage.

Humphries, B. (2008) *Social Work Research for Social Justice*. Basingstoke: Palgrave Macmillan. (Chapter 6: Case study research; Chapter 11: Evaluation research).

Humphries, B. and Truman, C. (eds) (1994) *Rethinking Social Research: Anti-Discriminatory Approaches in Research Methodology*. Aldershot: Avebury.

Ramazanoglu, C. and Holland, J. (2002) *Feminist Methodology: Challenges and Choices*. London: Sage.

Robson, C. (2000) *Small Scale Evaluation*. London: Sage.

Stanley, L. and Wise, S. (1983) *Breaking Out: Feminist Consciousness and Feminist Research*. London: Routledge and Kegan Paul.

Strauss, A. and Corbin, J. (1990) *Basics of Qualitative Research: Grounded Theory Procedures and Techniques*. Newbury Park, CA: Sage.

7 Traditional methods: Interviews, questionnaires and focus groups

Introduction

This chapter outlines three traditional methods used in empirical social work research. They are the interview, questionnaire and focus group. For most dissertations use of one of these methods will be enough to collect information or data to support a topic. However, there are times when two methods can be put together, such as by combining a series of individual interviews with a focus group meeting. Each method is explored in detail below.

The interview

In-depth interviews, usually with a small number of participants on a one to one basis, provide one of the most reliable means by which to build upon a literature review and explore the key themes and objectives of a research question. This is due to many factors, including a realization that through language people can often best articulate and explain their thoughts, opinions, emotions and experiences. As Darlington and Scott (2002: 48) suggest: 'The in-depth interview takes seriously the notion that people are experts on their own experience and so are best able to report how they experienced a particular event or phenomenon.'

Interviews are also one of the most popular means of data collection, principally because they provide a convenient, cheap, often uncomplicated and highly effective means by which to collect an extensive amount of data in a relatively brief period of time. Although most topics can be explored through interviews, there are particular research themes that are most suited to this approach. These include questions that aim to unravel the following:

- *Personal experience, emotions and feelings* Discussion of work experiences, day to day concerns or private or delicate matters for participants are likely to generate a lot of detail, and an interview can be an effective way to gather such rich sources of data.

- *Sensitive issues* Although rarely easy to delve into, social work practice (and therefore research) regularly confronts sensitive topics such as bereavement, loss, discrimination, prejudice, neglect or illness. Interviews may provide an ideal platform from which to investigate such issues, although the process usually demands ethical sensitivity and tact, as well as skill to facilitate any open discussion.
- *Privileged information* Following ethical and tutor approval, an interviewer may wish to explore restricted information from key participants. This may include other professionals, social workers themselves or possibly senior managers. Access to such 'key players' also offers an opportunity to gain insight on topics perhaps previously underexplored within research.

(Adapted from Denscombe, 2007: 111)

Qualitative interviewing usually differs considerably from the more formal and rigidly structured methods employed in surveys, and other quantitative approaches such as structured interviews or questionnaires. The emphasis tends to be more upon *depth* of investigation rather than a broad sweep of many sub-topics (Silverman, 1993). A yearning to investigate subjective dynamics, such as those that follow contemplation and personal reflection, tend to be prioritized by the researcher. Despite this the more mundane events or rituals in life can also be uncovered.

Before committing to the interview method, you will need to consider the *viability* or otherwise of interviews. Questions to ask prior to any commitment include:

- Will you be able to gain access to enough participants?
- If so how long will it take before formal permission is granted to approach or interview people?
- Will there be travel or any other costs involved?

If feasible the next step will be to speak to potential participants themselves. As any interviewer takes an interest in an aspect of participant's life it is often the case that people interviewed appreciate and enjoy the experience. The interview may also offer the participant an opportunity to take stock and reflect upon any issues explored. As Rapley (2004: 15) notes, if undertaken carefully and with skill, the interview can pervade 'our contemporary cultural experiences and knowledges of authentic personal, private lives'. The interview may also be therapeutic as well as stimulating and engaging for participants. Conversely it may simply represent another chore at the end of the day for the typically hard pressed social worker!

Interview formats

An interview for research is not simply a conversation or chat around a topic. As Denscombe (2007: 109) proposes: 'Although there are a lot of superficial similarities between a conversation and an interview, interviews . . . involve a set of assumptions and understandings about the situation which are not normally associated with a casual conversation.' Nearly always these assumptions and understandings emerge from delving into, and investigating, a research question and associated aims and objectives of a dissertation proposal.

In qualitative research two key formats of interview remain: unstructured and semi-structured. Both approaches take place with one person at a time, as interviews with groups of people tend to be difficult to organize and manage. With unstructured interviews there are some general pre-planned ideas or prompts regarding what may be discussed: however, considerable flexibility and discretion is allowed regarding what can be discussed. This freedom can be ideal in interviews where the emphasis is very much upon the participant guiding the conversation, while offering a detailed and open exploration of personal themes. For example, this approach is prevalent in narrative or life history research (explored in Chapter 8), in which a person may talk at great length and reflect upon prior life experiences. It is also the preferred method for undertaking forms of research influenced by interpretivist or postmodern theory, in which narrative or discourse analysis becomes the priority. However, notable drawbacks of unstructured interviews include that they can take considerable time to complete, and will tend to collect large amounts of data (that will need to be read, assessed and analysed).

Semi-structured interviews contain a combination of both pre-planned and unplanned questions, with the latter allowing the interviewer some discretion to create new questions in response to participant's answers. This format works well with social work students because the structured questions create a clear link to any research question, while the unplanned component of any interview permit room to query any issues raised by the participant. The use of questions that were not originally planned may help the interviewer probe a theme that the participant has unexpectedly raised, or alternatively allow the researcher to unpack and expand upon answers that were perhaps a little unclear. Semi-structured interviews can proceed with questions asked in any order depending upon circumstance – once again this allows more discretion.

An interviewer will need to decide at what location interviews will take place. This is very much up to you to decide. In my experience social work practitioners like to be interviewed somewhere private in their office environment and most people will not wish to travel to be interviewed. Some other groups may wish to be interviewed elsewhere and you may decide to give people a choice. It is generally ideal to find a room with privacy and away from any potential distractions, especially if you are tape recording the interviews. As for groups other than social work practitioners you will need to use your initiative and common sense and think carefully about people's mobility needs, personal requirements, and the possible impact that the environment may have on the nature of the discussion.

Finally, you may decide to undertake interviews over the telephone. This is possible but not ideal due to the lack of visual prompts and clues available, as well as the difficulty of note taking while interviewing. Advantages include any time saved travelling, and you may find it easier to gain access to a wider sample.

Interview questions

An initial priority is to think carefully about the types and number of questions to ask participants. Qualitative interviews are regularly dominated by *open-ended questions*, whereby interviewees are offered discretion regarding how to respond, and are also able to answer and explore any queries in their own words and style. Sometimes, however, one or more *closed-format questions* – whereby participants choose from a limited choice of answers – are included.

All interview questions should be clearly focused and link to any research question and related aims and objectives. It may help to initially construct a brief list of key themes to explore that relate to your topic, and then decide in which way each can be represented by suitable questions. It is also advisable to be careful not to ask too many questions. Try to keep questions to a minimum so that you do not collect too much information to process and analyse. Another option is to have pre-planned contingency questions in case a theme that links to a prepared question has not been adequately explored by a participant.

Below are some tips on how to construct your interview questions.

- Undertake an initial literature review and try to be clear about your research question and aims and objectives prior to constructing any questions.
- Ensure your questions closely link to a research topic and try to avoid asking too many questions.
- Try to keep questions short (ideally one sentence) as well as unambiguous and focused.
- Use simple and unpretentious language with familiar words drawn from everyday speech.
- Avoid jargon, acronyms or abbreviations, etc.
- Try not to ask questions which suggest that you hold strong opinions

and which may influence participants' responses. For example, 'Do you agree that social work practice is difficult, tiring and often quite boring?'

- Try to avoid ambiguous and difficult questions. For example, 'On how many occasions did you meet with "service users" last year?'
- Try to avoid questions with the word 'not' in the sentence as this is often confusing or provokes uncertainty for participants. For example, 'Is it *not* in the interest of service users to offer an assessment of need?'
- Avoid questions that are based on presumptions about participants. For example, 'Why have you always worked within a child protection social work team?'
- Avoid insensitive or offensive questions. For example, 'Are you also aloof when in the contact of service users?'
- Do not ask questions that assume prior knowledge as each can embarrass or make participants feel uncomfortable. For example, 'Do you agree with the recent reforms of the Mental Health Bill?'
- Avoid questions that prompt a particular answer as this will likely lead to significant bias regarding any response. For example, 'Do you agree that older people are always discriminated against by community nurses?'
- Ensure that you do not ask more than one question at a time. For example, 'Do you always feel tired after work and are also eager to watch television?'
- Avoid blatant discrimination such as prejudicial assumptions made about service users. For example, 'Do you feel that many "service users" are "demanding?'

(Adapted from Graham, 1994; Kumar 1996; Marlow; 2001; D'Cruz and Jones, 2004: 115; Denscombe, 2007)

In sum it is usually a priority to be clear, brief, unambiguous and avoid over-complicated or abstract words as part of any questions asked. Simplicity and clear links to a topic are imperative if you wish to reduce or avoid generating significant bias or poor quality data. It is also advisable to meet with a tutor so that they can check your questions prior to undertaking any interviews.

Core interview skills: approach and rapport

At first glance any interview process may appear to be relatively straightforward. However, interviewing participants is often much more complex and potentially hazardous, especially if prior planning and careful consideration is not undertaken. Denscombe (2007: 124–8) has provided a useful overview of some of the key skills to apply during any qualitative research interview process. They include a need for the following:

Be attentive throughout
Listen carefully to what is being said and try to minimize potential distractions (such as noise levels, possible interruptions, etc.). Try to also remain in the background and be careful about when to ask questions, and avoid unnecessary 'chatter' outside of any formal interview questions.

Remain sensitive to the feelings of the informant
You may not necessarily agree with the viewpoints being expressed but it is distracting if you emphasize any disapproval, such as with explicit gestures or noises. Try to manage and restrain your body language and not interrupt when a speaker is making a point.

Tolerate silences
Bear in mind that silences do not always mean that an interview has stalled but may instead allow the participant time to contemplate a question or possible response. Try not to be too eager to break silences – potentially this could disturb or even sabotage a good rapport!

Be adept at using prompts
Although silences can be productive sometimes prompts are necessary to move an interview along. Use your instinct and discretion. Also subtle tactics such as repeating a question or offering some examples from your own interpretation of an answer may help, especially if a participant's answer is unclear or if a response is unsatisfactory.

Use probes if appropriate
Again if an answer is unclear or too brief then the use of a subtle probe may help. Probes include asking for clarification of a participant's answer, or an example from a point raised or simply requesting more details.

Confirm responses if necessary
If a participant's response is unclear or vague you may need to verify the precise meaning intended by the participant. For example, you may wish to paraphrase or summarize any interpretation of answer(s) given, and await confirmation or correction as part of an interviewee's reply.

Remain non-judgemental
It is vital to respect each participant including if you disagree with their values or opinions. As stated above, you should persevere to avoid presenting any over-conspicuous projection of personal views. As Denscombe (2007: 126)

reminds us, being a good interviewer 'means not only biting your lip on occasion, but also taking care not to reveal disgust, surprise or pleasure through facial gestures'. Always remain as impartial as possible, unless your research question and methodology demand otherwise.

Use 'trigger' or stimulus material if necessary

There may be an aspect of your research topic that can stimulate interest and debate from the early stage of an interview or simply if a conversation begins to flounder. The advantage of such a mechanism is that the participant may be more engaged in the topic and forthright in opinion. Despite this, try to avoid stimulating unnecessary controversy for effect – this is likely to encourage bias in the overall findings, and may also deflect from any core themes.

Identify the main points being raised and isolate the underlying logic of what is being stated

Try to tease out the themes that are emerging as the interview proceeds, possibly bearing in mind the findings from any interviews previously undertaken. Another skill to develop is the capability to read between the lines – including to interpret what is really being stated 'beneath the surface' by a participant, and also suppose *what is not being said* and for what possible reasons.

Look for possible inconsistencies regarding the position of the participant

An interviewee may contradict themselves or generate paradoxes through key periods of the interview. It is a priority to make a written note of such occurrences if you are not taping the interview.

Be careful to check for exaggeration, boasting or attempts to please or fob off the interviewer

Inevitably people can become excited at times or animated when discussing something that is central to their life or self-identity. If you believe this is affecting any answers given you should make notes and think of possible ways to overcome such outcomes if it is a problem (such as changing the subject).

Try to maintain suitable eye contact and if necessary make notes on non-verbal communication

Body language often signifies the true feelings or beliefs held by a participant. Also a person may drop hints throughout an interview – remember you are likely to be a complete stranger from another organisation to a participant and the speaker may find it difficult to be open and honest at all times. Try not to maintain direct eye contact throughout, and avoid staring at a participant for long periods!

Try to contextualize the conversation
If you interview a social worker on a Friday afternoon when the working week is nearly complete you may get different answers to questions posed on a Monday morning. Recent or future events (such as a recent re-organization, staff shortages, imminent redundancies, impending policy reform, etc.) might influence the outcome of an interview and it will be worthwhile drawing reference to this within your methodology chapter, and recognizing it throughout any stage of data collection and analysis.

Inevitably there are many rules and conventions to follow and it will be difficult to abide by each in full – in practice there is unlikely to be such a thing as the perfect interview. The points raised above are *general* guidelines that should be considered rather than strict rules that you must always comply with! The extent to which you follow each will also differ from topic to topic and some conventions may counter your aspirations regarding the exploration of a research question.

Taping or note taking during interviews

The four options for gathering information during interviews are as follows:

1   Taping (and then transcribing) the conversation;
2   Making notes during the interview;
3   Making notes after the interview has finished;
4   A combination of both taping and note taking.

Each method has a number of advantages and disadvantages which include the following:

- Taping and transcribing may be indispensable for qualitative interviews because all of the conversation and verbal details are likely to be captured. There are problems, however, which include the significant time taken to tape record and transcribe an interview. Partial transcribing – such as of key points in an interview – remains another option. Potentially, however, tape recordings can be intimidating for participants which may affect any conversation.
- Making notes throughout an interview is cheap, relatively straight forward, and often effective. Nevertheless you will miss details and possible points raised and some participants may feel that you are not listening to them, or may be distracted while you write as they talk.
- Making notes after an interview has the advantage of not distracting the participant which can encourage a more 'honest' and open

account to emerge. However you are relying upon memory and inevitably there is a risk of losing important points raised.

• It is possible to tape record interviews and take notes, and often this is the ideal approach that professional researchers and academics follow. However, bear in mind that considerable work is likely to be generated which may take up many hours of precious time.

You will need to consider the most appropriate method available taking careful consideration of the topics to be explored, available time, participant needs, and so forth.

Figure 7.1 provides an example of a brief questionnaire to be completed by the researcher after each interview. This can be a useful instrument to collect minor details, remember and summarize key trends and outcomes, and also aid the process of analysis. This sheet can also be added to any dissertation as part of an appendix. Case study 7.1 gives an example of how interviews can be used as part of the research process.

Potential problems

Like all methods qualitative interviews are not without problems. These can include the sometimes potential difficulty of gaining access to enough suitable participants. Despite this, most social work students are usually in a relatively privileged position of having access to a potential sample through a previous, current or forthcoming work based practice placement. You may therefore wish to link your topic to any such placement, as many of my former students have in the past. If this is not an option then you will need to think carefully about whether or not access to suitable participants can be achieved, especially before committing time and effort to a particular project.

Alongside the problem of access there might also be times when participants arrive late or simply do not arrive for an interview, sometimes without any prior warning. This can be frustrating, but as a part of the culture of social work research we have to recognize the busy schedule that practitioners often have, and also the considerable commitments of carers, and so on. Therefore it may be advisable to organize some contingency plans, such as keeping space or additional dates in your diary for people who cancel or do not arrive.

There is also the possibility that an interview may not proceed according to plan for other reasons. For example, a participant might be unresponsive to questions, become upset during a conversation due to sensitive issues provoked, or leave halfway through an interview to attend another appointment, and so forth. Due to such 'human' and other unplanned factors (which often pervade qualitative research) it is advisable to begin with a slightly larger sample that may help make amends for other problematic interviews.

Interview date:

Name of participant:

Date of Birth:

Gender:

Status:

Time qualified as a social worker:

Participant's general answers to each question:

Question 1:

Question 2:

Question 3:

Question 4:

Question 5:

Underlying themes that emerged throughout the interview:

General comments about participants views:

Non-verbal communication:

Any additional information:

Figure 7.1 Example of a post-interview questionnaire.

Case Study 7.1

Topic: The changing needs of a local community and their impact upon social work services for older people

Paul wanted to look at the changing needs of older people that were linked to changes in a local community where he was based as part of a practice placement. He looked at the impact upon a social work department specializing in support for older people of changes that related to demographic trends linked to ageing, and other factors such as the impact of work and employment trends, housing needs, and so forth.

Paul focused his attention on six care managers who were in regular contact with older people. He scoured a variety of journals and textbooks to isolate key themes to explore within his research. His literature review included disciplines as diverse as social policy, sociology, social anthropology and social work, and he eventually isolated two core issues to explore. They included:

- attitudes among practitioners regarding change within a community setting;
- subsequent needs of older service users.

After considerable thought and a number of meetings with his tutor Paul eventually came up with five key questions. Each question would represent the most important asked during his individual one hour semi-structured interviews with practitioners, each of whom had 5 years or more experience of working in and around the local area where he was based. The questions were as follows:

1 Have you noticed any changes in the local area over the past 5 years (please detail)?
2 What do you believe are the main causes of such change in the local area during your time based here?
3 Have the general needs of [older] service users altered in anyway since you began to practise as a social worker?
4 Has your practice altered at all over recent years in response to any altered needs of your service users?
5 Would you like to see any changes in the way that service users' needs are met in order to better accommodate any possible changing needs?

As is apparent the questions were complex, multifaceted and somewhat broad, a point that was raised with the student by his tutor. Nevertheless (as is often the case) the student was certain that each point had to be addressed. Probably because of the complexity of the questions the interviews continued for an extended period of time. Also additional questions were asked within all but one of the interviews.

Each of the participants talked in great detail about community, change and the subsequent needs of older people. They also expressed, often in intricate detail, how their views about related themes such as risk management and crisis intervention had altered over time. In particular, each practitioner stressed the need to continuously update their knowledge base in order to be able to accommodate the changes that they identified regarding themes such as policy reforms, demographic trends, housing and employment needs, the expectations of supervisors, and so forth.

There was little need for prompting from Paul as the concepts of community and change generated considerable interest and discussion from each practitioner. The research findings both concurred with, and contradicted, many of the studies that Paul had previously discovered as part of his literature review. Although the questions asked were brief and easy to understand they took much time and great effort to construct. This effort was soon rewarded since each question was highly effective at stimulating the lively response gained from each participant, and which helped lead to a fruitful final stage of in-depth data analysis.

Finally, as Darlington and Scott (2002: 51, authors' emphasis) remind us, as with all methods there is an inherent flaw embedded within the culture of the interview. Alongside ethical concerns relating to power differentials between a researcher and participant, there is also the problem of limited access to people's actual, and, 'real life' *behaviour*: 'Interviews allow access to what people *say* but not to what they *do*. The only way to find out what "actually happens" in a given situation is through observation.'

Often it is also not possible to know whether or not all participants are telling the 'truth' at all times, and clearly there are people who may avoid factual accuracies at regular intervals during formal interviews for a variety of reasons. Once again use your discretion and also instinct, and look carefully at your notes or transcripts for possible inconsistencies if necessary.

Analysis

As was first discussed in Chapter 2, analysis is likely to precede any method such as the interview because it usually begins at any early stage, such as at the start of a literature review. As Walliman (2004: 188) reminds us, qualitative research is most distinct from quantitative methods at the point of analysis:

The essential difference between quantitative analysis and qualitative analysis is that with the former, you need to have completed your data collection before you can start analysis, while with the latter analysis is carried out concurrently with data collection. With qualitative studies, there is a constant interplay between collection and analysis [of information] that produces a gradual growth of understanding.

Despite this, analysis will almost certainly intensify once interviews begin, and especially when they are complete and you begin to reflect on any findings. Analysis is discussed in much more detail in Chapter 9; however, depending on your topic, the process can be summarized as fulfilling one or more of the following objectives during interviews:

- Try to tease out salient themes, trends, issues, and so forth that have emerged from each and every interview. This is an important process as such findings represent the 'evidence' upon which your dissertation is likely to rest.
- Identify and explore the extent to which such themes, etc., concur or differ from those discovered and discussed by other researchers within the literature review. For example, how do your own interview findings link to, or contrast with, the arguments presented by other researchers? Such similarities and/or differences are likely to make up much of the material explored within your analysis chapter, as well as contribute to your discussion and conclusion.
- Do any interview findings link to and answer your research question and subsequent aims and objectives?

Generally if interviews go well there is normally plenty of material to explore. You might decide to simply rely upon your notes when excavating the findings, or instead link the issues inherent within the notes or transcripts to a set of codes (discussed further in Chapter 9). The essence of most analysis is to compare and contrast themes to those of previous researchers, attempt to explain or contextualize your findings, including how they relate to relevant theories, and generate a discussion from conclusions and also potential recommendations that might emerge.

Interview checklist

Below is a checklist to consider prior to undertaking any interviews.

1   Based on the aims and objectives which relate to your research question decide *what it is you need to know*. Make a list of each requirement.
2   Decide if you really need all of this information. If not, then remove some requirements and concentrate on what is left. As Green (2005:

56) underlines, 'in an interview you want to generate data that, when analysed, will answer your research question – not generate a list of rather superficial thoughts on the answer to that question'.

3   From your list think carefully if interviews are the best format to collect this information. For example, might one focus group interview (discussed below) with all participants be better suited to your requirements?

4   Ensure that you have formal permission and also agreement to undertake research with a sample. *Try to secure both as early in advance as possible.* Also meet with your tutor prior to undertaking any interviews and show them the questions that you plan to ask.

5   Decide the format (face to face interview, telephone, etc.), method of data collection (tape recoding, note taking) and plan the best environment to undertake the research.

6   Carefully check the wording of your questions, being careful to be brief, clear, avoid ambiguity and link each question to your topic.

7   Decide the question types (for example, open ended, closed, etc.).

8   Write out a formal introduction to recite prior to the interview – *briefly* detailing the purpose of your study and overall intentions (especially if the participants have never met you before). You may also wish to provide candidates with other information such as the number of questions you wish to ask, the course you are studying for, etc., but always be brief and clear.

9   Add any instructions or reminders next to each question if necessary.

10 Always thank participants for their time and trouble after any interview. You may also wish to explain what you intend to do with the data.

Questionnaires

Another viable method used within qualitative social work research is the questionnaire. A questionnaire is a set of open and/or closed questions in a standardized format that participants complete by themselves. Occasionally, however, questionnaires can be completed by a researcher in the company of a participant. The many benefits of questionnaires include that they are typically convenient and exceptionally cheap to administer, can save considerable time and potentially may reach a larger audience. On the down side they do have a limited capacity to collect *precise* forms of information; and some topics and questions that are insensitive regarding issues and groups that social work students have access to may not be asked. However, and as Royse (1991: 129) points out, as with the interview the questionnaire represents one of the most common instruments that social workers utilize in their work. This might be through the initial 'intake' process following a referral to a social service department or more commonly as part of an assessment of need.

Questionnaires draw significantly from the tradition of quantitative and survey research, and usually most questions included tend to be presented in a closed format (with a limited and set number of possible answers). Despite this, for qualitative social work research it is possible, and indeed more probably essential, to utilize more open-ended questions so that participants can articulate and explore their views in more detail and depth. Therefore questionnaires for a social work dissertation will tend to be longer and ask more detailed questions than most used in survey research. Importantly you should always allow adequate space for completing open ended questions on a questionnaire.

Questionnaires are less likely to be completed and returned anonymously, although this is still an option and may be appropriate for exploring some sensitive or highly personal research topics. As with interviews the careful design of any questions is a priority for any questionnaire. In general the same rules apply for questionnaires as those for interviews (see pp. 198–200 above). In particular, a questionnaire should:

- include brief information clearly presenting a researcher's identity and general intentions. Participants should also be thanked for their time and effort in advance;
- offer simple and brief instructions on how to complete and return the document;
- be clear, unambiguous and easy to understand;
- not be too general and broad in either aim or questions asked;
- link clearly with research aims and objectives;
- allow adequate space for answers;
- contain only a relatively small number of questions that link to a research question;
- not ask any more than one question at a time;
- remain sensitive to participants' needs;
- avoid 'leading' questions (to encourage a particular answer).

It is vitally important to ensure that your questionnaire is as brief as is possible. This is because there is then much more chance of a document being completed to a satisfactory standard, as well as being returned. As many people do not like to engage with paperwork of any form, larger questionnaires rarely achieve a good response rate. Carefully ration your questions and ensure that they link to your original objectives. Sometimes a questionnaire will require more questions than the interview method. This is because when not in the company of a participant, it may take more questions to extract the information that you require. In general, however, completing a questionnaire alongside a participant is often a good procedure to follow. This is because a researcher's presence may help overcome potential difficulties such as the participant's uncertainty regarding the meaning of some questions.

The sequence of questions is also important. Ideally you should begin with a simple introductory question that is not too challenging. It is then possible to begin to *gradually explore* your topic over the course of any remaining questions. A common method used in questionnaire design is filtering. A filter question is closed (restrictive number of possible answers) and any answer then leads to either the next question being skipped or more details being provided. Figure 7.2 gives an example. The filter method is flexible and may be adapted to different versions and used for a number of purposes. For example, you may wish to target questions at people with particular attributes, and concentrate less on participants who are not as eligible for a research topic. This approach will be especially helpful if you have access to a larger sample. You may also wish to construct your questions to emphasize particular points or explore in much more detail specific questions. Although filter questions can be useful for some topics their construction is generally complex and they have to be especially clear so as not to confuse participants.

Questionnaires should always be tested prior to use in a research field. As Payne and Payne (2004: 189) observe:

---

1. Have you previously engaged in social work with children who have been adopted?

Yes (please go to the question 2)   **No** (please go to question 4)

2. Are there any specific ways in which this form of social work was different to other casework?

Yes (please go to the question 3)   **No** (please go to question 4)

3. Please briefly specify below any examples of ways in which social work with adopted children is distinct?

Figure 7.2   Part of a questionnaire with filter questions.

Designing questionnaires looks simple but it is not. A good rule of thumb is always to work in pairs, and then to use a couple of friends or family members as guinea pigs (they will be your sternest critics!). Even some professional survey researchers sometimes produce seriously deficient questions.

Finally, in my experience a brief questionnaire that is able be collect vital information from participants and which can be completed prior to, or after, an interview is often an extremely effective tool for social work research. This form of triangulation (merging more than one method) is especially useful for a dissertation, and such a combination of two methods is also adaptable. For example, you could merge a moderately sized questionnaire with brief interviews if your topic is suitable. However if you do lack time, and would ideally like to gain access to a larger sample, a qualitative questionnaire may be an ideal instrument by which to collect vital data over a short time period. Alternatively, well constructed questionnaires can also accommodate small numbers of participants and can ask and explore in-depth themes in a similar way to interviews. This process can also become anonymous, which may help you gain access to groups more difficult to reach, such as senior management or doctors, and so on.

Focus groups

Focus group research involves a *group* interview and discussion in which specific themes or issues are examined, often over an extended period of time. Typically the researcher acts as a 'moderator' and prompts or carefully leads any discussion by asking predetermined or spontaneous questions. Usually group participants have something in common and may also be in regular contact, such as employees or volunteers based within a social care organization. However, Kitzinger (1994) distinguishes between 'complimentary' and 'argumentative' focus groups, highlighting that different processes are likely depending on group members and related topics explored.

Complete strangers may be invited to a focus group meeting, but ideally there should be something that each participant has in common. In practice people of differing status or rank within an organization, or from different socio-economic or cultural backgrounds, are not merged for focus group research unless this is a priority regarding the aims and objectives of a dissertation.

Denscombe (2007: 178–81) isolates three attributes regarding focus group research. They include the following:

- There is a clear *focus* to any session based around status, beliefs or experience that all participants have in common. A group discussion will usually be triggered by a 'stimulus' – often a question that will encourage a lively debate or sometimes prompts can be used, such as a photograph or topical newspaper report to kindle a debate. A key priority for the moderator is that any discussion remains focused and at regular intervals.

- Interaction and lively talk between group members is ideal and will assist the task of eliciting information. In particular, the moderator should not merely seek to identify explicit *beliefs* or *attitudes* from participants, but should also look to unearth and explore any *reasons* for, or *causes* of, opinions expressed.

- The moderator should endeavour to *facilitate* the group. Strict control of participants' behaviour or talk is to be avoided – rather support and a delicate act of prompting, alongside the occasional steering of any debate if the original focus is lost, is paramount. The moderator may also subtly encourage quieter speakers, and tactfully discourage dominant or overbearing personalities, especially if they obstruct or inhibit other participants from contributing to a debate.

A moderator may also maintain field notes during or following any group discussion. The focus group meeting can be tape recorded and partially or entirely transcribed for analysis.

Regarding a sample size most focus group meetings tend to have between six and ten members. However, for a social work dissertation fewer may be more practical and appropriate. This will depend on factors such as available time, the topic of research under investigation, likely participants, a tutor's recommendations, course requirements, etc. Between three and four members is usually acceptable for many social work dissertations.

Another option is to run more than one focus group – for example, it could be possible to have two separate meetings in which different questions are provided to the same group. Alternatively two separate groups of people may be asked the same questions so as to increase the sample size. In practice, although such options remain and may be suitable, reducing potential work is always beneficial because it allows more time to concentrate upon any collected data. In my own experience social work students rarely have time on their hands to undertake more than one focus group meeting.

The length of time of any focus group meeting will differ depending upon factors such as the number and type of participants present, the research aims and objectives being explored, the response of group members to questions, and so on. Despite differences, however, it is advisable to try to complete the meeting within an hour. Typically focus group meeting are semi-structured, allowing the moderator and participants some discretion while ensuring that some structure and planning are in place. Questions will usually follow the same general rules as listed and explored earlier in this chapter. A good indicator of when to move onto the next question during any meeting is when initial points raised are repeated by participants.

Other points relating to focus group research include the following:

- The moderator should introduce themselves, thank people for coming, allow people to introduce themselves, and give a brief outline of their research.
- Some ground rules should be set, such as allowing people to finish speaking, only one person speaking at a time, etc.
- A general introductory question may be asked at the start of proceedings so as to 'warm up' participants.
- At least five key questions that directly link to any research aims and objectives should be prepared in advance and asked to the group.
- Questions can be used to break silences or bring the group discussion back to the initial research topic.
- Further questions may be asked by the moderator if points are unexplored or if a participant raises a pertinent issue that relates to the research question.
- Participants should be thanked at the end of any meeting and informed of what will happen to the findings.

(Adapted from Krueger and Casey, 2000)

One of the key benefits of focus group research remains its capacity to save both time and resources. This is because a considerable amount of information and other data can be collected during a brief meeting. As part of a social work dissertation a wide range of themes may be feasible for focus group research. Focus groups are especially viable for researchers wishing to explore peoples' motives, attitudes and opinions regarding a specific topic (for example, parenting, foster caring, service provision, empowerment, gender roles, and so on). Possible groups that can be interviewed include social work practitioners, managers, support workers, volunteers, health workers or other professionals such as teachers.

Linhorst (2002: 223) highlights the potential relevance of focus group research for social work. Reasons include:

- the diverse populations and issues covered by social work practice and research and the related flexibility and suitability of the focus group method;
- the method can support social work's 'unique person-in-environment perspective';

- the capacity of focus group research to be combined with other methods such as one-on-one interviews or questionnaires;
- the educational, therapeutic and empowering potential of focus group meetings for participants.

However the author also notes some limits which include:

- Focus groups can be difficult to organize and arrange.
- The numbers of potential questions to ask and issues to explore are often limited (especially in comparison to individual interviews) due to time constraints generated by group discussions and personal needs regarding confidentiality.
- The role of moderator can be stressful and difficult, especially for novices.
- Excess data can be collected making any analysis time consuming and difficult.
- Potential ethical and practical issues, particularly around maintaining confidentiality in a group setting or avoiding the possible exploitation of vulnerable participants, can persist.

It is imperative to raise or discuss any queries or concerns with a tutor prior to undertaking a focus group meeting. The analysis of research themes are generally the same as for other forms of interview and are explored in Chapter 9.

Summary

This chapter has looked at three distinct research methods – the interview, questionnaire and focus group. Each method offers a possible option for a social work dissertation, and each has the potential to help collect valuable data by which to explore a research question. In practice interview techniques tend to be the most popular among students. This is because they are able to collect large amounts of high quality data in a relatively brief period of time. Questionnaires again have the same benefit but are unlikely to be able to collect as much detailed information. Finally a focus group meeting will also have advantages and can often be ideal for exploring topics that people will be more comfortable discussing as part of a group; such as a social work role that requires a collective 'team' response at regular intervals or sensitive topics such as bereavement.

The next chapter looks at research methodologies relating to narrative research, discourse analysis and the life history approach.

Suggested reading

Bell, J. (2005) *Doing Your Research Project*, 4th edn. Maidenhead: Open University Press. (Chapter 7: Designing and Administering Questionnaires).

Darlington, Y. and Scott, D. (2002) *Qualitative Research in Practice: Stories from the Field*. Maidenhead: Open University Press. (Chapter 3: In-depth interviewing).

Gillham, B. (2005) *Research Interviewing – the Range of Techniques*. Maidenhead: Open University Press.

Krueger, R.A. and Casey, M.A. (2000) *Focus Groups: A Practical Guide for Applied Research*. London: Sage.

Linhorst, D.M. (2002) A review of the use and potential of focus groups in social work research, *Qualitative Social Work*, 1(2): 208–28.

Royse, D. (1991) *Research Methods for Social Work*. Chicago: Nelson-Hall Publishers. (Chapter 7: Questionnaire Design).

8 Alternative methodology: Narrative research, discourse analysis and life histories

Introduction

This chapter looks at three non-traditional or alternative forms of methodology. These are narrative, discourse analysis and life history research. Narrative based and life history research usually require some form of empirical research, which may include unstructured interviews. Discourse analysis is able to utilize either interviews or draw from material already published. Once again factors such as available time, potential sample group and the nature and context of the research question to be investigated all remain factors that can influence whether any such methodology is appropriate for intended research.

Each methodology is explored in detail below.

Narrative research

Since the 1990s narrative research has grown in prominence and is now established as a legitimate, if not mainstream, form of qualitative research (Reissman, 1993). Drawing from Mishler's (1986) influential book on interview methods, many advocates of narrative research propose that conventional approaches to the interview (structured and semi-structured) regularly restrict participants' responses. Consequentially, such traditional processes can reduce any capacity for the interviewee to express their real experiences or opinions, and also the interviewer may struggle to adequately unearth and explore research questions. It is proposed that although most forms of social work rely heavily upon the interview process as part of 'professional' procedure, such a *formal* cultural tradition restricts the capacity of employees to understand fully the sensitive and complex perspectives of service users. As Hall and White (2004: 379) underline, through traditions such as the assessment, the 'problems and interventions of social work are simplified, coded and cross tabulated, ignoring the complex and reflexive nature of such interactive encounters'.

Holloway and Jefferson (2000: 31) contend that the narrative researcher instead seeks to 'be a good listener and the interviewee is [recognized as] a story-teller rather than a respondent'. The research process then becomes 'open to development and change, depending on the narrator's experiences'. Narrative research concentrates upon the centrality of the stories generated by the teller and also the significance and meaning of the content of embodied responses. As Fraser (2004: 180) suggests: 'storytelling is such an important activity because narratives help people to organize their experiences into meaningful episodes that call upon cultural modes of reasoning and representation'. However narrative research can also be deeply political. For example, Plummer (2001) links a narrative approach to humanism and interpretivism, and encourages us to look at the *reasons* why stories are presented in the first place, their cultural and political significance, and how they might be utilized to reform society – particularly by drawing attention to the opinions of excluded voices.

Due to the interpretive stress upon exploring participants' understanding and meaning of their lives and self-identity, narrative approaches are often tied to a variety of disciplines, including theories of psychology, social anthropology and philosophy. Together these approaches look at themes such as memory and the construction of stories by use of a personal or culturally defined *identity*; and this process is seen as embodying the creation of the self. As well as interpretivism (and especially symbolic interactionism, see pp. 54–6), narrative research has also been strongly influenced by postmodern theory and especially the idea (drawing from the philosopher Friedrich Nietzsche) that 'truth' is unstable, ambivalent and should be left open to question. Indeed as Miller (2003: 208) argues:

> The narrative approach can be labelled 'post-modern', in that reality is seen to be situational and fluid – jointly constructed by the interview partnership during the conduct of the interview. The personal characteristic of the interviewer can constitute one of the main stimuli to the interviewee and there is not a blanket prohibition against the interviewer either reacting openly to the statements of the interviewee and/or revealing personal details of their own.

There is, however, a range of methods utilized in narrative research, and as with all research methodologies, different theoretical approaches can have an influence. For example, a more critical approach may seek to link the contents of any given narrative with the direct impact of seemingly dominant structural, ideological and cultural influences (schooling, the media, employment law, government policy, family traditions, language, etc.) upon the opinions of the speaker. Drawing from postmodernism, Coffey and Atkinson (1996) also explore the use of imagery and metaphor to convey shared meaning and understanding among participants. What these examples underline is the *flexibility* of the narrative approach, and therefore its capacity to be used within either critical, postmodern, or interpretive social work research, or a combined approach using different theories.

Fraser (2004: 181) identifies ways in which narrative approaches can have relevance to social work research. Narrative research can:

1. Provide a way 'to make sense of language', itself a core aspect of the social work task.
2. Permit a 'plurality of truths to be known' and presented within a thesis; especially those that are generated by the discretion offered to research participants themselves. This may also help link any discussion to contested aspects of social work practice, and, as a consequence, encourage democratic processes and more open discussion.
3. Allow the researcher to better understand and contextualize 'interactions that occur among individuals, groups and societies'. Through closer and more intimate contact encouraged through an exchange of language, it may also help the researcher better understand the people and topics that they are researching.
4. Permit different and less superficial discussions and opinions to prevail that contrast with the sometimes distant views of the trained expert or emotionless 'objective' researcher.
5. Encourage social work to move beyond the traditionally narrow focused 'problem solving' methods of the past (embedded in assessment procedures, legislation or systems theory), and instead engage more broadly with 'social phenomenon' such as during 'cross cultural work' with people from very different backgrounds.
6. Potentially offer a platform to 'excluded voices' and schemes to expand social justice; such as by encouraging the critical and emancipatory aspect of social work to be extended through a set of inclusive narratives.

It is likely that certain topics will be particularly feasible for the narrative method. This may include topics and related issues which the participant requires adequate time and space to explore in great detail and depth. This can include personally sensitive issues such as bereavement or addiction, or any other complex topic that is unlikely to be adequately explored following a series of brief and formal interviews or questionnaires. Because narrative can also utilize previously published material, this again increases the possibilities of the genre.

Fraser (2004: 184) offers the follow advice for researchers intending to undertake narrative interviews:

- First study the socio-historical contexts of participants' lives.
- Avoid interrogation and cross-examination style interview techniques.
- Be sensitive to the timing of questions and avoid unnecessary interruptions.
- Help to generate a 'climate of trust'.
- Allow participants to ask questions of their own.
- Be transparent and reveal your investment and motives for the research project.
- Share (with participants) some of the interpretations made regarding participants' views.
- Understand and appreciate the politics involved in knowledge generation.
- Be aware of, and try to respond to, different communication styles expressed during any interviews.

Reissman and Quinney (2005) offer a convenient list of four standards for good quality narrative research. They include the following:

1   *Detailed transcripts* It is necessary to accumulate as much detail as possible from interviews undertaken and also try to ensure that you have adequate source material available if using secondary sources.
2   *Focus on language and context of production* The use of language remains paramount to any narrative study and can link with a wide range of social work practices, such as relations with service users or other professionals, official procedures followed such as case reviews or diary accounts, and meetings between colleagues or with senior staff, and so on. Discussion of such 'real world' events and practices need to be identified, interpreted, contextualized or linked with, and analysed, regarding policy developments, legal practices and/or theoretical explanations that assess human behaviour and circumstance.
3   *Attention to structural features* It would be a mistake to concentrate entirely upon the use of language and projection of meaning by participants themselves – in contrast opinions must be explained and assessed regarding wider cultural and structural factors, and how they might influence or mould the narratives produced. It may therefore be helpful to ask one or two questions which help explore participants' background – for example, regarding themes such as number of years engaged in social work practice, socio-economic class background, reasons for entering social work, and so on.

4 *Acknowledgement of dialogic characteristics and a comparative approach (if appropriate)* It will help to make a note of emotional responses to any discussions or chat, for example if someone is upset when stressing a point. Also comparing different interviews can assist analysis, whether this includes previous research and/or different participants involved in your own research.

Based on personal experience Andrews *et al.* (2004) stress the variety of formats that narrative research can take. Three examples are presented that draw from personal encounters throughout the authors' careers. Among many others, they include:

Counter-narratives This approach aims to promote alternative voices regarding taken-for-granted assumptions and opinions, such as those imposed by a dominant ideology. Through use of the voices of people directly affected by a cultural or social phenomenon, an alternative set of views and arguments can be presented by participants and codified by researcher(s). As Molly Andrews states, 'people fashion stories that challenge – either implicitly or explicitly – those [dominant] master tales, revealing alternative versions of how ... stories *we* know best might be retold' (2004: 100). For example, the author details her research with protesters against the first Gulf War. By talking to people living in a military town in America (Colorado Springs) who engaged in counter-war activities during public demonstrations *supporting* the war, Andrews was able to explore 'what different meanings' the American flag represented to those who displayed it in public. Through their voices protesters questioned that in displaying the American flag at demonstrations their actions were unpatriotic and instead identified with different objectives: 'Far from being "unpatriotic" or "un-American", the peace protesters saw themselves as making an essential contribution to the democratic process and, as such, doing their duty as "good citizens".'
    The use of counter-narratives has great potential for social work. This might include the use of critical opinions expressed by students regarding aspects of their past experience; practitioners questioning a policy or service users' views on their support received or not; or informal carers' reflections on their role, and so on.

Subjectivity Narrative can also offer an opportunity to analyse the subjective personal experiences of participants, including responses to events that occur around the life cycle. Drawing from prior work as a lawyer specializing in divorce-related casework, Shelly Day Sclater offers a methodological template for narrative research that unearths 'how people frame, remember and report their experiences'. This allowed the researcher an opportunity to '[generate] knowledge that disrupts old certainties and allows us to glimpse something of the complexities of human lives, selves and endeavours'. It also offers a chance to not only explore individual lives and experience but bind these to 'broader social processes' (Andrews *et al.*, 2004: 103). Sclater interviewed people involved in the difficult process of divorce and encouraged participants to open up and explore their experiences. Extensive transcripts were then linked to a critical interpretation of a specific theory within psychology.

Perhaps more so than members of the law profession, social workers seek to explore personal qualities, viewpoints and needs, and also link these to wider cultural and structural dynamics during their daily routines followed in the workplace (Carey, 2004; 2008). Narrative research can exemplify this process through an examination and analysis of the detailed and rich accounts of participants' subjective experiences and opinions.

Autobiography By assessing autobiographical accounts, Corinne Squire and Maria Tamboukou have delved into the often deeply personal experiences of research participants through either in-depth readings of interview transcripts or published diary extracts. For example, in research with HIV positive women, Squire has highlighted the disparate and altering responses to the illness. This contrasts with the traditional emphasis within research (including some narrative based) which assumes that a person maintains 'consistent and coherent notions of identity' through periods of personal crisis or that subsequent participant stories follow a logical 'developmental or teleological frame'. In contrast, the use of a rich narrative stance that emphasizes discretion and openness for participants – while also exploring past lives – acknowledges instead the 'fragmented, indeterminate subject', and subsequently recognizes the importance of a variety of variant influences including personal identity and wider culture. This seemingly more detailed and intimate approach can also encourage critical self-reflection on behalf of both the researcher and participant.

By utilizing published diary extracts from women training to be teachers throughout the early twentieth century, Tamboukou has been able to again confront the limits of traditional research approaches and question established trends and taken for granted assumptions. For example, the author has stressed how such women cherished new found freedoms in the male dominated world of higher education and also began to question and resist established practices. Such previously neglected or denied outcomes were presented (and analysed) through the letters and diaries *of women themselves* (Andrews *et al.*, 2004: 104–9).

Any analysis of findings from the use of a narrative approach will be much the same as other forms of research. As detailed in previous chapters you should look to link your original research question, and subsequent aims and objectives, with any analysis. Typically it is a priority to tease out salient themes, trends, issues, etc. that have emerged from each interview, especially themes that cut across and link each interview as well as those that contrast. Similar and/or discordant themes are then typically compared with findings explored in other research and/or theory. Examples of some questions to ask within analysis might include:

- How do research findings link with and/or differ from other research findings explored throughout the literature review?
- Are there any issues that have emerged that need to be explored and unpacked further prior to a final write up?
- Are there any new findings identified that reveal something that has not been adequately explored elsewhere?

Potential problems and criticism of the narrative approach

If deciding to undertake narrative interviews then traditional problems relating to interviews – such as access to participants – again emerge. There are also likely to be longer periods of time spent involved with what are usually much less formal interviews; and such additional time should be accounted for, including a recognition that more time needs to be put aside to transcribe and analyse findings. Narrative interviews can also involve a more detailed exploration of interviewees' body language and emotional responses as part of the interview process – once again this aspect of the methodology may be time consuming and less straightforward than more traditional interview methods.

Despite its popularity narrative research has received significant criticism. One of the most pertinent points raised by detractors is the potentially conservative nature of the method. As Fraser (2004: 182) underlines:

> [T]he rise of the narrative movements has occurred during a sustained period of economic conservatism, at least in most of Anglo-American societies. Pointing out that governments have '... destroyed the social programs we cared about and re-channelled resources to the already rich', Laird (1994) wonders whether 'there is something "escapist" about the story metaphor?'

Finally, some concerns have been expressed regarding the potential bias inherent in interviews without any clear structure to support the process (Holloway and Jefferson, 2000). The downside of permitting so much discretion to participants is not merely the amount of precious time that this involves interviewing and transcribing, but also that this can mean that participants may drift away from any original topic while chatting. Again this very much depends upon your own interpretation and application of the methodology and processes followed. Narrative research does not have to be unstructured and you may decide to carefully plan ahead for subsequent questions asked because of limited available time. It will always help to explain clearly your motives and rationale for how you applied narrative research in the methodology section of the final dissertation. Case study 8.1 offers an example of how one of my students structured his dissertation according to the narrative approach.

Case Study 8.1

Topic: Communication and inter-professional practice during case conferences between health and social work professionals

Rob wanted to explore ways in which professionals *formally* communicate with one another as part of work within a joint social work and health care setting. He wanted to link this study to increasing numbers of debates around inter-professional working (for example, Reynolds, 2007). Rob eventually decided to focus upon the case conference as it represented a regularly formal ritual where different professionals discuss their own assessments and expectations of how a case should develop in the near and long term future.

Rob decided to interview three social workers and an equal number of health care professionals (two community nurses and one occupational therapist). He undertook an in-depth narrative based interview with each participant that lasted between an hour and an hour and a half. Rob tape recorded the interviews and then selectively transcribed sections (due to limited available time) that linked directly to his initial research aims and objectives. Rob's findings suggested both sites of conflict and consensus which led to an extensive discussion and numerous policy related and practice based recommendations in his final write up. Direct quotes from practitioners were used in the findings and analysis section of Rob's dissertation in order to emphasize points raised by the practitioners. Findings were also linked with a debate of previous research that had used symbolic inter-actionism to explore the benefits and flaws of inter-professional practices.

Discourse analysis

Another approach to social research that focuses upon the study of language is discourse analysis (DA). Like narrative research DA meticulously investigates the use of language within a social context. However, in drawing from Worrall, Jupp (1996: 300) underlines DA's wider ambitions as an approach that also prioritizes the structural, political and cultural consequences of language:

> Discourse embraces all aspects of a communication – not only its content, but its author (who says it?), its authority (on what grounds?), its audience (to whom?), its objective (in order to achieve what?) (Worrall, 1990: 8)

> Discourse encompasses ideas, statements or knowledge that are dominant at a particular time among particular sets of people . . . and which are held in relation to other sets of individuals . . . Implicit in the use of such knowledge is the application of power . . . discourse involves all forms of communication, including talk and conversation. In the latter, however, it is not restricted exclusively to verbalized propositions, but can include ways of seeing, categorizing and reacting to the social world in everyday practices. (cited in Punch, 2005: 221)

Although made up of language, discourse can translate into a wide variety of formats including theories, ideas, discussions, acts of legislation, rhetoric, traditions, organizational procedures, conversations, informal or formal rituals, and so on. The classic example of a discourse is that of the medical discourse generated by the medical profession, or the law discourse constructed, refined and developed by the law profession. Both represent belief systems, theories, traditions and specific attitudes, ways of viewing the world and behaving, and approaches which do not merely maintain their own interests, but also influence the opinions, choices and experiences of others (notably patients or clients but also other quasi-professions such as nursing, occupational therapy, social work, and so on). As Humphries (2008: 120, my emphasis) notes, as well as generating great consequence for us all, discourse is also versatile:

> DA sees language as *constitutive* – as actually creating, negotiating and changing meaning. It is not a static system but is located in ongoing interaction involving competing attempts to fix meaning and pin it down once and for all. The study of discourse, therefore, confronts debates about what constitutes reality and 'truth', what are social

problems and solutions and what is 'real', and about the very nature of meaning.

Discourse then, is identified as offering more than a mere exchange of words between people at a given time – it also embodies power, relationships, traditions, and assumptions, and more. Drawing from this assumption DA locates language with power relations by highlighting 'how language is used to produce versions of knowledge that then *gain legitimacy* in a political, social, cultural and professional sense' (D'Cruz and Jones, 2004: 156, authors' emphasis).

D'Cruz and Jones (2004: 156–7) discuss five traits relating to the DA approach. They include the following assumptions:

- Words represent and project interpretations of knowledge which 'also operate as devices of power'. This process may very much depend upon where words and language are used, and by whom and when.
- There are no fundamental 'truths' as such, yet it is likely that forms of truth (theories, attitudes, opinions, arguments, etc.) will be imposed through language and discourse by more dominant groups at a given time and place. This complex cultural and political process is often undertaken to subjugate and control less powerful people
- Discourses will differ and alter over time and place. This typically reflects the given interests of competing groups and, in particular, the need of dominant groups to always maintain their own interests despite changing social, economic and political trends. Within the boundaries of discourse 'participants actively engag[e] in relationships of power to give legitimacy to their version of knowledge and [to] discredit others' (p. 156).
- As with other professionals, social workers can utilize discourse (and especially professional or other 'expert' knowledge and related speech acts, procedures, and so on) to promote their own interests and possibly also dominate service users, informal carers, less qualified employees, etc. Often, discourse will also be utilized to gain specific privileges such as status, a higher salary, more discretion and control at work, and so on.
- However, social work researchers and practitioners can potentially use their attained linguistic and knowledge based power to highlight 'subjugated knowledge', such as the views and cultural traditions of service users, and the ways in which they have been marginalized or excluded.

Jupp (1996) (drawing from Foucault) extends these points and underlines that discourse has other features. For example, there is unlikely to be such a thing as a universal discourse (such as social work), and instead different discourses will be in competition with one another at any given time. Also, discourses may well be arranged in a hierarchy, such as regarding conflicting stances taken regarding beliefs about a social issue (such as the 'true' needs of older people or how to explain the causes and impact of poverty, etc). Inevitably more dominant voices emerge across and between discourses, such as the preferred and more legitimate and socially organized opinions of a doctor in contrast to a seemingly less knowledgeable patient. There typically also emerge competing views and camps within a discourse, such as differing views of how social work should be practised according to different ideologies, theories or policies. Once again such distinctions can be best explained through an analysis of conflict and power, and the ways in which the use of 'language' that is embedded in official reports and documentation, or conversations between people, etc., is often representative of differing power relations and competing interests. These can all provide potential data or evidence to the researcher.

As Crossley (2005: 61) underlines however, discourse is not necessarily consciously organized and planned by *individual* social actors, but instead may form over many generations and eventually become habitual:

> To refer to a 'medical discourse' or 'racist discourse' . . . is to identify a particular vocabulary, a set of norms or rules for defining (or 'constituting') and making sense of particular objects, and a variety of conventions and rhetorical techniques for settling disputes, making claims, researching issues, and so on. . . . The key critical import of this particular conception of discourse rests upon the assumption that those who partake in it are largely unaware of the system of conventions they habitually use and are perhaps also unaware of specific consequences that their way of speaking may have, such that an analysis which unearths and 'deconstructs' that system has a potentially liberatory value. Social agents are able, reflexively, to recognise that their way of seeing and thinking about the world is derived from a social structure (a discourse) that they have learnt and that they habitually rely upon.

The implications and possibilities of this approach are many for a social work dissertation. However, as with narrative research there is no definite or 'ideal' way to approach the DA methodology; instead a *variety* of formats and techniques is made *possible*. Although not offering a definite and clear method, the benefits to the student and researcher are many because of the flexibility and choice on offer regarding what research question, social issue and topic you can decide to pursue. Also, despite a variety of formats, clear trends and assumptions regarding DA have emerged, some of which are explored below.

Through research and analysis of dominant or subjugated ideas, routines, practices, conventions, etc., that are attached to a discourse (including a policy affecting social work or an aspect of social work education or practice), a student may be able to highlight competing interests, power differentials and their subsequent privileges or forms of exclusion, and the ways in which such processes are organized and made legitimate through language and discourse. As Alvesson (2002: 70) also suggests, a study of discourse can allow us the opportunity to 'rethink dominant and widespread assumptions of how language and social phenomenon interact, not only in our professional vocabularies, but also in our ordinary lives'.

Potter and Wetherall (1994) suggest three specific approaches regarding what they term critical discourse analysis:

1   *Locating talk and published material as social practices* Here the use of language is studied in order to unearth the social context and meanings attached. From a social work perspective this could involve the study of official documentation or procedure followed in a social care setting, including those that relate to the assessment process, supervision or team meetings, and so on.

2   *Identifying processes of action, construction and variability* This refers to the way in which a discourse is interpreted in actions and other human responses. Again this may involve a study of professional routines followed and how language might be utilized in the context of multi-disciplinary meetings or forms of social work education, etc. Why are these traditional uses of language constructed and followed, how do they present themselves and what interests are being maintained or excluded? Is any contact with service users influenced by a specific discourse; such as community care policy or a discourse held in law or medicine? Is there a variety of competing discourses attached to a specific act of social work practice, and which could be explored as part of a dissertation?

3   *Identifying the rhetorical or argumentative organisation of talk and text* An approach to this method might consider how the carefully constructed claims made in official reports, acts of legislation or policy documents may differ from aspects of social work practice. For example, are the claims in an official act of legislation that older peoples' needs are to be met *realized* in the practice arena of a social work department? If not whose interests are such seemingly false claims meeting and why? Perhaps you could compare the different arguments presented by competing voices held within the social work or inter-professional literature, and explore why such differences exist.

In advocating an alternative approach Jupp (2006: 75) has identified ten ways in which a policy document might be critically assessed through questions using discourse analysis. One or more may be used as a basis for a social work dissertation, and this approach can be applied to other documents such as academic, legal or organizational publications. The questions are as follows:

- What are the conditions out of which a text has emerged? What are the historical, social, cultural and political conditions which have made this text possible? For example, you may wish to consider some of the developments in ideas and practices that led to a particular policy being developed and later emerging.
- What traces of *other* text(s) are evident in the text, and how might this relationship be explored? What references do the author(s) cite and are such authors and the ideas presented balanced and representative of the time? If not, why have such references been emphasized and what interests may be being encouraged or suppressed?
- How consistent, contradictory or coherent is the text? How are con- tradictions managed? Are the arguments fluent, valid and do they give equal weight to all opinions? For example, in a policy document concerning carers' rights are all minority ethnic groups recognized as important? If not, why might this be the case?
- How are people, objects and thought categorized? Who or what are included/excluded? Again are there notable omissions throughout a text and is priority given to some people or sectors that may not necessarily be justified?
- Who and what are viewed as normal, natural and common sense? Does the nature of the text and style of writing assume too much regarding peoples' behaviour or are notable social trends denied or exaggerated? Perhaps some claims in a report contradict with other findings or your own experience?
- Are there any gaps, silences or 'absent presences' within the text?
- What is presented as legitimate/illegitimate? Again, through lan- guage, is any social issue or group given priority over others?
- Who are assumed to be the primary readers of the text? What assump- tions are being made about the audience? For example, is it clearly a document written with a specific set of people in mind, such as professional health employees? Does it neglect other important groups of people, including social workers or service users?
- What are the likely social (or political) effects of the text?
- What alternative readings might be made by different social groups?

Jupp's approach indicates an assumption that competing interests are held within most forms of discourse. Often, however, there are more than two camps held within any discourse. For example, within a discourse that pivots around social work with older people there will be different discourses generated – such as those represented by different social workers, team managers, informal carers, formal carers, service users, health professionals, and so on. Although dominant discourses emerge they are nearly always faced with forms of counter discourse or resistance.

Fairclough (2000; 2001: 229–30) offers another interpretation of DA that has commonly become known as critical discourse analysis (CDA). This approach looks at the specific links between language and 'its involvement in social processes', and seeks to link specific text to social interactions and processes. CDA is especially concerned with analysis of the ways in which language is used as a resource to maintain dominant power relations and/or to coerce or exclude social groups. Power is recognized as being yielded in a group or institutional form, and is also typically legitimated by legal or other discursive and ideological forms, such as those represented by the mass media, professional interests, the education system, and so on. Specifically CDA can be utilized as 'a resource which can be used in combination with others for researching change in contemporary social life – including current social scientific concerns such as globalization, social exclusion, shifts in governance, and so forth'.

Fairclough advocates five general processes to follow when applying CDA:

1 *Identify a social problem to investigate how it is influenced by discourse*, or more specifically semiosis (or the formation of meaning from verbal, visual or body language). Here a social issue or problem relating to social work would replace the traditional research question, but equally research aims and objectives will still need to be adopted to offer clarity to the project.

2 *Identify obstacles to alleviate the social problem*, and especially the impact that ideological or other dominant discourses have in *maintaining* any such social problem. Fairclough asks us to consider 'how does the problem arise and how is it rooted in the way that social life is organised?' The researcher can look at themes such as the network of practices the problem is located in, the relationship of semiosis to other elements within social practices, and semiosis itself (the order of semiosis, linguistic analysis, interactional analysis, interdiscusive analysis).

   Practically this might include critically analysing the linguistic and political structure of a wider social policy, or other rhetorical devices including business interests or the subtle demands of key professional groups (including social work) such as those articulated in textbooks, magazines or university lectures, etc. How does any such rhetoric device reveal itself, come about and how does it differ from the reality embodied in empirical evidence or the experience of the researcher?

3 *Detect whether politically dominant groups would benefit or not from a social problem being resolved, and what possible interests the problem may serve.* Who benefits most from the ways in which social life is now organized under the discourse and why do aspects of discourse maintain the problem? Here you may be looking for evidence to maintain your thesis, and look at who has generated the discourse that fuels the social problem identified – for example, is it the government, businesses or professionals, a combination of such groups or possibly another dominant group?

4 *Explore ways to overcome any obstacles relating to a social problem, including by providing resistance to a dominant discourse.* This section links to 2 above and in particular concerns new possibilities regarding how social processes (that link to discourse and semiosis) are organized. This might include more critical training as part of social work education, greater recognition and discussion of service user needs for support staff, a new legislation or policy structured around the needs of service users or informal carers, greater support services and resources provided and the development of a more confrontational and emancipatory approach as part of social work practice.

5 *Reflect critically upon any overall analysis undertaken since the start of the research.* This may include being reflexive about one's own stance. Where have we come from in our analysis and what is our social positioning now? Have our ideas changed since the research began and if so in what ways?

(Adapted from Fairclough, 2001: 236)

There are many possible areas to investigate for a dissertation that involves an exploration of DA and CDA. Obvious examples include the study of the changing use of discourse within social policy, social work or for a particular organization such as within the voluntary sector. More specifically, you might wish to explore a piece of legislation, a textbook or set of books and articles relating to a specific aspect of a discipline (for example, anti-oppressive or anti-discriminatory practice, the use of evidence–based practice or systems theory, etc.), diary notes kept by social workers, or another official document or processes. As discourse is, like social work, a broad and sometimes nebulous concept, it will help to define early on what it is you understand discourse to represent. Creating a clear working definition will help with this task, and it is essential to place this into any methodology section within your final write up. It will also help to define your overall methodology as early as possible, in particular how DA or CDA has been interpreted and applied. As ever it will also be of benefit to consult with relevant literature and a tutor regarding what it is you intend to do. An example of discourse analysis is provided in Case Study 8.2.

Case Study 8.2

Topic: A critical discourse analysis of social work with physically disabled adults

Bill wanted to examine the development of ideas regarding social work practice with physically disabled adults. He decided to concentrate upon (UK) published academic literature within 'the discourse of social work', and eventually focused upon the fifty year period from between 1940 and 1990. As a methodology he utilized the genealogical approach advocated and popularized by the French philosopher Michel Foucault. As Corrine Squire (Andrews *et al.*, 2004: 106) insists, a genealogical approach involves 'focusing on insignificant details, searching in the maze of dispersed grey and dusty documents to trace discontinuities, recurrences and play where traditional research sees continuous development, progress and seriousness'.

Bill spent most his time searching for, and reading, published literature by established authors. He concentrated upon textbooks and academic papers and quickly started to note a series of trends. Among others, they included:

1   the priority given to childcare within social work literature, and also child protection from the 1970s onwards;
2   the residual nature of much adult social work from the point of view of the priorities of many authors;
3   the gradual yet slow emphasis placed upon community care as a specific policy, and the significant periods at which this discourse in its own right, became prevalent (notably throughout the 1980s);
4   the dominance of bio-medical approaches within social work regarding disability, and the gradual increase in criticism of such a narrowly focused, seemingly pathological, approach.

The four areas identified above were then reduced to two by concentrating upon sections 1 and 2. A critical engagement with these two areas represented much of Bill's later research and his final write up. What had begun as a particularly broad topic eventually became more focused. Direct quotes from related textbooks and articles provided much of the data. This also represented a significant part of the analysis section of the final dissertation. There were many findings, including the rise in significance of adult social work over time, but also the increasing priority given to older people alongside child protection and the subsequent neglect of physical disability as a social work priority. Despite this, there was also evidence of a challenge to a dominant medical model of physical disability within social work, but this approach had also re-emerged under the guise of government initiatives such as evidence based practice. Bill felt that the intense reading and research benefited him considerably and he was able to apply his findings to his practice upon qualification.

Criticism of discourse analysis

One of the major criticisms levelled at DA is that there is too much emphasis placed upon language and text. For example, does such an assumption neglect the importance of human *action*, and also the moral choices that people often have open to them? In relation, some critical forms of DA seem to promote the importance of social structures, culture and language upon all else, and, unlike narrative research or the interview method, they may neglect *personal* perspectives.

More generally DA sometimes has no clear boundaries and techniques of practice, only general suggestions on how to undertake what can be a complex yet sometimes imprecise and therefore unclear method. By its very nature much discourse is dispersed and unseen, and therefore potentially it can be very difficult to research. There is also a wide variety of possible methods and topics to explore and potentially this can cause problems for students and researchers.

Despite such criticism DA offers a potentially fascinating option to the social work student. If concentrating upon a literature review dissertation it offers a wide range of possible topics to explore and clearly links to the critical tradition within sectors of social work academia. Again, defining a clear methodology as early as possible remains paramount, as does the importance of consultation with both relevant literature (including some suggested reading at the end of this chapter) and a personal tutor, so as to be clear about what it is you are doing from the outset.

Life history research

Many social research methodologies or methods seek to identify and unpack specific themes that link to events that occur or exist over relatively brief moments in time. In contrast, life history approaches try to examine extended periods of time and typically draw from the detailed and rich lived experiences of research participants. Often this methodology also seeks to delve into a wider set of inter-relating themes that draw not only on personal events but also broader occurrences (historical, cultural or political trends) which may, at the time, have had only limited influence from individual participants themselves (Miller, 2000). Life history approaches are linked to narrative research in their quest for deeper understanding and meaning from participants themselves. However, they also have distinct qualities, including a tendency to grasp the historical and the holistic.

As a part of life history research interviewees are encouraged to talk in general about their past. Here an exploration of 'what happened' to the 'eye witness' takes place alongside an endeavour to discover 'the inner experience of individuals, [and] how they interpret, understand, and define the world around them' (Faraday and Plummer, 1979, cited in Payne and Payne, 2004: 24). Typically this process follows an initial unstructured interview, although it is not uncommon for another interview with semi-structured questions exploring more specific topics to follow. Such a second interview can survey in more detail themes chosen and discussed by the participant themselves.

As with much narrative research there is a tendency to avoid interruption from the interviewer, and allow the participant as much space and time as is possible to talk. Traditionally, life history research has allowed any participant considerable control as part of the research process – this can include self-interviewing and extensive diary keeping and reflection (Plummer, 1983). Although this approach may be possible as part of a social work dissertation it is likely to be impractical and difficult to manage over the relatively brief period of time allowed for completion of a dissertation. In general, due to time and resource restrictions, a dissertation will require more control and leadership by the student throughout the research process.

The next stage of the research process involves linking interviewees' personal experience with other wider events, which may include the historic, the cultural and/or the political. As Plummer (2001: 39) notes, life histories seek to excavate a personal life regarding 'how it is lived over phases, careers, cycles, stages; and with time outside the life – of how the "historical moment" plays its role in any life's shape'. Here the researcher endeavours to link the micro (personal) with the macro (cultural, institutional, political, etc.), and therefore truly *contextualize* the conversations of participants. As Payne and Payne (2004: 24, original emphasis) confirm, the interviewee 'presents us with *both* a perception of self and the social world'. By integrating a distinct theoretical approach, for example a psycho-social perspective, the researcher will attempt to 'grasp the "whole person situation" ' and go on to interrogate 'the dynamics of a whole life and its institutional setting, while attending to inner worlds and personal disturbance' (Froggett and Chamberlayne, 2004: 73).

As well as exploring the findings held within interview extracts, life history researchers will also seek to delve into associated sources of 'evidence' so as to develop a thesis. These may include historical records, journals, monographs, newspaper articles, television archives, magazines or letters, among other relevant sources. It is not unusual for a disparity to emerge between seemingly 'official' reports – such as those presented in media outlets or even academic sources – and accounts given by research participants. Inevitably it is the researcher's job to develop any discovered 'gaps' between the micro and the macro, or contextualize and try to understand and explain disparities between participants' accounts and more formal reports of a time and era.

Analysis of family history research follows the same processes as most other forms of qualitative research. This will include drawing together issues explored by interviewees within conversation, and assessing how they link to a topic and previous findings and reports. Also aspects of themes extrapolated may be critically compared to other theoretical accounts as part of reflection and engagement with a thesis. A more deductive approach may instead seek to identify specific occurrences, categories or trends, and utilize these to build or test theory.

For a social work dissertation a single yet extensive life story interview with a participant *may* suffice regarding data collection. For example, a senior practitioner with many years experience in social work practice might be asked to reflect upon their career, and discuss in great detail an aspect of their practice which helps to substantiate analysis over the course of a dissertation. They may also be asked to consider and discuss some wider structural changes (social work legislation, policy, organizational, etc.) that have occurred as part of their role, and reflect upon their own personal responses and experience. It is not unusual to concentrate upon one case as part of a life history approach (see Plummer, 1983); however there are limitations with this methodology, most notably a lack of opportunity to compare different cases and experience, as well as the likelihood of generating significant bias.

Individual life histories can demand considerable time and commitment, so be careful not to be too ambitious – ideally between two and four participants is normally enough for a dissertation based on life history research. Possible research participants will vary, but as well as social workers other relevant interviewees may include health professionals or unqualified employees that work alongside social workers. Sometimes carers or service users may be interviewed, but this will depend upon questions of access, the nature of the topic being explored and possible ethical dilemmas and processes.

Plummer (1983) has helpfully proposed some boundaries regarding life history research. For example, he distinguishes between a 'retrospective' and 'contemporaneous' life history, with the former stressing past events and comparing those to the present feelings of a participant, and the latter instead closely exploring daily life today. In addition Plummer argues that a life history approach will usually concentrate upon one of three possible models – individual recollection, themes to explore which have been identified by the participant, or themes presented by any participant and which have then been distilled and interpreted by the researcher. There are five key stages to life history research:

1   *Preparation* This will involve the selection of a research question or social problem, and related decisions regarding likely participant(s), questions to ask, methods to deploy, location of interviews, and so on. A good working relationship between participant(s) and any

researcher is a priority, and trust and empathy as well as a general bond between both camps are often essential criteria.

2 *Data collection* Although the interview is likely to be the most common and convenient approach utilized there are other methods within life history research. As there is commonly a priority to build or extend a close relationship between participant(s) and researcher more informal approaches can be encouraged. For example, participant observation is not uncommon as is informal 'chatting' and note taking. Other sources of data such as diary notes, assessment documentation or even photographs are also possible.

3 *Data storage* The collection of extensive data is nearly always inevitable for most life history approaches. However due to time restrictions a social work student will need to control and limit this process, such as by asking more focused questions and being selective in notes taking. There must also be plans regarding where data is stored, and how it is to be transcribed if tape recordings are made. Due to ethical priorities the safety and security of data remain imperitive and pre-planning is usually necessary.

4 *Data analysis* Due to criticism of bias within life history research it is advisable to try to limit this wherever possible. One approach may be to compare any findings with other people's research, especially those that have accessed a larger sample. Another approach is to allow participants to read any notes or points identified from transcripts by the researcher, and then discuss these in detail with them such as during a second yet more informal interview. As with all analysis, however, the search for themes and issues that link to an initial or revised research questions remains a priority, as is a capacity to compare such themes with other research and/or theory.

5 *Data presentation* Three priorities are suggested regarding presentation. First, be clear about what you wish to accomplish and who it is you are writing about! Second, be careful regarding interpretation and editing as making false claims from collected data always remains a possible outcome. Always check and confirm with a participant if possible before formally writing up any research as authentic meaning from a participant remains imperative. Finally, always practise any writing wherever possible prior to a final write up.

(Adapted from Plummer, 1983)

Again, it is vital to construct a clear definition of the research question in advance of any interviews taking place. It is not enough to simply explore a person's previous life experiences or general attitudes – focus about what it is you intend to explore will be of benefit. Broad and general questions may lead to an excess of data being collected, which can mean a struggle to develop any analysis relating to a topic at a later period. Although this potential problem is apparent within all qualitative research, it is more likely within life history research because of the longer periods of time studied in relation to a participant's life experiences.

Regarding theory, each of the three main groups of social theories – interpretivism, critical and postmodern approaches (discussed in Chapter 3) – can be utilized within a life history methodology. For example, D'Cruz and Jones (2004: 120) highlight that life history approaches are particularly effective for critical social work research, and have proven especially suitable in attempts to 'restore lost voices and knowledge', including 'about colonized societies and peoples' such as aboriginal groups. Clifford (1994) has also championed the use of life histories in social work research: especially regarding approaches that highlight and challenge discrimination as well as allowing people previously ignored or neglected by formal power systems and dominant cultures to have a voice. The social anthropologist Pierre Bourdieu (1998) has also utilized critical life history research to explore the detrimental impact of social and government policy within France upon minority groups, especially as unemployed people, asylum seekers and low skilled employees.

The use of interpretive theory has also been influential in life history research; this is especially so when it is linked to narrative based approaches that stress the context of culture, understanding and meaning to participants themselves. In many respects interpretivism embodies and supports the core principles of both the life history approach, and qualitative research in general – emphasizing and allowing participants' vocal accounts to take precedence, while also contextualizing and framing these perspectives within a theory.

Potentially, a life history approach can be utilized to explore a wide range of possible research themes. For example, this may include a participant's recollection of childhood, schooling, life spent within an institutional setting, personal experiences of poverty, or of living within a particular urban setting. It might instead seek to explore people's careers, choices made, achievements, or more general reflections on specific themes embedded into the life cycle such as ageing or relationships.

The case study below draws from a complex thesis that I supervised and which was in part influenced by a life history methodology.

Case Study 8.3

Topic: A comparative analysis of social workers' emotional responses to changing legislation regarding child protection

Angela wanted to examine the life histories of two long-term practising social workers. She decided to interview and compare two practitioners employed in a busy 'child protection' team where she was based during a practice place-ment. *Initially* Angela wanted to explore, compare and contrast the two practi-tioners overall career development. However, following an extensive literature review, early placement experiences and brief consultation with a tutor, Angela eventually decided to concentrate upon the two practitioners' personal responses to changing child care *legislation*.

Interviews were ongoing during Angela's placement. The first practitioner had more than twenty years experience to draw upon, while the second had only recently been qualified – this disparity provided much of the foundation for com-parison. Following two brief interviews with each practitioner Angela's research objectives again became more focused, and she decided to be even more specific and concentrate upon the *emotional* responses to legislation of each practitioner.

Although the more experienced practitioner was able to draw upon more changes to legislation – including the substantial reforms of legislation embodied within 'case management' introduced more than a decade earlier – there were nevertheless similarities, as well as differences, in the responses from both people interviewed. For example, among many other findings, the experienced prac-titioner tended to be more reflexive; yet each agreed that the process of change was stressful and demanding, especially as the team or either practitioner had never been consulted prior to any changes taking place. The interviews were evocative and highly informative for Angela, and also allowed the student to better understand the use of theory during the research process. In particular she drew upon studies influenced by postmodernism that have explored stress, trauma and identity.

Criticism of life history research

Life history research has been criticized on numerous grounds, and three examples are provided. First, as with so much qualitative research that accommodates small samples, the potentially highly subjective nature of the approach has been questioned (Miller, 2000). Partly as life histories seek to reflect participant attitudes and beliefs the research processes may lack structure and planning. Consequentially there could be a lack of capacity to generalize about any findings.

Second, not everything can necessarily be understood and expressed through language and cultural conditioning alone, and such possible reduc-tionism can limit the potential claims made by researchers. For example, any interviewee may be prone to exaggerate or distort some points raised, and this response may reflect the personality traits of the person being inter-viewed as much as any influence of social conditioning. Finally, a participant's use of language may be ambivalent and unstable, and there are many different ways in which a narrative or biographical account can be interpreted and understood. By isolating purely vocal accounts – and possibly reading written documentation such as diary notes – the researcher is open to possible accusations of misinterpretation, inaccuracy or bias. Also, some critics of post-modernist approaches to social research argue that any subsequent stress upon language and narrative can draw attention away from themes that may have more impact upon service users, such as poverty, ideology or class. Again it will help to acknowledge any such limits when writing up this section for a dissertation.

Summary

This chapter has explored three methodologies that can be used as part of research for a social work dissertation – narrative, discourse analysis and life history research. Each methodology has unique qualities but they are also united by their capacity to explore social work related issues and topics *in great depth*. For example, narrative research is especially suitable for investigating topics or social issues that allow a research participant to take the initiative and also talk at length about something that they are willing or keen to express. Discourse analysis can be used to accommodate a wider variety of topics – including literature based themes – and does not necessarily require fresh data to be collected. Life histories look at themes embedded within a person's life course.

The next chapter looks in much more detail at qualitative analysis.

Suggested reading

Czarniowska, B. (2004) *Narratives in Social Science Research*. London: Sage.
Elliott, J. (2005) *Using Narrative in Social Research*. London: Sage.
Fairclough, N. (1995) *Critical Discourse Analysis*. London: Longman.
Fairclough, N. (2003) *Analysing Discourse: Textual Analysis for Social Research*. London: Routledge.
Giele, J.Z. and Elder, G.H. (eds) (1998) *Methods of Life Course Research: Qualitative and Quantitative Approaches*. London: Sage.
Millar, R.L. (2000) *Researching Life Stories and Family Histories*. London: Sage.
Perks, R. and Thompson, A. (eds) (2006) *The Oral History Reader*. Oxford: Routledge.

9   Qualitative analysis

Introduction

This chapter discusses qualitative analysis for a social work dissertation. It is divided into two main sections. The first section explores some of the *general* forms of qualitative analysis undertaken, and also considers some of the requirements for a social work thesis, such as the use of reflexivity and theory. The second section discusses more specific forms of qualitative analysis, which include documentary, thematic, comparative and critical analysis.

Qualitative analysis

When undertaking analysis the researcher attempts to generate *explanation, understanding* and *meaning* from research findings. Qualitative analysis within social work also demands a need to 'think creatively and conceptually' (Padgett, 1998: 72) and place *into context* what has been discovered. Meaning and understanding emerge from analysis due to different possible approaches – for example, identifying trends or occurrences in research findings and comparing these to other people's research and/or established theoretical perspectives such as systems theory or an interpretation of critical theory. Analysis will draw from different approaches and utilize a range of skills that can differ according to a researcher's personal values and beliefs, their research topic and subsequent aims and objectives, and any chosen research methodology and/or methods. The range of possible topics, approaches and interpretations means that – as Bryman (2004: 399) stresses – there are 'few well-established and widely accepted *rules* for the analysis of qualitative data'.

There are, however, general guidelines that assist any process of analysis, and some authors offer attempts to standardize possible methods. For example, Miles and Huberman (1994: 9) suggest core processes followed within forms of qualitative analysis. These include a tendency by a researcher to:

- identify similar phrases, relationships between topic-related patterns, themes, distinct differences and common sequences within research data;
- gradually elaborate a small set of generalizations that cover the consistencies recognized in the database and/or published material;
- confront generalizations with a formalized body of knowledge in the form of theories, constructs or models.

As part of the first approach patterns or trends are identified by the researcher, such as following interviews and the subsequent reading of transcripts with a small group of practitioners working in a day centre. Each practitioner may stress the importance of communication and empathy with service users, and explore ways of building a closer bond with clients within social work. There may be similar points raised in conversation by most if not all of those interviewed, and these allow generalizations to be made. Finally any such generalizations are then compared to other research and/or theoretical models.

Within this process there is also an ongoing attempt to *manage* and *reduce* data, which again is an aspect of social research that continues from an early stage and moves into later stages of a dissertation. As Huberman and Miles (cited in Marvasti, 2004: 89) summarize:

> With *data reduction*, the potential universe of data is reduced in an anticipatory way as the researcher chooses a conceptual framework, research questions, cases, and instruments. Once actual field notes, interviews, tapes, or other data are available, data summaries, coding, finding themes, clustering, and writing stories are all instances of further data selection and condensation.

Typically far more information and data is collected through reading or interviews, focus group sessions, etc., than can possibly be analysed or accounted for in a final write up; subsequently the researcher's capacity to excavate and 'pull out' key themes, such as those that most directly link with an initial research aims and objectives, remains the principal purpose. The research question or aims and objectives may also be fine tuned and made more specific if too much data still persists. In the final writing up of a dissertation research themes can be reduced further if necessary; such as by locating more specific themes from transcripts or information gathered during the literature review.

Alongside the identification and comparison of trends or themes, the unpacking of research findings is also a pivotal aspect of analysis. In particular, there is likely to follow techniques such as attaching meanings to new data, evaluating or assessing it, critically engaging with such findings, and trying to understand and locate any identified patterns. For example, a capacity to articulate and relate any findings to social work theory, historical trends, policy or practice, is likely to be important at this stage. Not unusually a theory may be criticized and reformed following analysis, or new recommendations made regarding how policy or practice might be changed to improve outcomes for service users. This is all part of the process of drawing conclusions from research findings, and it is here that the researcher will seek to create *meaningful statements* that draw directly from their data (observations, transcripts, notes, etc.) and related findings (Marvasti, 2004: 88–90). An example of a pair of meaningful statements (or 'codes') extracted and reduced from data is provided in Table 9.1.

The next key stage relates to how any data might be displayed. Typically qualitative data for a social work dissertation will be represented by textual information – such as verbal quotes from a practitioner interviewed or written observational notes made by the researcher when in the field or during reading. This will normally need to be highlighted, reduced and then organized – such as within a file of written notes – so as to make it easier to access and understand.

Once again, however, there are no concrete formats for this process, and it will be influenced by your own interpretation, reading, findings, objectives, values and beliefs; as well as ability to interact and critically engage with any pertinent issues that are discovered during any research process. In sum, then, analysis is a means by which to locate, gather, reduce, display

Table 9.1 Two codes drawn from interview data with a social work practitioner

Statement from interviewee (data)	Meaningful statement (codes)
. . . I wasn't really trying to upset the woman but she just kept asking me the same question time and time again and I had no choice but to answer in the most forthright way that I could. It was only in retrospect that I realized that that was not a good way to respond to the situation.	Sincere and emotive regret for unplanned verbal response to informal carer requests
I apologized that no more could be done for her son and also made it quite clear that in future I would argue the case for more support than what is currently being provided by this department. I have always argued the case for my most needy 'clients' and will continue to do so for as long as I practise!	Apology and insistence on practising altruistically despite difficulties sometimes generated

Source: Adapted from Marvasti, 2004: 88.

and evaluate data and general findings, which will then be utilized to draw conclusions – such as regarding a discussion of their relationship to service user need, theory, policy, legislation, and so forth.

Crucially these analytical processes and stages are not detached or separate from one another, or indeed any other stages of the research process such as reading or writing up. In contrast, they are all interrelated and supportive of one another. Boundaries are also often blurred within most if not all forms of qualitative analysis; this is because of the unpredictable and diverse nature of qualitative data itself, as well as the movement back and forth between different research stages which includes a 'repetitive interplay between the collection and analysis of data'. This is commonly known as an 'iterative' approach, in which cyclical movements back and forth between research stages leads to the development of ideas, and the transcending of raw information or data (Bryman, 2004: 399). This iterative process is summarized in Figure 9.1.

In contrast to Miles and Huberman's focused processes of qualitative analysis, Tesch (1990: 95–7) offers a somewhat broader definition of general approaches to apply. Processes that are relevant to social work research may include an attempt to do the following:

- *Begin analysis at an early stage and engage with a 'cyclical' process in which analysis moves back and forth.* As was explored in Chapter 2, in

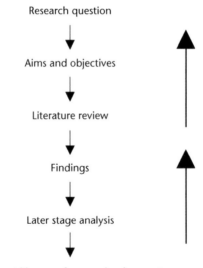

Figure 9.1 The iterative process in social research.

contrast to quantitative research, the qualitative approach is more difficult to predict. Analysis typically begins soon after a project starts, most notably during the initial literature review. Also any qualitative information or data gathering will induce a journey between different author's viewpoints, interviewee opinions and discoveries within the literature review, etc.

- *Try not to be rigid, 'mechanical' or defined by 'scientific' rules and laws.* Often in qualitative research a person will need to follow their intuition, instincts and also draw from practical experience and personal beliefs or values. Indeed many theorists such as some feminists question whether a detached objectivity is ethical or even possible within social research.
- *Endeavour to be systematic and comprehensive within analytic methods.* This is concerned with personal discipline and organization, as well as perseverance. Skills such as planning ahead and organizing any findings are essential, so as not to allow any analysis to become messy and incoherent.
- *Engage with critical reflexivity.* Again this is where the impact of the researcher's values, beliefs and possible prejudices are considered throughout the research process. This is explored further below.
- *Undertake necessary practical activities.* This will include reading, essential note taking, observations or interviews, and so on.
- *Engage with the 'main intellectual tool' of comparison.* Arguably one of the most important skills is a researcher's capacity to identify, understand, reflect upon and detail the *contrast* between different arguments, ideas and findings. Notable examples remain a student's capacity to compare different perspectives from participants or their own findings with previous related research or theory, especially any associated studies uncovered during the literature review. Comparison includes areas of disagreement or debate.
- *Generate debate, conclusions and recommendations.* Analysis should include conclusions that draw directly from findings, which may also encourage better social work practice. This may involve a change in the researcher's values and beliefs, as well as the day to day routines fulfilled as part of a social work job. As stated throughout this book recommendations regarding future social work practice, policy or legislation tend to represent a core component of many social work dissertations.

In a useful summary, Blaxter *et al.* (2006: 185) place four related words at the heart of qualitative analysis. They are:

Concepts Abstract or general ideas that help determine how we consider and critically assess subjects or ideas

Theories Suppositions that seek or help to explain something

Explanations Statements that clarify and explain 'why things are the way they are'

Understanding Our 'perception of the meaning of something'

Analysis regards a 'search for explanation and understanding', through which 'concepts and theories are likely to be advanced, considered and developed.' Concepts emerge from data and represent the foundation upon which a dissertation is built. From this foundation theories emerge or interact with concepts, and explanation and understanding should follow. Analysis is not simply a task that is stuck at the 'end stage' of a dissertation. As with related reading and writing. It should begin early, flow and be dispersed *throughout* a dissertation.

Analysis for a social work dissertation

Although analysis for a dissertation begins at an early stage and proceeds as a project gains momentum, there are points at which more intense forms of analysis evolve. For example, this may occur following interviews with participants, or when intense reading has taken place during a literature review. Just prior to the writing up stage is also a common juncture at which analysis intensifies. There are however research approaches and philosophies which are especially important to social work research, and which should be embedded implicitly throughout the research process. Each is discussed below.

Four core approaches within social work qualitative analysis

This section looks at four key approaches involved in qualitative analysis for a social work dissertation. They include:

1 Context

The placing of research findings *into context* represents a core component of any dissertation. Indeed a capacity to analyse would not be possible within qualitative research without an attempt to locate arguments, raise points, state and unpack issues addressed, etc., in the context of relating or attendant priorities. To contextualize means to place an argument, point raised, issue identified, interview theme acknowledged, academic paper read, and so forth, *into perspective* by assessing and evaluating it from one or more of the following perspectives:

- *Historical* A policy, theory or act of legislation, etc., may be considered and discussed with reference to the impact of *previous* legislation, social events, ideas or political circumstances.
- *Political* This is where an event or finding is explained through the lens of mitigating circumstances that might include the impact of government policy or legislation, or beliefs or ideas that are held by certain people at a given time. The status, gender or social class of a group being discussed may also impact upon research participants' attitudes or behaviour.
- *Cultural* This is closely related to political perspectives and considers how a topic might be better understood by looking at the context of the *place* and *time* in which they occur. For example, did the attitudes of social work practitioners based in a hospital differ to previous research undertaken because of the *institutional* environment in which they formed? Has social work practice been altered because of the setting and dominant health and medical model centred beliefs and ideology sustained in such a health centred institution? Were there dominant practices or ideas held at the time when a practitioner is reflecting that may have influenced perceptions or beliefs?
- *Comparison* As suggested, contrasting experiences, attitudes, forms of organization, case examples, theories, and so on, can permit greater understanding of anything being considered. For example, one person's experience of caring for someone with later stage dementia is likely to be better understood if it is compared to how four other people dealt with similar anxieties or events.

Context might also involve the use of a research methodology – for example by illustrating how your own research approach compares with, and possibly supports or extends, other similar methodologies used in previous research.

2 The use of theory

As first explored in Chapter 3, theory should support all forms of social work research. Holloway and Jefferson (2000: 58–9) identify two reasons why theory helps any process of analysis. First, a theoretical stance avoids largely futile attempts to simply 'tell it like it is'. Such an over pragmatic approach – also known as 'naive empiricism' – may encourage an over reliance upon pure description, as well as a likely haphazard attempt to position or understand any findings. Second, the use of theory encourages the researcher to interpret and critically understand their findings, rather than passively accept new observations or information without careful consideration.

Theory helps us to not only understand research findings, but also provides a *framework* around which to support and direct our research. Typically research findings, whether represented by sources of information or data, can be used to criticize or reform established theory, or develop new concepts or theories.

Potentially there are dangers inherent in any over-reliance upon any established theory. The risks are that such a theory may restrict any analysis by encouraging a limited view of the findings. In contrast, students should utilize theory but try to allow data to speak for itself wherever possible, while allowing any theoretical influence to be made explicit to the reader (Holloway and Todres, 2003).

3 Reflexivity

From a researcher's personal perspective key forms of analytic reflexivity can include:

- questioning preconceived assumptions made regarding any research topic;
- querying possible stereotypes or prejudices held about participants or related groups, such as those transmitted through norms, dominant values, language or through personal experiences with peers, or within the formal education system, forms of employment, etc.;
- reflections on personal 'life chances' and upbringing, including regarding how your gender, class, 'race', and so on may influence or affect your understanding of any interpretation of research findings;
- reflecting upon the learning process and findings as they evolve throughout the research process. How has any new information gathered altered your beliefs, values and possible future practice?

As has been detailed throughout this book research 'that looks back on itself' can greatly assist the process of analysis, such as by encouraging self critical thoughts and new understanding regarding highly personal and sensitive issues – in other words it provides depth and meaning to what could otherwise become a mechanical and arduous set of tasks attached to a demanding course.

Despite this, Alexander (2001: 355) warns that reflexivity also has potential dangers:

> At its best, [reflexivity] makes for better work (everything is stated, nothing, like the researcher's personal political beliefs, is left behind), and it can create a humbleness in researchers. At its worst, especially when researchers spend the entire write-up talking about themselves rather than their subjects, it can lead to intellectually boring work.

It is vital to remember that the exploration of an initial topic and aims and objectives must take priority. If reflexivity is tied to such priorities, and is used as part of a meaningful and engaged process that helps the author better understand and contextualize findings, then it usually maintains a supportive role. Along with theory, reflexivity should be a part of any methodology and analysis; but it should not saturate a thesis to the point where other key objectives are lost.

4 Critique, praxis and emancipation

This component of analysis draws from a wider philosophical tradition held within the thoughts and ideals of core philosophers such as Karl Marx, Friedrich Nietzche, Martin Heidegger, Max Horkeimer, among others. Such thinkers, loosely united within the tradition of what is now known as 'continental philosophy', together identified 'crisis' as an all present essence of (non-utopian) Capitalist societies. Although their reasoning differs somewhat, including any diagnosis of social and political crisis, they each nevertheless advocated an ethical and political response that should help us move 'towards a critique of present conditions', including an emancipatory zeal 'for a transformative practice of philosophy, art, thinking, or politics'.

Drawing from this attitude and culture in a field such as social work research can lead to the presentation and *critique* of evidence discovered in a non-ideal or even dystopian world – including findings gained and presented through ethically informed social research. This critique can then lead to *praxis*, or the merger of theory with practice as embodied within forms of direct social work practice influenced by critical knowledge. Eventually this should direct us towards forms of *emancipation* (such as of oppressed people) and the formation of a more ideal society. In stressing the significance of critique, praxis and emancipation, Critchley (2001: 74) argues that:

> [C]ritique is a critique of existing praxis because it is felt to be unjust, unfree, untrue, or whatever. Furthermore it is a critique that aims towards an emancipation from that unjust praxis towards another individual or collective praxis, a different way of conceiving of human life, whether that is a Nietzschean life of solitary nobility, the communist society envisaged by Marx, the multiple becomings described by Deleuze and Guattari, or something completely different.

Possibly a dissertation may well be somewhat less ambitious regarding practical outcomes; nevertheless it can still draw from the same cultural and political tradition of seeking to evaluate and critically assess whether or not overt or implicit themes within social research findings are fair, just, ideal, or contrary. For example, do your research findings suggest that service users are viewed as equals by their support workers or social workers? If not how might this outcome be explained, and possibly changed for the better within praxis? How might more just or ideal forms of practice be encouraged?

If a day centre is identified as not meeting the needs of its service users, then analysis will include both an attempt to understand and explain this outcome, as well as suggest possible new ways in which such needs might be better met. Suggestions or recommendations regarding how we might move to a state of better and more ethical practice – and towards more ideal outcomes for participants who engage with our research – might represent a core *aspect* of our analysis, even if it is perhaps a little less ambitious than the ideas of Nietzsche or Marx due to time and resource restrictions!

The second half of this chapter now considers more specific forms of analysis, one of which may be ideal in a quest to answer your research question.

Analysing documents

The analytical tradition within the social sciences is founded upon forms of critical investigation and insight. As May (1993: 138) suggests, from this culture of questioning and critical interrogation, published documents are often 'now viewed as mediums through which social power is expressed'. Therefore many qualitative researchers now tend to approach each 'in terms of the cultural context in which they were written', and they may also 'be viewed as attempts at persuasion'. It is imperative therefore not to merely read and describe published material that is encountered throughout a literature review, and beyond. Instead, as part of analysis regarding any published text, there should be a conscious effort to consider the following carefully:

- underlying assumptions and arguments presented;
- possible inconsistencies or paradoxes held within a debate or thesis;
- forms of possible bias;
- any personal interests that may be held by the author(s) and which may have influenced the findings;
- any notable strengths and weaknesses of the document, such as those relating to the methodology, general arguments, conclusions, etc.;
- the circumstances under which the document emerged and what impact this may have had on the content;
- who the document was produced *by* and *for*, and how this might have affected the subject matter and stance of the author(s);
- *why* the document was produced and whether this could have influenced any content and findings;
- whether there is sufficient evidence provided to support the claims;
- how convincing the arguments are;
- how the findings compare to or differ from arguments presented by other authors and research;
- whether the findings contrast with your own experience and views.

Clearly there is unlikely to be sufficient time to undertake all of these tasks for each and every document. Nevertheless, fulfilling some of these roles, especially those that link to your initial research question, will help to promote the process of critical analysis.

Taylor (1989, cited in Blaxter *et al.*, 2006: 217–18) highlights the most common responses to published documentation in the academic tradition. They include one or more of the following:

- defending or confirming a particular view;
- criticizing yet reformulating a particular view in order to improve the argument;
- dismissing arguments due to 'inadequacy, irrelevance, incoherence or by recourse to other appropriate criteria';
- reconciling two positions and proposing a compromise;
- proposing something different and original;
- revising a personal stance in the face of new evidence or arguments.

Once again, as part of any analysis general themes and patterns should be looked for within documentation. This may include issues that are raised consistently across several papers or articles. Such themes can include social trends explored, common behaviour patterns of a social group identified, typical or atypical attitudes and values noted of a social group or sub-culture, general meanings presented by participants and other possible trends.

Basic thematic analysis

Thematic analysis is a relatively common approach utilized within social work qualitative methodologies that involve empirical research. As Dawson (2006: 120) notes, this type of analysis is highly inductive as themes 'emerge from the data and are not imposed upon it by the researcher'. This approach looks to combine data collection and analysis; but, as is so often the case with inductive approaches *in practice*, analysis can also be generated around background reading undertaken prior to the collection of data.

Aronson (1994) offers a pragmatic definition of thematic analysis. Six processes are followed, and each is adapted to social work research below:

1   *Collect any data* This may include data from interviews, focus group meetings, and so on.
2   *Transcribe any conversations* Again the extent to which this is applied in practice will depend upon available times and the nature of the topic. A selective transcript – in which key aspects of the research are transcribed – can sometimes suffice for many dissertations.

3   *Identify themes from patterns within the transcriptions* These may include research participants' experiences, opinions, beliefs, etc. Typically themes are identified by 'bringing together [research participants] components or fragments of ideas or experiences, which often are meaningless when viewed alone' (p. 1).

4   *Themes are then 'pieced together to form a comprehensive picture of . . . [participants'] collective experience'* The researcher can identify themes as an interview progresses and may decide to adapt some questions to explore themes further. Themes are then bound together and reduced so as to reflect any findings in brief summaries such as statements or paragraphs.

5   *Build a valid argument for developing any themes such as by using each 'to develop a storyline'* This may involve reading relevant literature and formulating thematic statements that link to any excavated findings. Typically literature is interwoven with any findings to generate a discussion or critical discourse.

6   *Apply findings to practice* Because it operates as an applied discipline it is usually important to link any findings directly to social work practice. There are many ways to do this, but obvious examples include application to related aspects of policy, legislation, or specific practice based techniques (for example, casework, group work, etc.).

Thematic analysis can be applied to most topics that involve empirical research. Once again, small samples will typically be used (although this is not a requirement) and themes will tend to be rigorously explored. Despite the strong inductive emphasis upon data collection – and the related building up of an argument and thesis – the use of previously published material, as well as engagement with some kind of theoretical framework used to consider, assess and evaluate any findings, is usually central to thematic analysis for social work research.

Comparative analysis

As detailed throughout this book comparison remains at the heart of academic culture, writing and analysis – indeed this approach or technique will also play a role in essays, papers, reports and lectures or seminars. For a dissertation comparative analysis involves the researcher evaluating the contrast between two or more differing case studies, interviews, theories, practices, and so on. It can include comparison of two or more social policies or acts of legislation, such as those that impact upon a specific service user group, or are applied in different parts of a country. Comparison may also be made of different support services, including those applied in separate geographical regions, cities or countries. Indeed international perspectives – in which the experience of one country is contextualized and analysed by looking at related or diverging examples set in another country – have become increasingly popular within social work research (see for example, Ferguson *et al.*, 2005). Finally, comparative analysis may instead be used as an aspect of a dissertation, such as if comparing two separate interview outcomes as part of an attempt to tackle a broader research question.

Any policy, practice or interview, etc. compared with another will typically be viewed as a 'case' with its own distinct characteristics. Analysis of two or more cases will ordinarily seek to do the following:

- *Be clear from the outset what it is that is being compared and why.* For what reason(s) are two or more cases being compared and how does each case link to any motives for comparison?
- *Establish one or more themes around which any comparison will pivot.* This may include an argument, problem, theory or specific area of interest to the researcher. Any identified theme(s) should hold together a thesis and provide a focal point for discussion and analysis.
- *Develop a thesis that relates to any cases explored.* For example, what is the relationship between each case and is there a clear argument or theory that links to each? Again, as with identified themes, any thesis will help to connect each case and also hopefully provide coherence and fluidity to the task in hand. A unifying thesis helps us to avoid any risk of *separation* between cases within analysis; in which there may be little if any link provided during any discussion and critical examination.
- *Provide basic details relating to each case but avoid merely describing any cases under investigation.* The reader will need to be made aware of any background introductory information relating so that any analysis which takes place is better understood.
- *Seek to explore similarities and/or differences relating to each case.* By its very nature comparison should stimulate consideration of parallel attributes and disparities regarding each case. Potentially this task can be exhaustive, and it is likely that any possible similarities or differences for discussion will need to be reduced, most likely at an early stage in the research.
- *Aim to establish firm conclusions and recommendations relating to any findings from each case examined.* What has been learnt from the process of comparison and how might any findings assist any understanding of each, and potentially other, related cases?

Walk (1998: 1) also details the benefits of a 'lens' or 'keyhole' comparison. This is where the usual method of comparing two cases equally, or with a slant towards one, is replaced by a challenge to instead 'weight A less heavily than B' while also 'us[ing] A as a lens through which to view B'. Therefore, one case is presented and then utilized to contextualize and critically explore another in more depth.

Walk also highlights that all forms of comparative analysis should seek to use reliable sources as evidence, such as key authors relating to a case and sources of data. Also, many forms of comparative analysis will tend to precede *point-by-point*, in which a different issue relating to each case is discussed, then analysed and followed by the next. Alternatively a researcher may decide to progress *text-by-text*, in which one theme within a paper or book is first explored followed by the next, but with each being assessed according to a similar set of criteria and literary sources.

Critical analysis

Another distinct approach within qualitative research is critical analysis which draws from a variety of theoretical sources. These include feminism, Marxism, postmodernism, and anti-oppressive practice. Harvey (1990: 14–32) pinpoints a number of qualities that are rooted within critical analysis. Within social work these will include a tendency to engage with one or more attributes, including:

- to be sceptical or deny that research can be objective and scientific;
- to question taken for granted assumptions in an attempt to 'get beneath the surface of [theoretical or empirical] appearances' (p. 21);
- to locate a research concept and thoroughly investigate and explore their relevance, purpose and possible ulterior interests;
- to explore critically social inequalities and forms of social injustice, especially those relating to class, gender, 'race', disability, and so forth;
- to investigate the means by which forms of social inequality and power are established; including through the application of prevailing and dominant ideologies and other belief systems (rhetoric, ideology, myth, theory, discourse, etc.);
- to question established and prevailing legislation, policy and subsequent 'traditional' social work practices including the assessment, professionalism, managerialism, reliance upon the medical model, the application of punitive interventions against women or other minority groups, and so on;
- to examine the *context* of, and the *fundamental nature* of, social phenomena;
- to explore critically abstract generalizations such as those embedded

within social theory, policy or legislation, and *how practice or day to day 'reality' compare and contrast.*
- to look at the 'totality' of social phenomena or the 'view that social phenomenon are interrelated and form a total whole'. This is a philosophy that stands against 'micro-analysis' or observing and assessing complex social dynamics and themes *in isolation*. For example, racism or sexism may need to be considered regarding their 'holistic' social, political and cultural complexity, and their relation to the role of governments, the education system, the mass media, the institutional make up of the family, and possible personal roles in perpetuating and enforcing forms of oppression;
- to engage critically with forms of knowledge while also 'questioning the nature of knowledge' and how knowledge is produced and applied. This will include personal reflexivity regarding prior and current beliefs and taken for granted assumptions, the relevance or otherwise of specific theory to practice and the possible interests that lie behind claims to professionalism and claims to expertise.

Potentially any topic can be analysed using this approach, although in general themes that link to issues regarding inequality and poverty, class, race and ethnicity, and gender or disability are likely to be most suited. As an analytical approach it defies tradition and looks to question taken for granted assumptions, traditions, norms or values, as well as established knowledge and forms of practice. Despite this, there are still 'traditional' skills necessary in order to undertake any form of analysis. Once again critical qualitative analysis will begin at an early stage, rely upon extensive yet focused and directed reading, and note taking and reflection throughout. Because it deals explicitly with forms of injustice and discrimination, critical analysis is also closely tied to ethics and moral philosophy – in particular an endeavour throughout research to draw attention to forms of inequality and injustice, and wherever possible confront them.

Ramazanoglu and Holland (2002: 159–61) highlight key approaches used as a part of critical analysis. In particular they emphasize a need for the following:

- Be creative and use your imagination so as to make 'your data speak'. As there are so many potential ways of interpreting data or other information it is imperative to think laterally regarding how such data may be evaluated and made accessible to the reader.
- Compare your previous views and ask whether these have now changed and why this might be so.
- Look for discernible patterns and trends, and in particular seek to distinguish data which provides 'evidence' regarding answers to your

research question from general information or 'ideas' that do not strictly relate.

- Carefully consider any claims made that draw from research findings and ask whether or not a different perspective may be possible. Ask whether or not any conclusions can be fully justified. For example, would research participants agree with your interpretation of their opinions or experiences? Would other researchers have sympathy with your interpretation of any findings? If there are tensions, taking time to explore each can be useful to help better understand and convey data and other information such as that unearthed during the literature review.
- Drawing from literature based and/ or empirical sources, ask yourself whether or not there is enough 'evidence' available to sustain your attempt to answer the research question. Can the findings be used to make generalizations regarding more people or trends? If not make clear to the reader any potential hazards attached to the findings.
- Try not to get lost within any process of analysis and try to have confidence in your eventual conclusions. As the authors warn: 'there is no point at which the possibility of competing interpretations and analyses [of research findings] stops, but there will be pressure on you to come to a point of decision'.

Since the 1970s critical analysis has been extensively explored within social work literature and research and can be seen as offering a distinct method-ological approach. The writings of key authors – including Lena Dominelli, Sue Wise, Jan Fook and Beth Humphries, among others, have set a precedence regarding how to analyse social work practice and research critically. It is advisable to look at some literature relating to these authors to get a feel of how this approach can be applied within a dissertation. Some related reading is also identified at the end of this chapter.

Summary

This chapter has concentrated upon qualitative analysis. This should provide a crucial component of any social work dissertation and ideally analysis should begin at an early stage. There are many forms of qualitative analysis but all share similar attributes. Among others, these include the identification of underlying research themes or issues, the need to critically explore and unpack these, and, if appropriate, apply the findings from each to a form of social work practice.

Specific forms of analysis can be used for a social work dissertation, includ-ing general, thematic, comparative and critical approaches. Again, however, there is still an attempt made to unearth and locate relevant themes, critically engage with each, and eventually seek to find possible ways of reforming and improving social work theory and/or practice. The most basic forms of analysis include *comparison* (differences/similarities between two or more cases and how findings compare with other peoples' research findings and/or theory) and *contextualization* (how findings relate to established theory, historical trends, political processes, and so on). Typically each represents the most common and sometimes the most effective forms of analysis for a dissertation.

The final chapter looks at the writing and dissemination of research findings.

Suggested reading

Bryman, A. (2004) *Social Research Methods*. Oxford: Oxford University Press. (Chapter 19: Qualitative data analysis)

Denscombe, M. (2007) *The Good Research Guide For Small Scale Research Projects*. Maidenhead: Open University Press. (Chapter 15: Writing up the research)

Harvey, L. (1990) *Critical Social Research*. London: Unwin Hyman. (Chapter 1: Basics)

Humphries, B. (2008) *Social Work Research for Social Justice*. Basingstoke: Palgrave Macmillan. (Chapter 7: Critical Social Research)

Humphries, B. and Truman, C. (eds) (1994) *Re-Thinking Social Research: Anti-discriminatory Approaches in Research Methodology*. Aldershot: Avebury.

Marvasti, A.B. (2004) *Qualitative Research in Sociology*. London: Sage. (Chapter 5: Data analysis)

Padgett, D.K. (1998) *Qualitative Methods in Social Work Research – Challenges and Rewards*. London: Sage. (Chapter 7: Data management and analysis)

Ramazanoglu, C. and Holland, J. (2002) *Feminist Methodology: Challenges and Choices*. Sage: London. (Chapter 8: Choices and decisions: doing a feminist research project)

10 Writing up and dissemination

Introduction

This chapter explores the process of writing up a social work dissertation. It considers when to begin writing, different writing styles and how to maintain critical engagement throughout the writing process. The various possible structures of a social work dissertation – including the differences in organization between an empirical and literature based dissertation – are also discussed. In addition, suggestions are made regarding how to improve the content and presentation of a final document. Finally, ways in which research findings might be disseminated – including after a social work course has finished and qualified practice begins – are also presented.

When to write

As is often the case with the process of analysis, it is sometimes assumed that the writing up of a dissertation takes place towards the end stage of a dissertation. However, writing should ideally begin as early as possible, with core sections such as the literature review and methodology typically able to be completed in draft form early on. There are several advantages to beginning the process of writing earlier rather than later. To begin with, this will help you avoid the emotional stress, anxiety and panic associated with being faced with the daunting task of needing to write up a 12,000 word (or more) dissertation in a relatively brief time frame. Starting early will also provide an opportunity to develop your writing skills – like many things in life, writing improves with practice. Moreover, a number of research stages, such as data collection, are inadvertently connected to the process of writing. As Marvasti (2004: 130) warns:

> Do not approach writing and data collection as separate parts of your
> research paper. Write everything down as you collect your data. . . .
> Much of this material may not be included in the final draft of your
> paper, but at the very least, the continuous recording of all this
> information will hone your writing skills. If you don't begin writing
> until the data collection is complete, your original research question
> might seem like a needle in a haystack of data. Continuous writing
> helps you stay on track and focused.

Writing from an early stage will also help you to remember key points
unearthed during the literature review and develop aspects of the thesis such
as research aims, objectives and methodology.

Ideally the writing of a social work dissertation should not only start early
but also proceed in tandem within a more holistic and interrelated research
process. For a literature based dissertation writing can also begin and proceed
as your reading and ideas progress and cultivate. As Blaxter *et al.* (2006: 208)
point out, in practice writing for a dissertation is usually a cyclical process in
which a student will 'draft a section or chapter, then move on to some
other activity, and return one or more times to redraft [the] original version'.
Such an iterative journey back and forth occurs due to the impact of new
findings, further reading or personal reflection, all of which may lead to a
reform or extension of earlier arguments. This sometimes introspective and
symbiotic culture of social work research can also support the research process
by encouraging analytical techniques such as reflexivity and contextualization
from an early stage.

Style and critical engagement

Initially it can be difficult to decide upon a particular style of writing in relation to a dissertation topic. Styles will differ according to personality, degrees
of flair, a topic explored, eventual findings uncovered, and so forth. Despite
this, there are some general tips and loose knit traditions attached to the writing up of much qualitative research. As well as beginning as early as possible,
Padgett (1998: 105) recommends looking at other examples of writing styles.
This will include previously published qualitative literature, such as presented
in books and journals, and previous dissertations relating to your field of
enquiry. Checking or skim reading any such material is useful because it can
help you to recognize the variety of writing styles and formats of presentation
available 'which can [all] help you to develop your own presentation style'.

The title of a dissertation should be brief yet reflect the work's content,
and the final document should be divided up into clear sections using headings and sub-headings. In general academic prose is 'detached' and 'passive'

(Swetnam, 2000: 100) so you should try to avoid strongly opinionated (and usually highly subjective) rants or emotional outbursts. One area where quali- tative research is quite distinct from quantitative research regards the absence of any standard formats for writing. As Padgett (1998: 105) notes, this may be liberating but can also place added pressure upon a student. Despite this variety, clarity and consistency remain crucial, as does avoiding over-elaborate sentences or arguments. For example, Swetnam (2000: 101) laments that even 'a sophisticated audience finds excessively long sentences difficult to absorb'. As noted in Chapter 8, Crossley (2005: viii) offers a more critical inter- pretation, and suggests that deliberately complex arguments, or convoluted theoretical propositions, sometimes conceal a lack of creativity and ideas. It is always beneficial to present arguments and findings so that they are coherent, lucid and as accessible to the reader as is possible. More often than not this will lead to more empathy with a dissertation work from an examiner as there is little danger of a thesis – and many good points and ideas – becoming 'lost' among too many arguments.

Other concerns regarding style include using the third person (avoiding the use of 'I', 'my', and 'we') wherever possible, and being consistent with the use of tense. The example below is written in the first person and present tense:

> I was a little surprised to have discovered that many children in care tend to prefer having more time to spend with their social worker. I have also just discovered through my interviews that . . .

The following example demonstrates a more appropriate writing style employ- ing the third person and past tense:

> The research findings suggest that children in care prefer having more time to spend in the company of their social worker. It was also discovered that . . .

There should also be clear links between each chapter and each section of the dissertation, and a consistent and coherent flow to arguments and presenta- tion of findings. One argument or theme should proceed after another and each argument – or author's work cited – should be adequately explored and unpacked. Critical engagement with previous related research is essential within qualitative research and should be sustained throughout. This means trying to avoid passively agreeing with each and every other author – an outcome that seems unlikely with the variety of often conflicting opinions held within most debates and discourses. Taylor (1989) suggests a number of possible responses to academic material that can include:

1 agreeing with or confirming a stance;
2 accepting many of the argument(s) presented by author(s) but suggesting additional points and/or disagreeing with some issues raised;
3 revising a general point of view and thereby improving the argument(s), ideally with a rationale for any such revision;
4 dismissing argument(s) or a thesis and underlining the weaknesses inherent in the work;
5 accepting much within two opposing ideas or theories but offering an alternative stance that accommodates the best aspects of both viewpoints;
6 acknowledging the weaknesses of your own research or arguments and identifying ways in which this may be revised.

In social work, you may also look more generally at accepted beliefs and applied practices or policies. As Padgett (1998) notes, a relatively common stance is to encourage the reader to reconsider an accepted belief or practice. This may include the merits of an established support service such as residential or respite care. When confronting a traditional viewpoint or practice it is vital to provide clear evidence for any critical claims so as to sustain and support your arguments – this may come from alternative research sources, your own empirical findings or a combination of the two.

Denscombe (2007: 318) also underlines the importance of the following:

- *Being selective about what is included and presented in the final document* Not everything discovered can be discussed due to limited available space so try to prioritize material to include and decide what might be omitted. It will always help to be as succinct as is reasonably possible.
- *Avoiding unashamed bias but at the same time trying to be positive about your findings* As the author emphasizes: 'without resorting to deceit or untruths, the account of research will almost certainly entail some upbeat positive filtering. The point, after all, is to justify the procedures as "good" research'.
- *Recognizing the impact of your own norms and values upon any research and making this explicit in sections such as the methodology, discussion and/or concluding chapters* Within qualitative research any personal account offers only one possible interpretation of any findings and therefore it will help to acknowledge your own cultural influences and possible prejudices.

Typically universities, colleges and tutors will provide clear guidelines regarding essential criteria such as referencing, style and presentation. Originality can be gained from any empirical or conceptual findings which throw new light upon the behaviour or attitudes of social groups or traditional assumptions or practices, or which revise arguments or theories or make new recommendations that relate to social work practice based on your own research.

Key sections – an empirical based dissertation

For an empirical based dissertation there is a relatively standard means by which to present findings during the write up. Core sections will usually include the following.

Introduction

This is a foreword in which the reader is presented with initial information. This might include the focus of the study and/or a brief overview of the topic or a recent or pertinent theme (such as a recent policy initiative) that links and which may offer an insight into why the research question is being addressed as part of a dissertation. You may also wish to use this space to explain more explicitly why the topic was chosen for study and outline your general interest and relationship to the topic. For example, the choice of topic may be linked to past work experience in social work or social care. This section can also be used to introduce the research question – what is it that you are trying to find out and why? Typically the introduction should be brief and make up approximately 5 per cent of the overall content of the dissertation.

Literature review

This is an overview of your background research, or sources of literature, such as academic papers, textbooks and relevant reports, etc., that link to a topic. Usually a literature review will begin with a wide gaze and then narrow in focus closer to a specific topic as it proceeds. You may also wish to draw on non-traditional sources, such as publications that cite service user group opinions (for example, advocacy magazines, Internet sites or meetings or conversations you have engaged in) or which reflect the interests of non-professional employees. Ideally there will be balance to your literature review in that it reflects different stances while allowing the reader to:

- become aware of the range of opinions and debates relating to a topic;
- become aware of key pertinent themes and issues that have been identified as linking to a research question.

The literature review not only offers an opportunity to summarize your reading and research undertaken prior to empirical research; it also allows you to reveal to the reader the key debates that link to any later empirical research. The literature review also offers an opportunity to place into context the topic under investigation, and this is likely to support any analysis later on.

Depending on the topic a literature review can take up anything from between 20 to 35 per cent of the total word length – inevitably this is not likely to be enough to cover every previous theme and argument in depth so it is always important to be precise and succinct in your writing style, and also to use your references well.

Methodology

This section identifies, describes and attempts to justify both your methodology and the methods utilized to collect data. For example, were you influenced by a theory as part of the selected methodology? Did you use a 'mixed method' approach? How was your methodology brought to life – how did you collect and analyse the necessary data? Was it by interview, focus group, or some other method? Finally, you should endeavour to acknowledge any advantages and disadvantages attached to the research methodology and methods utilized. In general a methodology section of a social work dissertation will represent around 10 per cent of the total word length.

Findings and analysis

For qualitative research this section will provide an opportunity to present exactly what it is you have discovered. This may include details of issues or themes unearthed, such as how participants have responded to and addressed questions that you have asked by detailing pertinent opinions or raising specific concerns. A common question to ask is how best to present extensive data – such as field notes or interview transcriptions – with only limited word length available? It is important to be detailed but succinct and also selective about what it is that will be admitted and omitted in the findings chapter. Only material that connects directly with either the research aims or objectives should be included. Some findings can be condensed or discussed less explicitly to make more space for supplementary findings if they have a function regarding the overall study. Despite these intentions you will still need to be careful not to cram too much information into this chapter as an avalanche of findings may confuse or even confound the reader. Try to decide what takes priority and always think carefully about what will be included and how this links to your principle research ambitions. As discussed in the previous chapter, regarding the specifics of analysis, there are many differing ways to approach this section. They are likely to include one or more of the following: comparing and contrasting your findings to other research findings; looking at the theoretical implications of your data; considering your findings in relation to other people's research and past or current social work practice or policy; or more generally contextualising what you have discovered regarding how it links with wider social, historic or political trends. It always helps to compare your findings to previous research. As well as helping the reader better understand the structure and coherence of any thesis overall, this approach will also help bring back into focus references and themes first introduced in a literature review chapter. The findings and analysis chapter will typically take up between 20 to 25 per cent of the overall word length.

Discussion

A separate discussion section is not compulsory but in some cases it may help to isolate and provide space to better explore certain pertinent themes that have emerged from the research. This may include special points that are especially pertinent to social work practice. Ideally the discussion should be a relatively brief section that links together both the analysis and conclusion. It is unlikely to constitute more than 20 per cent of the total word length.

Conclusions and recommendations

Any conclusion is helpful because it should be able to tie together and unite previous sections of a dissertation. Preferably you should be able to draw from your research and make clear unambiguous statements regarding what you have learnt and also how this might influence policy and practice. Recommendations are not compulsory and may not fit some forms of research. When they are suitable they are best presented as possible directions in which both policy and practice may steer. They can be represented and codified as suggestions, statements or identified themes that need to be addressed by practitioners, associated organizations, policy makers, and so forth. This final section will vary in size but typically will be around 10–15 per cent of the total word length.

In practice, once you begin to develop your writing style word space tends to be used up very quickly – all space is precious within any academic work that has a ceiling regarding word length. Try to be as succinct and clear as possible and keep a careful check on the word length as the dissertation progresses.

Key sections – a literature based dissertation

As discussed in Chapters 2 and 6, there are different ways in which a literature based dissertation can be structured. This depends upon the topic, the results of the findings and also the decision of the author regarding how best to structure the dissertation in order to present and unpack the findings effectively. In general, literature based dissertations begin with an introduction and proceed with a methodology, findings, discussion, conclusion and recommendations section. It is how the findings are presented as chapters that tend to differ. Below is one example. See Levin (2005: 84–9) for helpful examples of differing structures depending upon the topic, complete with general chapter headings and content.

Introduction

Again this is a brief outline and offers a summary of initial information regarding the topic, research question and any reasons you may have had for its selection. This section is unlikely to take up more than 5 per cent of the total word length.

Methodology

This section explains to the reader what it is you have been trying to achieve and specifically how the information relating to the literature search on which your work is founded was collected, processed and analysed. For example, the reader may be informed that an attempt was made to explore conflicting perspectives in related literature regarding a specific topic; such as the differing ways in which older people are assessed by health and social care professionals or the potential relevance of the ideas of R.D. Laing to mental health related social work. The reader will want to know how and why any related material was selected by a student to explore these topics. The student may have looked at specific journals that relate to each topic and also searched for well known authors who specialize in research relating to the topic. This initial research strategy may then have led to academic papers that directed the student to other related publications, and so on. The student may also be influenced by a particular theory, author, or approach literature that links to a research topic while reflecting upon personal experience. Such explicit details reveal to the examiner that there has been adequate planning undertaken and a clear strategy has unfolded as part of any search for literature. This is in contrast to a more cavalier search for any publications that might happen to be stocked in the nearest library!

You should also discuss the type of analysis undertaken as part of any literature review. For example, has a critical or comparative analysis been undertaken of the literature, or has some alternative approach been applied that links to post-modern theory? In sum, how was information collected and evaluated? An attempt to be reflexive and critical in your findings is usually an expectation. The size of the methodology chapter will usually be no more than 10 per cent of the total word length.

Literature review – previous research and trends

This chapter is similar across all dissertations. It is sometimes called a foundation chapter as it supports all others. As stated earlier, this section will usually begin with a wide gaze of relevant literature (journal articles, reports, text books, etc.) and then start to focus upon any selected topic. The examiner will want to know what the current state of the literature is regarding a topic, and also what are the key themes relating to any research aims and objectives. The size of this chapter will depend on the topic.

Literature review – key themes and topics

This chapter addresses some of the key themes that link to a research question and topic. In particular, it presents the findings relating to the aims and objectives of the research. As part of this process it has presented a critical interpretation of the views of key authors in the field and other differing stances regarding the topic. It should also seek to present what has been discovered and any notable points of contention. It is imperative that a thorough overview of relating themes and debates is addressed in the literature, generating a debate and discourse held around the initial research aims and objectives. In this example this chapter is the most significant in size, and constituted 40 per cent of the total word length.

Discussion and analysis

Although a discussion section is not compulsory regarding empirical research, this is usually advisable for a literature based dissertation. This allows you to identify and unpack pertinent themes from the previous chapter and perhaps also discuss uncertain or ambiguous themes discovered. In general, analysis occurs throughout the write up but there may be themes that require specific attention in this chapter. In this example this chapter constituted 20 per cent of the word length.

Conclusion and recommendations

This chapter will typically tie together and summarize findings as well as draw recommendations, some of which may directly influence social work practice. It will usually constitute around 10 per cent of the total word length.

Possible ways to improve your dissertation

Most pieces of academic work can be improved in some way. Sometimes relatively small changes can make a big difference when viewed from the perspective of an examiner. Below are some suggestions for where a little extra attention or care can potentially make a significant difference to the overall impression that a dissertation makes.

Meet regularly with a supervisor and carefully consider their advice

As identified earlier a tutor should be able to offer indispensable information relating to the research process, relevant reading, how to engage with research methods, and so forth. A tutor may also be willing to assess some of your ideas and check some of your writing. Many students of all ability avoid supervision. This is a pity as the supervisor is usually also the examiner and a handful of brief meetings will often improve the quality and grade of a dissertation.

Try to avoid citing a publication yet revealing very little about it

Relevant reading always constitutes a core component of any dissertation and integrating a variety of authors and their published works into a thesis that contrasts with, compliments or strengthens an argument or debate, is always beneficial. However, there may be occasions when a publication is cited but not explored in any depth. It will help to offer adequate detail relating to many publications such as a summary, and possibly a direct quote, that accurately reflects work being cited. From an examiner's point of view it can be frustrating to note that significant works have been cited within a dissertation, but then discover that only one or two teasing sentences deal with these works before the author swiftly moves to the next point!

Always seek to unpack arguments and points raised

If a pertinent point is raised that fits with an overall thesis try to explore and unpack that issue in some detail. For example, it may help to generate a brief debate around the point, or bring in other authors to throw new light on any discussion. Perhaps an example from your own practice experience may also help to sustain an argument?

Try not to laboriously recite or rehash other people's ideas

An examiner is unlikely to be impressed with attempts to simply regurgitate other people's work and offer little that reflects your own experiences, thoughts and ideas. Although reference to other publications will impress an examiner (assuming such work links with a thesis), this technique should be applied with a careful and critical overview of any such work. Publications should also not be described one after another without a link or clear purpose. Ideally such research should be assessed and examined with a critical eye that carefully considers its strengths, relationship to your own findings, possible weaknesses, and so on.

Provide adequate evidence of points raised

It is a researcher's responsibility to support claims made by presenting to the reader sources of evidence that can include other people's research, your own arguments and logic or empirical data.

Endeavour not to over-rely upon a handful of sources

Sometimes this is unavoidable, such as when exploring a topic that has been under-researched. If this is the case then this point should be made explicit to the reader – otherwise it may give an impression of superficial and inadequate research undertaken. Try to find as many reliable and varied sources that are suitable as possible and integrate them into your writing.

Make an effort not to over-rely upon the internet and core textbooks

As discussed in Chapter 5, Internet sources should be used in moderation. This is because unlike most academic journals and textbooks, Internet sites tend to lack regulation and a peer review culture meaning that the reliability of information held is sometimes open to question. Although general course textbooks can be extremely useful in offering a reliable introduction to a subject, they are often less likely to be able to explore the nuances of a topic. Other sources, such as specialist journal articles or published monographs, are more likely to offer such a service.

Integrate personal experience

Within an applied discipline such as social work personal experience can be extremely valid, especially if past experience fits with a thesis being explored. Experience might also provide 'evidence' to support a claim or argument. Ideally this should not be anecdotal, histrionic or of only limited relevance to a thesis.

Avoid repetition

Typically, some points will need to be raised on more than one occasion, and in some dissertations this will be essential to exploring ideas or theories. However, continued repetition, as well as potentially undermining a dissertation, will almost certainly dilute your arguments and may also annoy the examiner!

Proof-read and edit a dissertation prior to submission: no academic work should be submitted before reading thoroughly at least twice. It is nearly always the case that errors regarding grammar, spelling, consistency or coherence of argument will be found in some parts of a document. Correction will almost certainly lead to a better standard of work and therefore a higher grade.

Dissemination

Although never a compulsory aspect of a social work dissertation, dissemination – or the distribution, 'spreading out' and/or direct application of research findings – can represent a crucial element of the research process. Dissemination can take many forms that include:

- discussing research findings with social work colleagues or service users and carers;
- allowing research findings to directly influence social work practice;
- writing an article for a social work magazine such as *Community Care* or an academic journal;
- presenting a paper at a conference;
- integrating findings within future research, such as for an MPhil or PhD.

It is likely that social work practitioners will be interested in your research findings. Dissemination may have the potential of improving the quality of their practice and the outcomes for service users and carers. Corby (2006: 152–3) has argued that dissemination can also promote closer links between the theory and practice of social work. In particular, he notes that there are dangers in 'trying to make too clear a distinction between theory and practice and assuming that because theorists are into ideas and practitioners into action and that never the twain should meet'. In contrast, dissemination of research is one means by which theory can move closer to practice while also helping to reverse the long held tradition of researchers 'communicating with other researchers and policy makers, but not more directly with those at the front-line of practice'.

When it is linked to moulding practice, involving service users, and potentially influencing other people's beliefs, a thesis can sustain a social and political impact far beyond the latter stages of a formal course. What becomes of research findings after a dissertation is submitted is really at the discretion of the student. However, with increasing pressure to integrate research into social work practice, it is likely that dissemination will continue to expand as a priority for most of us. Dissemination may also be a way of raising consciousness and awareness, particularly regarding issues where there is little available information for practitioners to draw from. There are therefore potential ethical and moral benefits attached to dissemination, including its possible capacity to support and empower service users through increased knowledge and understanding.

Dissemination is not necessarily a set of tasks to engage with after a dissertation has been completed. Instead, as with analysis, dissemination can begin early – such as within a practice placement or by discussing aspects of your research within a seminar, essay or presentation. Dissemination can also have an impact many years after a dissertation module or course has ended, and may prove to be the most tangible and lasting component of a social work dissertation.

Summary

The final chapter has drawn attention to the importance of writing up a dissertation and any subsequent dissemination of findings. The use of reliable references that link to a thesis is especially significant in order to help adequately articulate opinions or general findings. Clarity, coherence and brevity are also of importance regarding style. Other techniques or approaches have also been highlighted, and, among others, these include the role of structure, avoiding any over repetition of findings or points raised, and also being succinct and focused when presenting data or related arguments.

Although dissemination is not compulsory for some dissertations (such as many Bachelor degrees) for an applied discipline such as social work this stage of the research process can be the most beneficial regarding any future practice. For some factions within social work – such as many critical feminists – dissemination is considered to be the most significant stage of the research process.

Suggested reading

Becker, H.S. (1986) *Writing for Social Scientists: How to Start and Finish Your Thesis, Book or Article*. Chicago: Chicago University Press.

Blaxter, L., Hughes, C. and Tight, M. (2006) *How to Research*. Berkshire: Open University Press. (Chapter 8: Writing up)

Levin, P. (2005) *Excellent Dissertations!* Maidenhead: Open University Press. (Part 4: The End Game)

Marvasti, A.B. (2004) *Qualitative Research in Sociology*. London: Sage. (Chapter 6: Writing)

Padgett, D.K. (1998) *Qualitative Methods in Social Work Research – Challenges and Rewards*. London: Sage. (Chapter 9: Telling the story)

Royse, D. (1991) *Research Methods in Social Work*. Chicago: Nelson-Hall Publishers. (Chapter 13: Writing research reports and journal articles)

Taylor, G. (1989) *The Student's Writing Guide for the Arts and Social Sciences*. Cambridge: Cambridge University Press.

Appendix

Websites to support a social work dissertation:

www.socscidiss.bham.ac.uk/s1.html An excellent site that provides information on research methodology, methods and all the key stages of any dissertation.

www.radstat.org.uk The radical statistics group (Radstats) was established in 1975 and aims to critically assess and question the government and institutional representation of official statistics, especially for political purpose. The site is invaluable, providing free access to a journal and other resources, often with contributions from leading experts in a range of academic and practice based fields.

http://www.lwbooks.co.uk/journals/soundings/contents.html The *Soundings* journal offers critical analysis regarding many issues relating to social work and social policy research. Some are free to read and print off.

http://www.socwork.net/ This site deals specifically with critical research relating to social work and is free to access. This is an essential resource for students and practitioners.

http://www.socialworkfuture.org/ The social work action network (SWAN) is a loose knit collective of (mostly) academics, alongside some students, practitioners, managers and service users within social work. The website provides a lively forum for critical and political debate, and principle members also have their own manifesto! This site offers a valuable resource.

www.rip.org.uk This site is dedicated to social work research dissemination.

www.jrf.org.uk The Joseph Rowntree site disseminates research findings and reports relating to the alleviation of poverty.

www.communitycare.co.uk The weekly social care magazine has its own website which is continuously updated and includes weekly articles. It also has an archive article search section which is extremely useful for researchers.

http://www.jiscmail.ac.uk This intends to 'facilitate knowledge sharing within the UK centred academic community'. Resources include forums for discussion (including social work and social welfare).

www.All4one This is a 'meta search engine' which combines different search engines (for example, Google, Excite, etc.) to offer a comprehensive and broad trawl for relevant websites, articles, etc.

www.vts.rdn.ac.uk Among other facilities the Virtual Training Suite offers advice on social work resources and free online tutorials for different subject areas.

www.vts.intute.ac.uk/he/tutorial/social-worker Part of the Virtual Training Suite, this site includes forums for discussion around social work related issues. This is also a possible site to gain access to participants for empirical research.

www.sosig.ac.uk This offers a comprehensive and precise search engine in specialist subjects, including social policy and social work.

www.bubl.ac.uk A wide catalogue of academic links and resources is on offer, including a section dedicated to social work research.

www.hero.ac.uk This is an excellent resource that provides links to key social work resources, university facilities, groups and organizations, etc.

www.loc.gov/ The American Library of Congress claims to be the largest library in the world. Among other resources this site offers a powerful search engine that scours books and manuscripts published in every country in the world.

www.bl.uk/ The British Library website boasts a catalogue of over 13 million books and 920,000 journal and newspaper titles. This is particularly useful for gaining access to obscure or out of date publications.

www.ilo.org The International Labour Organisation is a tripartite United Nations agency that 'brings together governments, employers and workers . . . to promote decent work throughout the world'. Among other things, this site offers annual reports and working papers related to work, industry and employment.

http://europa.eu.int/comm/eurostat/ The main gateway to statistical data regarding the European Union; it also accommodates policy and legislation. It may be of particular use if engaging in a comparative study of two European countries.

www.data-archive.ac.uk/ Again this site offers a rich source of statistical information across Europe and also provides other resources such as online learning and teaching programmes.

www.statistics.gov.uk This government site disseminates statistical data relating to social trends in the UK.

www.essex.ac.uk/qualidata/index.htm This site – based at Essex University – offers a wealthy source of primary data gathered from qualitative social research undertaken over the years. Potentially some of this data could be used to undertake secondary analysis as part of a social work dissertation.

www.mimas.ac.uk This site, which is based at Manchester University, provides data and information resources 'to support teaching, learning and research across a wide range of disciplines'. It also provides staff contact details for help and assistance.

http://qb.soc.surrey.ac.uk/ The question bank is an information resource geared towards quantitative research and questionnaire surveys and structures. Despite this, the guidelines and examples from prior questionnaire designs can offer extremely useful pointers to designing your qualitative research questionnaire and may also be a good guide for appropriate interview questions. A number of topics related to social work research are covered.

www.natcen.ac.uk/ The National Centre for Social Research is the 'largest independent social research Institute in Britain' which carries out and 'analyse[s] research studies in the fields of social and public policy'. This site is excellent for examples of qualitative methodology that link to social work.

www.publist.com/ This site offers a database of over 150,000 magazines, journals, newsletters and other periodicals.

www.lse.ac.uk/IBSS/ The International Bibliography of the Social Sciences offers access to articles, papers, abstracts books and reviews, and also offers tips for using the site for dissertations and an online thesaurus among other resources.

www.oclc.org/firstsearch/ Among other services this site offers access to multidisciplinary databases.

www.lib.gla.ac.uk Proceedings First is based at Glasgow University and offers access to e journals, newspapers, exam papers, etc.

www.worldcat.org/advancedsearch This site is a union catalogue that itemizes the collection of over 10,000 libraries based in more than ninety countries.

Bibliography

Adams, R., Dominelli, L. and Payne, M. (eds) (2005) *Social Work Futures*. Basingstoke: Palgrave Macmillan.

Alexander, V.D. (2001) Analysing factual accounts, in N. Gilbert (ed.) *Researching Social Life*. London: Sage.

Alston, M. and Bowles, W. (1998) *Research for Social Workers: An Introduction to Methods*. Australia: Allen and Unwin.

Althusser, L. (1971) *Lenin and Philosophy and other essays*. London, NLB pubs.

Alvesson, M. (2002) *Postmodernism and Social Research*. Buckingham: Open University Press.

Alvesson, M. and Skoldberg, K. (2000) *Reflexive Methodology*. London: Sage

Andrews, M., Day Sclater, S., Squire, C. and Tamboukou, M. (2004) Narrative Research, in C. Seale, G. Gobo, J. Gubrium and D. Silverman (eds) *Qualitative Research Practice*. London: Sage.

Aronson, J. (1994) A pragmatic view of thematic analysis, *The Qualitative Report*, 2(1): 1–3.

Balloch, S., McLean, A. and Fisher, M. (eds) (1999) *Social Services: Working Under Pressure*. Bristol: Policy Press.

Banks, S. (2002) *Ethics and Values in Social Work*, 2nd edn. Basingstoke: Macmillan.

Banyard, P. and Hayes, N. (1994) *Psychology: Theory and Application*. London: Chapman and Hall.

Baines, D. (2004) Pro-market, non-market: the dual nature of organisational change in social services delivery, *Critical Social Policy*, 24(1): 5–29.

Barker, K. (1998) Toiling for piece-rates and accumulating deficits: contingency work in higher education, in K. Barker, K. Christensen (eds) *Contingent Work: American Employment Relations in Transition*. New York: Cornell University Press.

Becker, H.S. (1967) Whose side are we on? *Social Problems*, 14.

Becker, H.S. (1982) *Art Worlds*. London: University of California Press.

Becker, H.S. (1986) *Writing for Social Scientists: How to Start and Finish Your Thesis Book or Article*. Chicago: Chicago University Press.

Bell, J. (1987) *Doing Your Research Project*. Milton Keynes: Open University Press.

Bell, J. (2005) *Doing Your Research Project*, 4th edn. Maidenhead: Open University Press.

Bishop, R. (1996) Postmodernism, in D. Levinson and M. Ember (eds) *Encyclopaedia of Cultural Anthropology*. New York: Henry Holt.

Blaxter, L., Hughes, C. and Tight, M. (2006) *How To Research*. Maidenhead: Open University Press.

Bloor, M. (1978) On the analysis of observational data: a discussion of the worth and uses of induction techniques and respondent validation, *Sociology*, 12(3): 545–52.

Bloor, M. (1993) Addressing social problems through qualitative research, in D. Silverman (ed.) *Qualitative Research – Theory, Method and Practice*. London: Sage.

Bourdieu, P. (1977) *Outline of a Theory of Practice*. Cambridge: Cambridge University Press.

Bourdieu, P. (1984) *Distinction: A Social Critique of the Judgement of Taste*. Cambridge, MA: Harvard University Press.

Bourdieu, P. (1998) *Acts of Resistance – Against the New Myths of Our Time*. Cambridge: Polity Press.

Bowles, W., Collingridge, M., Curry, S. and Valentine, B. (2006) *Ethical Practice in Social Work*. Maidenhead: Open University Press.

Brewer, J. and Hunter, A. (1989) *Multi-Method Research: A Synthesis of Styles*. Newbury Park: CA, Sage.

Brewer, J. (2000) *Ethnography*. Open University Press: Buckingham.

Brewer, J. (2003a) Positivism, in R.L. Miller and J.D. Brewer (eds), *The A to Z of Social Research*. London: Sage.

Brewer, J. (2003b) Discourse analysis, in R.L. Miller and J.D. Brewer (eds), *The A to Z of Social Research*. London: Sage.

Brewer, J. (2003c) Ethnography, in R.L. Miller and J.D. Brewer (eds), *The A to Z of Social Research*. London: Sage.

Brewer, J. (2003d) Induction, in R.L. Miller and J.D. Brewer (eds), *The A to Z of Social Research*. London: Sage.

Bryman, A. (2004) *Social Research Methods*. Oxford: Oxford University Press.

Butler, I. (2002) A code of ethics for social work and social care research, *British Journal of Social Work*, 32: 239–48.

Cancian, F.M. (1993) Conflicts between activist research and academic success: participatory research and alternative strategies, *The American Sociologist*, 81: 92–106.

Carey, M. (2003) Anatomy of a care manager, *Work, Employment and Society*, 17(1): 121–35.

Carey, M. (2004) The Care Managers – Life on the Front-Line after Social Work. Unpublished PhD, University of Liverpool.

Carey, M. (2008) Care management unleashed: enduring ethical tensions twenty years after the Griffiths Report 1988, *Ethics and Social Welfare*, 2(3): 308–16.

Carey, M. (2009) The order of chaos: exploring agency care managers' construction of social order within fragmented worlds of state social work, *British Journal of Social Work*, 39(3): 556–73.

Chaiklin, S. (1993) Understanding the social scientific practice of understanding practice, in S. Chaiklin and J. Lave (eds) *Understanding Practice: Perspectives on Activity and Context*. Cambridge: Cambridge University Press.

Clark, W. (2001) Being here – Bob Holman interview, *Variant*, 13: 1–5.

Clifford, D. (1994) Critical life histories: key anti-oppressive research methods and processes, in B. Humphries and C. Truman (eds) *Rethinking Social Research: Anti-Discriminatory Approaches in Research Methodology*. Aldershot: Avebury.

Coffey, A. and Atkinson, P. (1996) *Making Sense of Qualitative Data*. London: Sage.

Coffey, A. (1999) *The Ethnographic Self – Fieldwork and the Representation of Data*. London: Sage.

Cohen, L., Manion, L. and Morrison, K. (2007) *Research Methods in Education*, 6th edn. London: Routledge.

Colaizzi, P.F. (1978) Psychological research as the phenomenologist views it, in R.S. Valle and M. King (eds) *Existential Phenomenological Alternatives for Psychology*. Oxford University Press: New York.

Corby, B. (1982) Theory and practice in long term social work: a case study of practice with social service department clients, *British Journal of Social Work*, 12: 619–38.

Corby, B. (2006) *Applying Research in Social Work Practice*. Maidenhead: Open University Press.

Critchley, S. (2001) *Continental Philosophy – A Very Short Introduction*. Oxford: Oxford University Press.

Crossley, N. (2005) *Key Concepts in Critical Social Theory*. London: Sage.

Crotty, M. (1998) *The Foundations of Social Research*. London: Sage.

Czarniowska, B. (2004) *Narratives in Social Science Research*. London: Sage.

Daly, M. (2003) Methodology, in R.L. Miller and J.D. Brewer (eds) *The A–Z of Social Research*. London: Sage.

Darlington, Y. and Scott, D. (2002) *Qualitative Research in Practice: Stories from the Field*. Maidenhead: Open University Press.

Davies, L. and Leonard, P. (2004) *Social Work in a Corporate Era – Practices of Power and Resistance*. Aldershot: Ashgate.

Dawson, C. (2006) *A Practical Guide to Research Methods*, 3rd edn. Oxford: How To Books Limited.

D'Cruz, H. and Jones, M. (2004) *Social Work Research – Ethical and Political Contexts*. London: Sage.

De Laine, M. (2000) *Fieldwork, Participation and Practice*. London: Sage.

de Montigny, G. (2007) Ethnomethodology for social work, *Qualitative Social Work*, 6(1): 95–120.

Dellgran, P. and Hojer, S. (2003) Topics and epistemological positions in Swedish social work research, *Social Work Education*, 22(6): 565–75.

Denscombe, M. (2007) *The Good Research Guide For Small Scale Research Projects*, 3rd edn. Maidenhead: Open University Press.

Department of Health (2001) *Research Governance Framework for Health and Social Care*. London: Department of Health.

Dey, I. (1998) *Grounding Grounded Theory: Guidelines for Qualitative Inquiry*. San Deigo: Academic Press.

Dominelli, L. (1988) *Anti-racist Social Work*. London: Macmillan.

Dominelli, L. (2002) *Feminist Social Work Theory and Practice*. Basingstoke: Palgrave.

Dominelli, L. (2004) *Social Work – Theory and Practice for a Changing Profession*. Cambridge: Polity.

Dominelli, L. (2005) Social work research: contested knowledge for practice, in R. Adams, L. Dominelli and M. Payne (eds) *Social Work Futures*. Basingstoke: Palgrave Macmillan.

Drake, B. and Jonson-Reid, M. (2007) *Social Work Research Methods: From Conceptualisation to Dissemination*. New Jersey: Allyn and Bacon.

Eagleton, T. (2007) *Ideology: An Introduction*. London: Verso.

Eichler, M. (1988) *Non-Sexist Research Methods*. Boston: Allen and Unwin.

Elliott, J. (2005) *Using Narrative in Social Research*. London: Sage.

Emerson, R.M. (2004) Working with 'key incidents', in C. Seale, G. Gobo, J. Gubrium and D. Silverman (eds) *Qualitative Research Practice*. London: Sage.

Evans, T. and Harris, J. (2004) Street-level bureaucracy, social work and the (exaggerated) death of discretion, *British Journal of Social Work*, 34(6): 871–95.

Ezzy, D. (2002) *Qualitative Analysis: Practice and Innovation*. London: Routledge.

Fairclough, N. (1995) *Critical Discourse Analysis: The Critical Study of Language*. London: Longman.

Fairclough, N. (2000) *New Labour, New Language?* London: Routledge.

Fairclough, N. (2001) The discourse of new labour: critical discourse analysis, in M. Wetherall, S. Taylor and S.J. Yates (eds) *Discourse Theory and Practice: A Reader*. London: Sage.

Fairclough, N. (2003) *Analysing Discourse: Textual Analysis for Social Research*. Oxford: Routledge.

Ferguson, I., Lavalette, M. and Whittmore, E. (eds) (2005) *Globalisation, Global Justice and Social Work*. London: Routledge.

Fernandes, L. (2003) *Transforming Feminist Practice – Non-violence, Social Justice and the Possibilities of a Spiritualised Feminism*. San Francisco, CA: Aunt Lute Books.

Fetterman, D.M. (1998) *Ethnography – Step by Step*. London: Sage.

Feyerabend, P. (1975) *Against Method*. London: Verso.

Fink, A. (2005) *Conducting Research Literature Reviews – From the Internet to Paper*. London: Sage.

Flyvberg, B. (2004) Five misunderstandings about case-study research, in C. Seale, G. Gobo, J. Gubrium and D. Silverman (eds) *Qualitative Research Practice*. London: Sage.

Foddy, W. (1994) *Constructing Questions for Interviews and Questionnaires*. Cambridge: Cambridge University Press.

Fook, J. (2002) *Social Work: Critical Theory and Practice*. London: Sage.

Forte, J.A. (2001) *Symbolic Interactionist Translations*. Lanham: University Press of America.

Foster, V.L. (2007a) Painting a picture of Sure Start Parr: exploring participatory arts-based research with working class women. Unpublished PhD thesis, University of Liverpool.

Foster, V.L. (2007b) The art of empathy: employing the arts in social inquiry with poor working class women, *Social Justice*, 34(1): 12–27.

Foucault, M. (1977) *Discipline and Punish – The Birth of the Prison*. London: Penguin.

Fraser, H. (2004) Doing narrative research: analysing personal stories line by line, *Qualitative Social Work*, 3(2): 179–201.

Froggett, L. and Chamberlayne, P. (2004) Narratives of social enterprise, *Qualitative Social Work*, 3(1): 61–77.

Furedi, F. (2002) Don't rock the research boat, *Times Higher Education Supplement*, 11 January: 20.

Gash, S. (1999) *Effective Literature Searching for Research*. Aldershot: Gower.

General Social Care Council (2004) *A Consultation on the Structure of a New framework of Post-Qualifying Social Work Education and Training*. London: GSCC.

Gibbs, A. (2001) The changing nature and context of social work research, *British Journal of Social Work*, 31: 687–704.

Gibson, B. (2003) Grounded theory, in R.L. Miller and J.D. Brewer (eds), *The A to Z of Social Research*. London: Sage.

Giele, J.Z. and Elder, G.H. (eds) (1998) *Methods of Life Course Research: Qualitative and Quantitative Approaches*. London: Sage.

Gilchrist, R. and Jeffs, T. (eds) (2001) *Settlements, Social Change and Community Action*. London: Jessica Kingsley.

Gilgun, J.F. (1994) Hand into glove: the grounded theory approach and social work practice research, in E. Sherman and W.J. Reid (eds) *Qualitative Research in Social Work*. New York: Columbia University Press.

Gillham, B. (2000) *Developing a Questionnaire*. London: Continuum International Publishing Group.

Gillham, B. (2005) *Research Interviewing – The Range of Techniques*. Maidenhead: Open University Press.

Glaser, B. and Strauss, A. (1967) *The Discovery of Grounded Theory*. Chicago: Aldine.

Gomm, R. (2003) *Social Research Methodology – A Critical Introduction*. New York: Palgrave Macmillan.

Gomm, R., Hammersley, M. and Foster, P. (eds) (2000) *Case Study Method*. London: Sage.

Goppner, J.H. and Hamalainen, J. (2007) Developing a science of social work, *Journal of Social Work*, 7: 269–87.

Gough, I. (1979) *The Political Economy of the Welfare State*. Basingstoke: Macmillan.

Graham, A. (1994) *Teach Yourself Statistics*. London: Hoddler Headline Arnold.

Green, J.C. (2000) Understanding social programmes through evaluation, in N.K. Denzin and Y.S. Lincoln (eds) *Handbook of Qualitative Research*, 2nd edn. Thousand Oaks, CA: Sage.

Green, J. (2005) Qualitative interviewing, in J. Green and J. Browne (eds) *Principles of Social Research*. Maidenhead: Open University Press.

Greene, J. and Browne, J. (2005) Framing a research question, in J. Green and J. Browne (eds) *Principles of Social Research*. Maidenhead: Open University Press.

Grundy, S. (1990) Three modes of action research, in S. Kemmis and R. McTaggart (eds) *The Action Research Reader*, 3rd edn. Victoria, Australia: Deakin University Press.

Guba, E. and Lincoln, Y. (1989) *Fourth Generation Evaluation*. Newbury Park, CA: Sage.

Gubrium, J.F. and Holstein, J.A. (2001) *Handbook of Interview Research*. London: Sage.

Hall, D. and Hall, I. (1996) *Practical Social Research – Project Work in the Community*. Basingstoke: Macmillan.

Hall, C. and White, S. (2004) 'Editorial – looking inside professional practice: discourse, narrative and ethnographic approaches to social work and counselling, *Qualitative Social Work*, 4(4): 379–90.

Hammersley, M. and Atkinson, P. (1995) *Ethnography – Principles in Practice*. London: Routledge.

Hammersley, M. (2003) Social research today, *Qualitative Social Work*, 2(1): 25–44.

Harding, S. (1986) *The Science Question in Feminism*. New York: Cornell University Press.

Harrison, J., Hepworth, M. and de Chazal, P. (2004) NHS and social care interface: a study of social workers, *Library and Information Needs Journal of Librarianship and Information Science*, 36(1): 27–35.

Hart, C. (1998) *Doing a Literature Review – Releasing the Social Science Research Imagination*. London: Sage.

Hart, C. (2001) *Doing a Literature Search – A Comprehensive Guide*. London: Sage.

Harvey, D. (1989) *The Condition of Postmodernity: An Enquiry into the Origins of Cultural Change*. London: Blackwell.

Harvey, L. (1990) *Critical Social Research*. London: Unwin Hyman.

Healy, K. (2005) *Social Work Theories in Context – Creating Frameworks for Practice*. Basingstoke: Palgrave Macmillan.

Healy, K. and Meagher, G. (2001) The reprofessionalisation of social work: collaborative approaches for achieving professional recognition, *British Journal of Social Work*, 34: 157–74.

Hitchcock, G. and Hughes, D. (1989) *Research and the Teacher: A Qualitative Introduction to School-based Research*. London: Routledge.

Hindess, B. (1973) *The Use of Official Statistics: A Critique of Positivism and Ethnomethodology*. London: Macmillan.

Hine, C. (2005) *Virtual Methods: Issues in Social Research on the Internet*. London: Berg.

Holloway, I. (1997) *Basic Concepts for Qualitative Research*. Oxford: Blackwell Science.

Holloway, W. and Jefferson, J. (2000) *Doing Qualitative Research Differently – Free Association, Narrative and the Interview Method*. London: Sage.

Holloway, W. and Todres, L. (2003) The status of method: flexibility, consistency and coherence, *Qualitative Research*, 3: 345–57.

Holstein, J.A. and Gubrium, J.F. (1997) Active interviewing, in D. Silverman (ed.) *Qualitative Research: Theory, Method and Practice*. London: Sage.

Hood, S., Mayall, B. and Oliver, S. (eds) (1999) *Critical Issues in Social Research: Power and Prejudice*. Buckingham: Open University Press.

Howe, D. (1987) *An Introduction to Social Work Theory*. Aldershot: Wildwood House Limited.

Hughes, J.A. (1990) *The Philosophy of Social Research*. London: Longman.

Hugman, R. (1991) *Power in Caring Professions*. Hampshire: Macmillan.

Humphries, B. (2008) *Social Work Research for Social Justice*. Basingstoke: Palgrave Macmillan.

Humphries, B. and Truman, C. (eds) (1994) *Rethinking Social Research: Anti-Discriminatory Approaches in Research Methodology*. Aldershot: Avebury.

Johnston, T. (1972) *Professions and Power*. London: Macmillan.

Jones, C. (1983) *State Social Work and the Working Class*. Basingstoke: Macmillan.

Jones, C. (1996) Anti-intellectualism and the peculiarities of British social work education, in N. Parton (ed.) (1996) *Social Theory, Social Change and Social Work*. London: Routledge.

Jones, C. (2001) Voices from the front-line: State social workers and New Labour, *British Journal of Social Work*, 31: 547–62.

Jones, P. (1993) *Studying Society – Sociological Theories and Research Practices*. London: HarperCollins.

Jupp, V. (1996) Documents and critical research, in R. Sapsford and V. Jupp (eds) *Data Collection and Analysis*. London: Sage.

Jupp, V. (2006) *The Sage Dictionary of Social Research Methods*. London: Sage.

Kitzinger, J. (1994) The methodology of focus groups: the importance of interactions between research participants, *Sociology of Health and Illness*, 16: 103–21.

Krueger, R.A. and Casey, M.A. (2000) *Focus Groups: A Practical Guide for Applied Research*. London: Sage.

Kumar, R. (1996) *Research Methodology: A Step-by-Step Guide for Beginners*. Melbourne: Longman.

Kunda, G. and Ailon-Souday, G. (2005) Managers, markets and ideologies – design and devotion revisited, in S. Ackroyd, R. Batt, P. Thompson and P.S. Tolbert (eds) *The Oxford Handbook of Work and Organization*. Oxford: Oxford University Press.

La Fontaine, J. (1985) *What is Social Anthropology?* Arnold: London.

Lather, P. (1991) *Getting Smart*. New York: Routledge.

Layton, R. (1997) *An Introduction to Theory in Anthropology*. Cambridge: Cambridge University Press.

Leach, E. (1982) *Social Anthropology*. Glasgow: Collins.

LeBesco, K. (2004) Managing visibility, intimacy, and focus in online critical ethnography, in S.C. Shing-Ling and G.J. Hall (eds) (2004) *Online Social Research – Methods, Issues and Ethics*. Oxford: Peter Lang.

Lemert, E. (1951) *Social Pathology*. New York: McGraw-Hill.

Levin, P. (2005) *Excellent Dissertations!* Maidenhead: Open University Press.

Linhorst, D.M. (2002) A review of the use and potential of focus groups in social work research, *Qualitative Social Work*, 1(2): 208–28.

Lynch, K. (2000) The role of emancipatory research in the Academy, in A. Byrne and R. Lentin (eds) *Researching Women: Feminist Research Methodologies in the Social Sciences in Ireland*. Dublin, Institute of Public Administration.

Mann, C. and Stewart, F. (2000) *Internet Communication and Qualitative Research Online*. London: Sage.

Marlow, C. (2001) *Research Methods for Generalist Social Work*. Belmont, CA: Wadsworth.

Marvasti, A.B. (2004) *Qualitative Research in Sociology*. London: Sage.

May, T. (1993) *Social Research: Issues, Methods and Process*. Buckingham: Open University Press.

McCauley, C. (2003) Ethics and the academic community, in R.L. Miller and J.D. Brewer (eds) *The A to Z of Social Research*. London: Sage.

McLaughlin, H. (2007) *Understanding Social Work Research*. London: Sage.

McLeod, E. (1982) *Women Working: Prostitution Now*. London: Croom Helm.

McNiff, J. (2000) *Action Research in Organisations*. London: Routledge.

Menabney, N. (2003) Internet, in R.L. Miller and J.D. Brewer (eds) *The A to Z of Social Research*. London: Sage.

Miles, M. (1993) Towards a methodology for feminist research, in M. Hammersley (ed.) *Social Research – Philosophy, Politics and Practice*. London, Sage.

Miles, M.B. and Huberman, A.M. (1994) *Qualitative Data Analysis*. Thousand Oaks, CA: Sage.

Miller, R.L. (2000) *Researching Life Stories and Family Histories*. London: Sage.

Miller, R.L. (2003) Narrative analysis, in R.L. Miller and J.D. Brewer (eds) *The A to Z of Social Research*. London: Sage.

Miller, R.L. and Brewer, J.D. (eds) (2003) *The A to Z of Social Research*. London: Sage.

Mishler, E.G. (1986) *Research Interviewing: Context and Narrative*. Cambridge, MA: Harvard University Press.

Morrow, R.A. and Brown, D.D. (1994) *Critical Theory and Methodology*. London: Sage.

Nielson, J.M. (1990) *Feminist Research Methods*. Boulder, CA: Westview Press.

Norris, C. (1995) Postmodernism, in T. Hoderich (ed.) *The Oxford Companion to Philosophy*. Oxford: The Oxford University Press.

Oakley, A. (1974) *The Sociology of Housework*. Oxford: Martin Robertson.

O Dochartaigh, N. (2001) *The Internet Research Handbook: An Introductory Guide for the Social Sciences*. London: Sage.

Padgett, D.K. (1998) *Qualitative Methods in Social Work Research – Challenges and Rewards*. London: Sage.

Parton, N. (1994) The nature of social work under conditions of (post) modernity, *Social Work and Social Sciences Review*, 5(2): 93–112.

Parton, N. (ed.) (1996) *Social Theory, Social Change and Social Work*. London: Routledge.

Parton, N. and O'Byrne, P. (2000) *Constructive Social Work – Towards a New Practice*. Basingstoke: Macmillan.

Payne, M. (2005) *Modern Social Work Theory*, 3rd revised edn. Basingstoke: Palgrave Macmillan.

Payne, G. and Payne, J. (2004) *Key Concepts in Social Research*. London: Sage.

Perks, R. and Thompson, A. (eds) (2006) *The Oral History Reader*. Oxford: Routledge.

Pink, S. (2001) *Doing Visual Ethnography – Images, Media and Representation in Research*. London: Sage.

Plummer, K. (1983) *Documents of Life: An Introduction to the Problems and Literature of a Humanistic Method*. London: Allen and Unwin.

Plummer, K. (2001) *Documents of Life 2 – An Invitation to Critical Humanism*. London: Sage.

Porter, S. (2003) Critical theory, in R.L. Miller and J.D. Brewer, *The A to Z of Social Research*. London: Sage.

Potter, J. and Wetherall, M. (1994) Analyzing discourse, in A. Bryman and R.G. Burgess (eds) *Analysing Qualitative Data*. London: Routledge.

Punch, K. (2005) *Introduction to Social Research – Quantitative and Qualitative Approaches*. London: Sage.

Quality Assurance Agency for Higher Education (2000) *Benchmark Statement: Social Policy and Administration and Social Work*. Gloucester: QAA.

Radnor, H. (2002) *Researching Your Professional Practice – Doing Interpretive Research*. Buckingham: Open University Press.

Ramazanoglu, C. and Holland, J. (2002) *Feminist Methodology: Challenges and Choices*. London: Sage.

Rapley, T. (2004) Interviews, in C. Seale, G. Gobo, J. Gubrium and D. Silverman (eds) *Qualitative Research Practice*. London: Sage.

Reason, P. and Bradbury, H. (eds) (2000) *Handbook of Action Research: Participatory Inquiry and Practice*. London: Sage.

Reinharz, S. (1983) Experiential analysis: a contribution to feminist research, in G. Bowles and R.D. Klein (eds) *Theories of Women's Studies*. London: Routledge and Kegan Paul.

Reinharz, S. (1992) *Feminist Methods in Social Research*. New York: Oxford University Press.

Reissman, C.K. (1993) *Narrative Analysis*. London: Sage.

Reissman, C. and Quinney, L. (2005) Narrative in social work: a critical review, *Qualitative Social Work*, 4(4): 391–412.

Reynolds, J. (2007) Discourses of inter-professionalism, *British Journal of Social Work*, 37: 441–57.

Ridley, D. (2008) *The Literature Review – A Step by Step Guide for Students*. London: Sage.

Roberts, B. (2002) *Biographical Research*. Buckingham: Open University Press.

Roberts, B. (2006) *Micro Social Theory*. Basingstoke: Palgrave Macmillan.

Robson, C. (2000) *Small Scale Evaluation*. London: Sage.

Rogers, A. and Pilgrim, D. (2001) *Mental Health Policy in Britain*, 2nd edn. Basingstoke: Palgrave Macmillan.

Rosen, A. (2003) Evidence-based social work practice: challenges and promise, *Social Work Research*, 27(4): 197–208.

Rosenthal, G. (1993) Reconstruction of life stories. Principle of selection in generating stories for narrative biographical interviews, in R. Josselson and A. Lieblich (eds) *The Narrative Study Lives*. London: Newbury Park.

Royse, D. (1991) *Research Methods in Social Work*. Chicago: Nelson-Hall Publishers.

Salkind, N.J. (2006) *Exploring Research*. New Jersey: Pearson.

Sanders, P. and Liptrot, D. (1994) *An Incomplete Guide to Qualitative Research Methods for Counsellors*. Manchester: PCCS books.

Sapsford, R. and Abbott, P. (1996) Ethics, politics and research, in R. Sapsford and V. Jupp (eds) *Data Collection and Analysis*. London: Sage.

Scott, J. (1995) *Sociological Theory – Contemporary Debates*. Aldershot: Edward Elgar Ltd.

Scourfield, J. (2001) Interviewing interviewers and knowing about knowledge, in I. Shaw and N. Gould (eds) *Qualitative Research in Social Work*. London: Sage.

Seale, C., Gobo, G., Gubrium, J. and Silverman, D. (2004) Inside qualitative research, in C. Seale, G. Gobo, J. Gubrium and D. Silverman (eds) *Qualitative Research Practice*. London: Sage.

Shaw, I. (1999) *Qualitative Evaluation*. London: Sage.

Shaw, I. and Gould, N. (2001) *Qualitative Research in Social Work – Introducing Qualitative Methods*. London: Sage.

Sheldon, B. and Chivers, R. (2000) *Evidence-based Social Care: A Study of Prospects and Problems*. Lyme Regis: Russell House Publishing.

Silverman, D. (1993) *Interpreting Qualitative Data*. London: Sage.

Skeggs, B. (2001) Feminist ethnography, in P. Atkinson, A. Coffey, S. Delamont, J. Lofland and L. Lofland (eds) *Handbook of Ethnography*. London: Sage.

Social Care Institute for Excellence (2004) *Knowledge Review – Improving the Use of Research in Social Care Practice*. Bristol: Policy Press.

Spence, G. (2001) *A Simple Guide to Internet Research*. Harlow: Prentice Hall.

Stake, R.E. (1995) *The Art of Case Study Research*. Thousand Oaks, CA: Sage.

Stanley, L. and Wise, S. (1983) *Breaking Out: Feminist Consciousness and Feminist Research*. London: Routledge and Kegan Paul.

Stanley, L. and Wise, S. (1993) *Breaking Out Again: Feminist Ontology and Epistemology*. London: Routledge.

Stenson, K. (1993) Social work discourse and the social work interview, *Economy and Society*, 1: 42–76.

Strauss, A. and Corbin, J. (1990) *Basics of Qualitative Research: Grounded Theory Procedures and Techniques*. Newbury Park, CA: Sage.

Stroobants, V. (2005) Stories about learning in narrative biographical research, *International Journal of Qualitative Studies in Education*, 18(1): 47–61.

Sumner, C. (1994) *The Sociology of Deviance*. Buckingham: Open University Press.

Swetnam, D. (2000) *Writing Your Dissertation*. Oxford: How To Books.

Symonds, A. and Kelly, A. (eds) (1998) *The Social Construction of Community Care*. London: Macmillan.

Taylor, G. (1989) *The Students Writing Guide for the Arts and Social Sciences*. Cambridge: Cambridge University Press.

Taylor, S. and White, S. (2000) *Practising Reflexivity in Health and Welfare: Making Knowledge*. Buckingham: Open University Press

Tesch, R. (1990) *Qualitative Research – Analysis, Types and Software Tools*. London: Falmer Press.

Thomas, J. (2004) Re-examining the ethics of internet research: facing the challenge of overzealous oversight, in S.C. Shing-Ling and G.J. Hall (eds) *Online Social Research – Methods, Issues and Ethics*. Oxford: Peter Lang.

Training Organisation for the Personal Social Services (2002) *The National Occupational Standards for Social Work*. Leeds: TOPPS.

Trinder, L. and Reynolds, S. (eds) (2000) *Evidence Based Practice: A Critical Appraisal*. Oxford: Blackwell Science.

Truman, C. (2003) Ethics and the ruling relations of research production, *Sociological Research Online*, 8(1): 1–15.

Vesey, G. and Foulkes, P. (1999) *Dictionary of Philosophy*. Glasgow: HarperCollins.

Walk, K. (1998) *How to Write a Comparative Analysis*. Cambridge, MA: Harvard University, Writing Centre.

Walliman, N. (2004) *Your Undergraduate Dissertation – the Essential Guide for Success*. London: Sage.

Walliman, N. (2006) *Social Research Methods*. London: Sage

Warburton, N. (2004) *Philosophy: The Essential Study*. London: Routledge.

Webb, S. (2001) Some considerations on the validity of evidence-based practice in social work, *British Journal of Social Work*, 31: 57–79.

Wetherall, M., Taylor, S. and Yates, S.J. (eds) (2001) *Discourse as Data: A Guide for Analysis*. London: Sage.

Whitmore, E. (2001) 'People listened to what we had to say': reflections on an emancipatory qualitative evaluation, in I. Shaw and N. Gould (eds) *Qualitative Research in Social Work*. London: Sage.

Wilkinson, D. (2005) *The Essential Guide to Postgraduate Study*. London: Sage.

Williams, F., Popay, J. and Oakley, A. (eds) *Welfare Research: A Critical Review*. London: UCL Press.

Willis, U.W. (2007) *Foundations of Qualitative Research – Interpretive and Qualitative Approaches*. London: Sage.

Wilson, T.D. (2002) Alfred Schutz, phenomenology and research methodology for information behaviour research. Paper presented at Fourth International

Conference on Information Seeking in Context, Universidade Lusiada, Lisbon, Portugal, 11–13 September.

Wise, S. (2001) Auto-ethnography as reflexive inquiry: the research act as self-surveillance, in I. Shaw and N. Gould (eds) *Qualitative Research in Social Work*. London: Sage.

Wodak, R. and Meyer, M. (2001) *Methods of Critical Discourse Analysis*. London: Sage.

Wolcott, H.F. (1999) *Ethnography: A Way of Seeing*. London: Sage.

Worrell, A. (1990) *Offending Women: Female Lawbreakers and the Criminal Justice System*. London: Routledge.

Yin, R.K. (1994) *Case Study Research – Design and Methods*. London: Sage.

Index